The Examined Run

The Examined Run

Why Good People Make Better Runners

SABRINA B. LITTLE

OXFORD
UNIVERSITY PRESS

OXFORD
UNIVERSITY PRESS

Oxford University Press is a department of the University of Oxford. It furthers
the University's objective of excellence in research, scholarship, and education
by publishing worldwide. Oxford is a registered trade mark of Oxford University
Press in the UK and certain other countries.

Published in the United States of America by Oxford University Press
198 Madison Avenue, New York, NY 10016, United States of America.

Library of Congress Cataloging-in-Publication Data
Names: Little, Sabrina, author.
Title: The examined run : why good people make better runners / Sabrina Little.
Description: New York, NY : Oxford University Press, 2024. |
Includes bibliographical references and index.
Identifiers: LCCN 2023043714 | ISBN 9780197678695 (paperback) |
ISBN 9780197678688 (hardback) | ISBN 9780197678701 (epub)
Subjects: LCSH: Running—Psychological aspects. | Runners
(Sports)—Psychology. | Runners (Sports)—Conduct of life. |
Athletes—Conduct of life. | Conduct of life. | Character.
Classification: LCC GV1061.8.P75 L57 2024 |
DDC 796.4201/9—dc23/eng/20231025
LC record available at https://lccn.loc.gov/2023043714

DOI: 10.1093/oso/9780197678688.001.0001

Paperback printed by Sheridan Books, Inc., United States of America
Hardback printed by Bridgeport National Bindery, Inc., United States of America

To David, Lucy, and Frances
my loving family
and to the seven pairs of running sneakers I wore out
during the writing of this monograph

Contents

Preface   ix
Acknowledgments   xv

1. Pride Ran-eth Me into a Shed: An Introduction to
   Running and Virtue Ethics   1

2. Practicing Courage in My Sneakers: Virtue and
   Development   31

3. Feeling *Good*: Running on Emotions   68

4. The Runners I Look Up To   93

5. Good and Fast: Performance-Enhancing Virtues   118

6. Bad Competition: Performance-Enhancing Vices   139

7. The Happy Runner: Running and the Good Life   180

8. Limitless: The Pitfalls of Faustian Running   209

Conclusion   228

Notes   231
Works Cited   257
Index   269

Preface

During graduate school, there was a hill where I used to run repeats. Sometimes I would set a timer and run up and down the hill as fast as I could until the timer ran out. Other times, I would aim to run a set number of ascents up the hill, finishing the last one faster than the first. Occasionally, I ran intervals up the hill—from fifteen seconds to two minutes in length—with equal recovery before restarting my next ascent. I ran that hill every week, sometimes twice a week, for years.

There is at least one thing that trail runners and philosophers hold in common. This is a preoccupation with ascent. Trail runners scale mountains. They record vertical gain in their training and speak blithely about "earning their views." Likewise, philosophers turn their eyes heavenward and ask big questions. Plato's Socrates described Diotima's ladder, a stepwise ascent from appreciating particular beautiful bodies to contemplating the Form of Beauty itself,[1] which Plotinus, a neo-Platonist, later named as the One, or God.[2]

About a millennium later, Italian poet Dante Alighieri (an admirable choice for one's favorite endurance athlete) described in both geographic and internal terms his soul's journey to ascend to God. Dante first descends into hell, on what only can be described as the most terrifying trail running course I have ever read about, due to demons and jagged terrain. Then he climbs a mountain heavenward—an ascent that redeems and restores his soul.

As both a philosopher and a trail runner, I love to ascend. Maybe I *need* to ascend—on average twice weekly in my running sneakers, and figuratively every day in my philosophy shoes (tasteful loafers).

Throughout my time in graduate school, the hill I ascended never changed. It remained steep and uncompromising, with divots up the center, broken asphalt along the perimeters, and an incline that steepened before it leveled off near the top. But I changed. Over the years as I trained on the hill, I became a person more capable of ascending it. My heart and lungs grew stronger. My legs toughened. I could sustain harder efforts for longer intervals, and my ascents grew consistently faster.

But it was not just my body that changed. My character was edified, too. I grew in courage on that hill, as I took risks in pacing that I was not sure I could sustain. I learned perseverance by remaining on-task during difficult workouts. I developed patience when I was not where I wanted to be, fitness-wise, and I became a grittier, more resilient, and more confident version of myself.

Over the past couple of years since finishing graduate school and moving away from the hill, my fitness has waxed and waned. But what is interesting is that the internal changes that occurred alongside of my physical development have remained and revealed themselves in areas of life beyond running. When I think back to graduate school, it is clear to me that I received an education on that hill—if not commensurate to the learning I did in my graduate courses and research, certainly a nontrivial addition to it. The hill served as an occasion for my formation as a person. Ascending it shaped my character in manifold and mostly constructive ways.

The Purpose of This Book

Over the past few years, I have noticed two rising tides in athletics.

The first is a curiosity for the internal work required to sustain peak performance. This curiosity is often framed as conversations about performance psychology and mental health in sport, and recently new support has been extended to athletes in these areas. For example, in 2020, the United States Olympic and Paralympic

Committee (USOPC) launched a mental health task force for the first time in the organization's history, providing mental health services for athletes in recognition of the fact that mental health conversations are integral to conversations about physical performance.[3] And recently, athletes such as Olympians Simone Biles (gymnastics), Michael Phelps (swimming), and Gracie Gold (figure skating) publicly disclosed their personal histories with depression, anxiety, and performance anxiety, helping to destigmatize mental health issues in sport.[4] There is a momentum in athletics around discussing athleticism beyond the physical dimensions of performance.

The second rising tide in athletics—which is an extension of something seen culturally, beyond sport—is an impoverished moral vocabulary. Very few athletes have a language for discussing the good-making features of persons, or virtues relevant to sport. In part, this seems due to the fact that, much of the time when ethics is introduced into athletic conversations, it is because of transgressions: someone took performance-enhancing drugs, cheated, or violated the spirit of the sport in some significant way. Stated differently, ethical conversations in sport are often framed in terms of the *negative*—what one *ought not* do, without providing a vision for what one ought to *do* or *be* instead.

This wholly negative framing is a mistake because it offers an asymmetrical picture of what athletics—and a good life more generally—consists. A good life is not merely the absence of bad actions, such as stealing or lying. It also consists of the good actions we do perform, such as acts of justice or courage. Likewise, a good athlete is not the athlete who simply fails to cheat or disrespect competitors. The good athlete is also marked by great feats, perseverance, courage, and a dedication to "not letting one's capacities lie fallow."[5]

Interestingly, virtue ethics—a moral theory that emphasizes virtues and moral character—answers both of these tides. First, a concern for the internal condition of an athlete can be made richer by reference to character. This is because having virtue and vice concepts is like being given spectacles that help an athlete to better see herself. It permits an athlete to name her excellences and deficiencies, identify patterns of action, and develop clarity about what she is accountable (and not accountable) for changing. Having this moral language can also be valuable for helping an athlete to clarify the nature of a struggle.

An example is that, early in my running career, I often had difficulty sustaining longer efforts. I readily attributed this difficulty to a deficiency in fitness. I thought that I just needed to become physically stronger to perform better in long runs. Then I read about the vice of *acedia*, or sloth. Sloth resists necessary work and cannot stay in place. It has two manifestations—despair and frenetic busyness. Learning about this vice helped me to understand that the deficiency I was experiencing on long efforts was not physical, or not *merely* physical; I also had a character issue—the busyness manifestation of sloth. During difficult efforts, I wanted to flit off and do something else to distract myself from difficult work, rather than to remain in place. Having a vocabulary of virtue and vice helped me to see myself more clearly and to be honest about what I needed to do to improve. I needed to acquire the virtue of perseverance.

There are numerous other examples I could provide. Virtue ethics has a tradition of inquiry about flourishing and suffering that I have been both chastised by, and found solace in, during my time as an athlete. It has helped me to understand the difference between productive and unproductive forms of pain, and between ordinary suffering and disorder. Studying virtue ethics has positioned me to inquire about what a good life consists of and to evaluate the ways athletic training might contribute to, and detract from, a good life. It has also helped me to think more critically about the ends toward which my actions are directed and the importance of refining the motivations of my actions. In the face of contemporary athletics' asymmetrical focus on *ought-nots* over *oughts*, virtue ethics has refined my vision for what a rich athletic life can look like.

With these things in mind, I wrote this book to welcome other athletes into a tradition of inquiry about character, flourishing, and suffering so that we can ask better questions together about our sport and ourselves and share a common vocabulary of virtue and vice. My hope is that others' experiences in running can be enriched and humanized in the ways that mine have been, through an exposure to virtue ethics.

Acknowledgments

I am very grateful to my editors, Bryon Powell, Meghan Hicks, and Sarah Brady, at iRunFar.com. Since 2018, they have given me a platform to engage philosophically with the sport of ultrarunning in a monthly column. They have been a great source of encouragement as I have grown as a public philosopher. I am also grateful for their permission to engage with some of the stories and ideas I have written about for iRunFar.com more formally in this book.

I am grateful to the editorial team at Oxford University Press, particularly Peter Ohlin for taking on this project. Thank you for the thoughtful feedback and support you have provided throughout the book-writing process.

I am thankful for the encouragement I have received from the many excellent teachers and mentors in my life. These include the great C. Stephen Evans, my dissertation director, as well as Christian B. Miller, Michael Beaty, Anne-Marie Schultz, and the rest of Baylor Philosophy. Thank you for modeling excellent scholarship, directing me to the Great Books, challenging me, and teaching me how to write. Any bits of clarity are thanks to their guidance.

Thank you to my many running friends for sharing miles and teaching me so much about character, courage, and the good life. Thank you especially to the Live Oak Classical School cross-country team for learning, growing, and practicing virtues alongside me. I am grateful for your hard work, and I am not sorry for making you do hill repeats.

Lastly, I could not have written this book without the support of my friends and family. Most of this book was written in the months prior to and following the birth of my second daughter, Frannie.

Thank you to my philosophical best friend, Maria Waggoner, for long phone calls and encouraging text messages. Thank you to my family—Theodore Moran, Teddy Moran, Amanda Nguyen, Mary Elena Moran, Katrina Watson, Kaky and Louie Little, and Katie and Bryan Haring—for your support and help with the kids. Thank you, Lucy and Frannie. You two are my greatest joys. Most of all, thank you to my wonderful and kind husband, David Little, for his support and encouragement. David, thank you for modeling virtue and showing me how to live a good and honorable life.

1

Pride Ran-eth Me into a Shed

An Introduction to Running and Virtue Ethics

There was a boy in my fourth-grade class who once brazenly announced that he was faster than me. "No, you are not," I assured him. Nevertheless, we lined up to race at recess, surrounded by classmates. A friend yelled "Go!" and we took off across the pavement. The first person to the equipment shed would win.

My competitor got tripped up in a jump rope en route. It really was not fair. But rather than restarting the race, I ran backward to gloat and misjudged my distance to the shed. I turned around just in time to strike it full force with my face. This was a bloody incident, spectated by many of my peers, and I still have a chin scar to remember it by. Afterward, the boy walked me to the nurse's office to patch up my face. I sheepishly thanked him. I also assured him that I would have won the race, regardless of any complications from jump ropes.

Pride go-eth before a fall. Pride ran-eth me into a shed.

Running has been the source of a lot of my life lessons, and it has shaped my character, for both good and for ill. My misadventure at recess that day was not the last one of its kind, but it was a solid, palpable strike to my hubris (and to my face). When I recall the event, I still feel the reverberations on my chin, mixed with a tinge of regret for having been so proud. It's like my body holds the lesson that my heart learned. It's like my legs—running forward, backward, and into a shed—were the means by which I grew as a person.[1]

The Philosophical Context

The idea that athletics can shape a person's character is not a new one. It was articulated as early as 375 BCE by Plato and Aristotle. In Plato's *Republic*, Socrates famously describes the education of the guardians in his "City in Speech."[2] The guardians are professional soldiers whose task is to protect the city from injustice. Their education has two components: gymnastics (or athletic training) and poetry. Gymnastics is used to cultivate spiritedness, which manifests as "savageness and hardness,"[3] and poetry softens and humanizes them. These two components are to be applied immediately from youth without delay and dispensed in proper proportion so that a guardian becomes neither too hard nor too soft. They are to be "tuned to the proper degree of tension and relaxation,"[4] similar to the way one tunes a violin. The strings need to be taut, but not so taut that they snap or fail to produce the right sound. If their educations are carried out correctly, the guardians develop well-ordered souls and can fulfill their function in the hypothetical city.

In Plato's *Protagoras*, we find gymnastics named again in a conversation between Socrates and Protagoras about the possibility of an education preparing a student for virtue.[5] Protagoras describes how gymnastics instructs young men in courage and self-control so that their "bodies may better minister to the sound mind."[6]

Gymnastics appears a third time in Plato's *Laws*.[7] In the *Laws*, an unnamed Athenian names riding, archery, javelin-throwing, dancing, and wrestling specifically as athletic activities suited for educating students' souls. The Athenian—like Socrates in the *Republic*—affirms that these educative tools need to be applied immediately from youth before any bad habits are in place. It is crucial that the youth participate in athletics for the sake of their souls! For the Athenian, the primary objective of education is not the acquisition of technical skills but the formation of virtue.[8] Poetry and gymnastics are used to teach learners to love the right things, in the right ways.

Likewise, Plato's student, Aristotle, describes poetry and gymnastics as imperative from youth onward. He writes, "[I]t is plain that education by habit must come before education by reason, and training of the body before training of the mind."[9] For Aristotle, gymnastics serves as a *propaedeutic*, or preparation, for education. Alongside poetry, athletics helps a learner to form good habits and to live a well-ordered, disciplined life so that he is teachable and can self-govern well.

The point is that conceiving of athletics as a tool to direct and discipline learners is not a new idea. Following the ancients, a similar idea was found in the monasticism of the Desert Tradition, between the third and fifth centuries of the Common Era. Monks such as Evagrius of Pontus and John Cassian emphasized internal transformation through perseverance. They regarded staying in place during manual labor—neither idling nor "acting as busybodies"—as a treatment for vice. Physical actions were used as a means of interior transformation.[10]

This idea that physically "staying in place," or persevering, is both utterly difficult and deeply transformative is one that should resonate with a distance runner. Staying in place is a description of endurance, and enduring through difficulty often refines us.

An additional example of using physical work as a means of internal change is *kaihōgyō*, or "circling of the mountain." This is an ascetic practice—a practice characterized by self-denial—used by a sect of Buddhist monks in Japan. This sect, popularly known today as the "marathon monks," journey by foot around Mount Hiei in an attempt to attain enlightenment.[11]

The marathon monks are a good example of a pattern found across many religious traditions—a reliance on physical touchstones and bodily actions to facilitate internal transformation. Many faiths use practices such as fasting and prayer to assist practitioners in decreasing their reliance on material comforts and focusing on divinity. Religions also often employ liturgies, that incorporate bowing, singing, and kneeling. These physical actions gesture toward something beyond them. They are performed with some degree of automaticity or habit, and they refocus one's attention on the subject toward which they are directed—namely a god, gods, or God. They facilitate transformation through worship.

Of course, using physical practices as a means of interior transformation is neither distinctly religious nor an antiquated way of approaching character. Rather, it is distinctly *human*. It recognizes something true and obvious about human nature, which is that we are embodied. And where our bodies go, our minds go, too.

The reality of being human is that how we move our bodies, particularly in the habitual way we do as athletes, has a direct bearing on who we are as people. For example, every day I wake up and put my sneakers on. I run some predetermined distance from my training schedule, sometimes fast and other times less so. I watch some numbers grow smaller (pace and heart rate) and some numbers grow bigger (mileage and aerobic capacity). But it is not just my body that changes. It could not be just my body. This is because I am not a physical shell—like a chocolate bunny with an unincorporated ghost floating inside. I am both fully embodied and fully an agent, and what I do with my body impacts who I am. Running provides an occasion by which my body is submitted to disciplines, and this changes the way I am inclined to think, act, and feel.

Furthermore, this should not be surprising. While we read much less Plato these days, we still often think and speak as the ancients did about athletics. If you ask any parents why they drive their children to athletic practices multiple times per week, they often say something along the lines of wanting their children to learn the value of hard work or to help them develop discipline. And this is true. They do often learn discipline, and they are transformed in certain ways. However, there are many questions we should ask about the process by which character formation occurs in sport, including whether this formation is, in every instance, productive.

Athletics Gone Awry

If the only thing character formation required were a spot on a Little League team, everybody would sign up their children (and themselves) to play. Furthermore, if that the only thing character formation required were committed participation in a sport, we would expect the World Cup, National Football League, and World Athletics (the international governing body for running) to be bastions of virtue. They are not.

It may be the case that we are shaped by athletics, but there is more than one shape in the world. There are circles, triangles, and octagons. And it is possible that, despite the good intentions we enter sport with, we come away from sport changed for ill. This is something we should consider as athletes, as parents of athletes, and as partakers in athletics. Culturally, we are often inclined to speak of athletics as an unqualified good for character development. We make proclamations about how placing ourselves in difficult situations or "doing hard things" is sufficient for building character. But it is not repeatedly "doing hard things" that develops a good character; it is practicing being a certain type of person and acting from the right motivation during those hard things that helps us to cultivate virtue.

Aristotle writes, "Again, it is from the same causes and by the same means that every virtue is both produced and destroyed, and similarly every art; for it is from playing the lyre that both good and bad lyre-players are produced. And the corresponding statement is true of builders and of all the rest; men will be good or bad builders as a result of building well or badly."[12] That is, it might be the case that every day, a runner wakes up and covers miles. But if her pacing is imprudent, her desires intemperate, her inclinations uncourageous, or her motivations awry, she is practicing disagreeable qualities that she will very likely carry into the rest of her life.

The focus of this book is the formation of virtues through distance running. This requires a background in virtue ethics and its connection to running. In this chapter, I provide an overview of virtue ethics and defend the value of placing it in conversation with distance running. This will provide a framework for addressing the specific questions of virtue, vice, development, happiness, and other considerations of virtue ethics found in later chapters.

One caution about the forthcoming section is that—in the same way that you need to adjust your pace when you run a rocky, technical trail—you may need to *slow down* to adjust to the level of difficulty. Often when my students encounter philosophy for the first time, and it takes them longer to read it, they think something is wrong with them. Nothing is wrong with them! It takes me longer to read philosophy texts, as compared to novels and other kinds of books, too. Also, the more practice we have in reading difficult passages, we grow more capable of reading at faster paces. So, imagine you are in philosophy training. Consider this section of the chapter the rocky trail equivalent of reading. Enjoy the views, and adjust your speed accordingly.

What Kind of Thing Is Virtue Ethics?

The field of ethics has three branches: (1) metaethics, (2) normative ethics, and (3) applied ethics.

Metaethics

I tell you that cutting corners on a cross-country course is wrong. You answer, "What makes it wrong? Is it wrong just because you say so?" Suddenly, we are doing metaethics at a cross-country meet.

Metaethics addresses the meaning of moral language, or what someone means when they say that one 'ought' to do or be one thing rather than another. It asks what exactly a 'value' is and what metaphysically grounds a value, or any obligations and responsibilities we perceive ourselves as having. Metaethics raises epistemic (knowledge) questions about morality, such as whether and how one might know what is good, bad, right, or wrong. It asks whether there are moral facts, in the same way there are facts about physical objects like trees and rocks, or whether morality is an expression of our own preferences or feelings. And it examines semantic features of morality, or how we speak about goodness and badness.

One example of a metaethical position is natural law—the view that 'good' and 'bad' are facts of our human nature that are binding and can be learned as we learn other natural facts, by close observation. For example, lying is bad because of the kind of creatures that we are—social beings who depend on speech. Cheating on the cross-country course is bad because, again, we are social creatures. Cheating undermines trust in one another. A second example of a metaethical position is moral relativism—the view that 'goodness' and 'badness' are the subjective preferences of individuals or groups. On this view, there is nothing inherently good or bad about cheating, for example. Cheating is not for *me*; I would not cheat. But *you* define your own terms of morality.

Normative Ethics

I assert that we ought to speak well of our competitors. You rebut, "Why should we be kind in competition? Why can't we be malicious when we play sports?" In this exchange, we are discussing normative ethics at a track meet. We are talking about virtues and vices.

Normative ethics is also called moral theory. This is the branch of ethics concerned with what makes actions right and wrong. There are three dominant approaches to normative ethics. These are deontology, consequentialism, and virtue ethics. Deontology focuses on duties, rights, and responsibilities. (*Deon* means "duty" in Greek.) Consequentialism is concerned with the results of one's actions. Virtue ethics is the theory for which virtue and vice are foundational concepts of morality, instead of duties or consequences. Virtue ethics principally examines the *person* performing the good or bad action.

While these are three distinct approaches, they are not wholly discrete in practice. First, regardless of where these theoretical fault lines fall, common discourse about moral affairs often draws on all three ways of speaking—duties, consequences, and features of persons. Nonethicists are not ordinarily inclined to pull exclusively from one normative view when they address right and wrong. For example, in the same conversation, a coach might scold an athlete for failing to clean up the training room after weight training (duty). They might note that this makes the athlete seem unconscientious (feature of persons), then let them know about the negative repercussions this action had on the entire team (consequences).

Second, there are many hybrid accounts of morality. Philosopher Julia Driver's consequentialist virtue theory is an example. For Driver, virtues are character traits that consistently produce good consequences, regardless of the motivations of the agent.[13] A second example is that Immanuel Kant (whose ethical theory is a primary example of deontology) also exercises the language of virtue. For Kant, virtue is duty-driven resolve—"the moral strength of a man's will in fulfilling his duty."[14] For Kant, motivation is what matters for a good action; consequences do not. For Driver, motivation is a black box; we are concerned with consequences. For both, virtues feature strongly in their accounts.

Furthermore, in virtue ethics, there is an interesting literature on the nature of the moral 'ought'—whether we are obligated to acquire certain character traits because of natural law or divine command, or whether the obligation to acquire certain traits is binding in any real sense at all.[15] If the nature of one's obligation is law-based, this is a deontic feature of one's virtue ethics. So these are three separate traditions, which lend themselves to different kinds of questions. However, in many cases, the variations we identify among accounts only amount to a difference in emphasis—trait-focused, consequence-focused, or duty-focused.

Applied Ethics

At a road race, you discuss with a friend whether or not carbon-plated racing shoes are fair, since they enhance athletic performance, yet runners have unequal access to them. Your inquiry is an example of applied ethics.

The final branch of ethics is applied ethics. This subfield of ethics addresses specific moral problems—or the moral prohibitions against, obligations to, permissibility for, or acceptability of certain actions. Examples of topics include the following: What qualifies as performance enhancement in sports, and are all forms of enhancement equally problematic? Is it morally permissible to eat meat? Under what conditions would it be acceptable to lie to an elderly parent with dementia? Do we have obligations to care for the poor? If so, what are these obligations?

Putting It All Together

While metaethics, normative theory, and applied ethics are three separate branches of ethics, they are not separable in practice. It helps me to think of these positions like this: *Normative theories* (like virtue ethics) are trees. Trees need to be rooted in something, or else they fall over. These roots are *metaethical theories* (like natural law). The fruit that falls from a tree are *applied ethical questions* (like whether performance-enhancing drugs are fair).

Let's start with the tree and its roots. Normative theories stand on the answers we provide to metaethical questions. This is called metaethical grounding.[16] For example, a deontologist must answer the question of what makes an action obligatory. Is the obligation an expression of personal preference, with no fact of the matter? Are we obligated by social contract, or by agreements held among members of a society? Is it possible that, when I say something is right, I am wrong?

Relevant to virtue ethics, we may wonder whether the goodness of certain traits is grounded in human nature as moral facts—that having certain virtues (like kindness) is fitting for the kind of beings we are, in the same way that there are certain goods (like aviation and sense of direction) for birds. Alternatively, perhaps these traits are good because a god or God recognizes them as such. Or maybe both of these are true, as Thomas Aquinas thought. Without first supplying an answer to the metaethical question about the source of normativity, moral theories are like trees without any roots. We are at a loss for explaining which traits are good and why.

Now let's look at the tree and its fruit. How we approach an applied ethical question depends on the normative system assumed. An example is that a consequentialist running coach may be faced with the question of whether to permit doping on his team. As a consequentialist, he weighs predictive results of doing so. Maybe performance-enhancing drugs will increase marketability and generate excitement because of unbelievable performances (if the athletes are sneaky and people do not discover they are taking drugs). But if the public finds out, they may become jaded or angry. Furthermore, there are serious negative health repercussions for athletes who dope. Doped performances will feel less meaningful because they will be predicated on a lie, and the presence of doping will make the sport less hospitable to those who choose not to partake in drugs. The consequentialist track coach weighs these potential outcomes.

Conversely, a deontologist track coach considers whether drugs violate the spirit of the sport. He asks whether we have a duty to honor other performers, and whether he can conceive of a world in which everyone cheats. Lastly, a virtue ethicist track coach may ask what kind of person would take performance-enhancing drugs. He may inquire about what it means to be an athlete with integrity.

To answer the applied question about what we ought to do in a specific situation, we first need to establish the terms of goodness or badness of an action—that is, adopt a normative theory. The (applied ethical) fruit we gather depends on the kind of (normative) tree it came from.

Our Theory in Focus

To summarize, virtue ethics is a normative theory, or a means of approaching questions of good, bad, right, and wrong. It is concerned with virtue and vice, or qualities of persons. It can be applied to specific moral situations, or applied ethical questions. Moreover, virtue ethics is anchored by our metaethical assumptions.

Regardless of these assumptions, there are certain virtues and vices for which there is broad consensus about their goodness or badness. For example, most people would agree that kindness and honesty are virtues, and they make one's life better. But when it comes to virtues and vices of lower consensus, as well as the nature of one's *ought* regarding the acquisition and expression of virtues, and questions such as the character of happiness, we cannot rely on broad agreement. In Chapter 7, "The Happy Runner: Running and the Good Life," I address considerations of the happy life and how running might fit in—considerations that require more discussions about metaethics.

Why Virtue Ethics?

One might wonder why I have chosen virtue ethics, rather than deontology or consequentialism, for a project of this sort. This is a great question.

Frankly, a book on distance running, paired with any of these approaches, would be interesting. For starters, a deontology book would raise great questions. We may wonder whether we have certain duties toward our competitors, such as by not cheating or harming others. We might wonder whether athletic inclusion is a right for all people, and whether athletes have other rights owed to them, such as safety or access to training resources.

In a deontology book, we could also examine questions such as the presence of deception in certain sports. For example, in soccer and basketball, players often fake right and then move to the left. They signal a lie. Surely, this violates Kant's categorical imperative against lying, since we cannot at the same time both (a) deceive in this way and (b) will that everyone else use their bodies in deceptive ways. There are interesting questions to ask about how Kant's ethics might transform how certain sports are played.[17]

Additionally, the World Anti-Doping Agency (WADA)—an agency that regulates performance enhancement in global sport and issues a list of prohibited substances and methods—frames their doping criteria deontologically. Under WADA code, a substance or method is prohibited if it (a) has the potential to enhance or enhances sport performance, (b) represents an actual or potential health risk to the athlete, or (c) violates the "spirit of the sport."[18] "Spirit of sport" is described as an intrinsic value to uphold regardless of consequences. As far as I know, there is no sustained analytic treatment of what this 'intrinsic value' amounts to in practice, and whether it has any teeth in guiding ethical policy in sport.

A book on consequentialism and running would be interesting, too, and would likely counter the conclusions of the deontological one. If consequences are what are most salient for the moral decisions we make, then one may be willing to tread upon any assumed intrinsic values of sport to accomplish results deemed preferable. In fact, presumably, athletic doping *is* justified on consequentialist grounds. The end (winning) justifies the means (doping). This book could also touch on pragmatic features of sport, such as marketing and monetization, safety issues, and maximizing participation or the audience of the sport to achieve the greatest good for the greatest number of people.

Both books would be interesting. Regardless, I wrote about virtue ethics and distance running because there is a natural kinship between athletics and virtue development.

First, character development is often described as involving a practice-based approach to acquiring the virtues. We become virtuous by doing virtuous actions, repeatedly, until they define our second nature.[19] Likewise, the idea of a 'practice' is natural to an athlete. Alongside music, athletics is a domain in which people actively think in terms of practice and set out nearly every day with the intention of getting better. Structurally, then, there is a kinship between athletics and virtue development. It is also relatively easy to incorporate character practice into athletic practice, but we do not often think in these terms. This is a missed opportunity. Furthermore, the kind of questions virtue ethics raises can enrich athletic practice. For example, thinking about specific virtues and vices can provide a means of understanding ourselves, our strengths and vulnerabilities as athletes. A vocabulary that captures our dispositions of thinking, acting, and feeling is an important complement to—if not more valuable than—words such as VO2 max, aerobic efficiency, cadence, *fartleks*,[20] and numerous other terms we learn and exercise regularly in our sport.

Virtue ethics also has a tradition of inquiry about flourishing and suffering that I have been both chastised by, and found solace in, during my time as an athlete. It has helped me to understand the difference between productive and unproductive forms of pain, and between ordinary suffering and disorder. It also taught me to inquire about suffering's impact on my existence in more global terms—considering the entirety of my life—rather than only now, in this limited time when I am still competing at a high level in the sport.

Studying virtue ethics has positioned me to inquire about what a good life consists of and to evaluate the ways athletic training might contribute to, and detract from, a good life. It has also helped me to think more critically about the ends toward which my actions are directed and the importance of refining the motivations of my actions. Virtue ethics has refined my vision for what a rich athletic life can look like.

So why virtue ethics? It has made my running a lot richer.

Why Running?

One might also wonder why I have chosen distance running, rather than other sports, or sports in general, for a project of this sort. This is another great question.

The short answer is that my commentary on gymnastics would be very bad. It would likely be as bad as my cartwheels, which are so bad that you almost need to squint while watching them in order to make them look normal. There is also no need to stay tuned for my Kantian book on football because I am neither a Kantian nor a football player. My greatest contribution to the football literature would be to ask why they are called "linebackers" instead of "line-segment-backers."

I wrote about distance running because this is the sport I know best. I have run track and cross-country for my whole life—more recently at a high level in trail running and ultramarathoning. I follow and have competed in elite and professional racing for several years. I also have a background in coaching. I coached middle and high school track and cross country and mentored collegiate distance runners, prior to and during my doctoral program. I run every day, often twice a day, so I know I can write with integrity and insight on the subject matter.

Additionally, focusing on distance running alone, rather than sports in general, permits me to address some of the idiosyncratic features of the sport in the virtue developmental process. First, distance running is a lifelong sport, rather than one that athletes regularly need to quit after school ends. This means it is a physical practice that can have a formative impact on us throughout our lives. Furthermore, at various stages throughout a person's life and however fit they happen to be, there is always an occasion for internal growth because running never becomes easier. For everyone, there are moments of feeling overwhelmed. For some people this feeling of being overwhelmed just occurs at a faster pace than it does for others. Stated differently, fitness is feeling like you are dying at a much faster pace than you used to feel like you were dying at.

Also, distance running has a competitive structure that is edifying. Runners run alongside one another, and their intention is to outdo one another, rather than undo one another. This mirrors the structure of the virtue friendships that Aristotle, C. S. Lewis, Kierkegaard, and other thinkers describe. This means we can get the best out of each other, and that is something worth talking about.

Running is also a sport that offers training in the downregulation of our heightened emotions, more than most other athletic activities. For example, sports like football and sprinting are more spirited, or *thumos*-based, sports. They are explosive and may reward impulsivity and immediate reactions in the field of play. In distance running, as in other endurance sports such as distance biking or swimming, emotional control features more centrally. The objective is to stay calm while under distress, in order to mete out our energy evenly throughout the race. In distance running, there is an expression: "Emotions can cook your food or set your kitchen on fire." Being able to downregulate arousal and rationally superintend emotions to use that energy productively is an asset as a distance runner. Being able to do so is also conducive to the development of certain virtues, since virtues consist, in part, of well-ordered emotions.

Certainly, many other sports can also have constructive impacts on our characters. I encourage someone to write those books.

Key Concepts in Virtue Ethics

In the West, Plato and Aristotle are called the founders of virtue ethics. In the East, the founders are Mencius and Confucius.[21] Naturally, when many Westerners think about virtue, they are inclined to think in terms of the Western origins of these concepts, and philosophers such as Plato, Aristotle, Aquinas, the Roman stoics, and contemporary neo-Aristotelian philosophers such as Elizabeth Anscombe, Philippa Foot, John McDowell, and Michael Slote.[22] But it is important to remember that virtue, character, and the good life are not purely Western notions. These concepts are also present in Islamic, Jewish, Buddhist, Chinese, and Hindu cultures.[23]

In this book, I focus on broadly neo-Aristotelian considerations of virtue and vice. So, in this section, I describe key concepts of Aristotle's theory.

Defining Virtue

Often when friends learn that I study the virtues, the feedback they give me is that they have no interest in the topic, for reasons similar to those that philosopher Susan Wolf gives in her memorable essay, "Moral Saints." She writes, "I don't know whether there are any moral saints. But if there are, I am glad that neither I nor those about whom I care most about are among them."[24]

Wolf defines the moral saint as "a person whose every action is as morally good as possible."[25] She describes this maximally good person as so preoccupied with being good that they would be unable to enjoy life. They would be humorless and bland, sanctimonious, and almost inhuman. They would lack all color and personal interests of their own.

Yes, this sounds like a pitiable existence. If the goal of virtue development were to become this kind of person—an austere, morally perfect floating angel—then virtue would not appeal to me either.[26] But this image is not what I intend, nor is it the picture we receive from the classical tradition.[27] I cannot become a floating angel because I have no capacity for flight. I am a human.

Virtues are excellences suited to the kind of being we are, and, in the classical tradition, they are constitutive goods of our nature.[28] They are a means of becoming higher versions of ourselves, rather than turning us into something else.[29] To be clear, this is not to say acquiring virtues won't turn our affections toward the right things, or make us less selfish, more patient, or more humble. I hope these things happen. They need to happen so that I will not get in my own way of living a full, happy life, in which I can self-govern effectively and invest well in my community. But in my case, when I say I want to become more virtuous, I mean I want to be a more excellent version of *me*—a sneaker-wearing, distance-running, philosophy-teaching human. The only time I float is in the swimming pool.

By definition, a *virtue* is a kind-specific excellence. The Greek word for virtue, *aretḗ*, means excellence. Maybe there would be less confusion if, instead of telling my friends I wanted virtues, I told them I wanted to be excellent. By 'kind-specific,' I mean that there are certain excellences suited to different things. A good cat is fluffy, for example. A good tree is not fluffy, since this quality is not relevant to what makes trees excellent. Fluff does not help a tree to fulfill its function as a tree.[30]

Aristotle identifies the virtues of a thing by asking what something's *ergon*, or function, is. This is called his *Function Argument*. For example, the function of a table is to support objects. The qualities that help it to fulfill that function (or to be a good table) include a level surface and sturdy legs. These are two of the table's virtues.

Consider a second example—a school bus. The function of a school bus is to transport students safely from home to school and back, on time. Thus, the virtues of a school bus include a strong engine and ample seating, among other things. Virtues are kind-specific because not all excellences are relevant to the good in question. It would be odd if the good qualities one sought in a pet cat, for example, included a level surface or a strong engine. These are not excellences suited to cats.

Answering the question of function becomes more challenging when it comes to people. This is because it depends on what kind of thing a human is, or what one thinks people are *for*. Are humans *for* garnering praise, acquiring material goods, looking fabulous, or accruing prestige? These are answers often supplied by popular culture, sometimes explicitly in advertisements or implicitly in terms of cultural values. And if you pay attention to sports marketing and media, you will find athlete-specific answers to this question, too.

Often what athletes are *for* is described in exclusively body-focused or performance-relevant terms—winning races or occupying a smaller body, depending on the source. These are the terms of success. There are at least two problems with these answers.

The first is that, if winning races is the *ergon*, or function, of an athlete, this restricts the set of virtues to only those qualities that make one more likely to win. This means qualities like gentleness, kindness, and justice may be excluded in the set of virtues, whereas unfavorable traits such as aggression, certain forms of intemperance, and selfishness may be included because these can help people win. These unfavorable traits—the vices or bad qualities of persons that sustain performance—may support winning but are at odds with a happy life in other ways.[31]

A second problem is that the two objectives I named—winning and shrinking—are nearsighted and, frankly, short-change the richness of a happy life. For example, if we orient ourselves exclusively, or even largely, in terms of winning, at the expense of other things in life (such as community or intellectual goods), this can lead us to feel unfulfilled. This is because winning is not a good suited to the kind of being we are. And if we lose the ability to win (or never have that ability in the first place), we feel the loss of our great purpose—something that could never actually satisfy us.

There are many other big questions to ask about human function and sport. For example, what might it look like to have running well as a lesser purpose in one's life, or a good subordinated to a higher or more complete end? Is it okay if long-term considerations of happiness are compromised in the life of a high-level or Olympic athlete? Or should having a good character always be the primary objective of sport, even if it costs us in terms of performance? I address these questions—and Aristotle's answer to the question of our greatest good (an activity he calls *eudaimonia*)—in Chapter 7.

Two Kinds of Virtues

Chances are, you can already name several virtues. If I asked you to name the traits you admire in your favorite athlete, you might start with physical characteristics—speed, strength, or agility—but you would probably list virtues, too—dedication, perseverance, or bravery. Our admiration of others is often a means by which we identify virtues, a phenomenon I describe in greater detail in Chapter 3.

Following Aristotle, there are two kinds of virtues: moral and intellectual.[32]

A *moral virtue* is a *hexis* of the soul. It is an active disposition to feel, choose, and act well, defined with respect to an emotion. For example, fortitude concerns fear. Temperance concerns the pleasure we take in food and drink. Wittiness concerns the amount of pleasure taken in a joke.

For Aristotle, moral virtues involve hitting the mean with respect to this emotion. This is called the *virtue mean*. Every virtue is a mean between two *vices*—a vice of excess and a vice of deficiency. For example, a witty person is not humorless. She takes fitting pleasure in jokes. Her pleasure is neither excessive, such that she is a buffoon (vice of excess), nor deficient, such that she is a boor (vice of deficiency).

In this way, moral virtue for Aristotle is not ascetic, in the sense of self-denial. For example, the objective of temperance is not to deny oneself the experience of pleasure altogether, in the way that many people conceive of virtue. It is just taking fitting pleasure in food and drink. This virtue frees us to direct our attention at worthier things, such as the people present at meals.

By contrast, *intellectual virtues* are excellences of thinking. Philosopher Nathan King defines them as traits that assist us in "*getting* truth, knowledge, and understanding, but also to our *keeping* and *sharing* them."[33] Examples of intellectual virtues include wisdom (an excellence of knowing what is of value) and practical wisdom (right thinking plus action). Unlike moral virtues, intellectual virtues do not, for Aristotle, have a virtue mean.[34] This is because, for example, there is no such thing as being *too* wise. There is no excess of intellectual virtue. There is only deficiency.

Both moral and intellectual virtues are *acquired* rather than natural. This means that they are not qualities we are born with. They are not a consequence of a person's biology or qualities that have been manipulated or have been developed in a person apart from the participation of his or her will. Rather, a virtue is a kind of achievement. It is a trait "possessed by someone who has cooperated in its formation."[35]

While both kinds of virtues are acquired, they develop in different ways. Aristotle writes that "intellectual virtue . . . owes both its birth and its growth to teaching (for which reason it requires experience and time), while moral virtue comes about as a result of habit, whence also its name *ethike* is one that is formed by a slight variation from the word *ethos* (habit)."[36] Intellectual virtues develop through teaching and experience. Moral virtues develop as habits do—by repeated practice.

This is one of the most helpful features of virtue ethics. There is clear guidance for how to develop a good character, and it is guidance that will especially resonate with an athlete: We develop good characters in the same way that we become better runners. We practice. Aristotle writes, "For the things we have to learn before we can do them, we learn by doing them, e.g., men become builders by building and lyre players by playing the lyre; so too we become just by doing just acts, temperate by doing temperate acts, brave by doing brave acts."[37]

Stated differently, if I would like to become more humble, courageous, witty, or better in command of my appetites, it is not enough to just recognize my deficiencies in these respects. I also need to practice virtuous habits until they define me in a stable way.

Practicing the Virtues

Throughout graduate school, I coached a middle and high school track team. Having attended graduate school in central Texas, I can tell you that youth runners down there are tough. The humidity is heavy, and there is an oppressive heat that starts in April and does not usually abate until November. The atmosphere feels like you are being hugged--like you are running while embraced by an unwelcome, unescapable hug. Texas running feels like you are preheating the oven to cook a chicken, and then you find out that the chicken is you. The foliage is prickly, sparse, and defiant. It offers little respite from the sun. But every practice, we brought our best attitudes. And, every practice, we rode a fine line between remaining humans and becoming steamed asparagus.

To avoid the afternoon sun, I often met with my team before school. There was a local track where we met twice weekly before sunrise. Certain sections of the track were lit by nearby streetlamps, while others were enshrouded in darkness. It was so dark that we could not see our hands or one another, but we ran shoulder to shoulder like a Greek phalanx, passing alternately between blackness and light, and we got our work done. We developed a confidence forged in darkness, in the invisible hours of morning.

Running involves a lot of passing in and out of darkness. Racing is visible. People gather to watch and cheer, albeit not in the droves they come to watch football. But a lot of the sport is hidden from view. Runners run in the early mornings when people are sleeping, and many of their miles are solitary. They stretch and lift on their own initiative, and if they surge during a run, rather than ease off the gas, they are the only ones who will ever know that. Running is difficult, and runners encounter that difficulty daily and bodily. It is how runners manage themselves through that difficulty that determines the sort of character they develop over time.

For three years, I also taught in the school that my runners attended. Character development was part of the curriculum there, so, for fifteen minutes each morning, we had virtue education lessons. Students memorized virtue concepts, read stories about people exemplifying these virtues, and reflected together about how to implement these virtues in their present context.

This was a valuable time in terms of the self-honesty it afforded my students. Acquiring a vocabulary of virtue and vice is like being given spectacles that help you to see yourself—*really* see yourself—blemishes, excellences, mediocrities, and all. But the work of virtue education was incomplete in the classroom. This was because, it is one thing to sit comfortably in a chair and think about perseverance as a concept. It is another thing to do the hard work of developing perseverance, in the way that my team did during our morning sessions at the darkened track. In a classroom, perseverance seems nice; it sounds like a trait one might like to have. On the track, it exhausts and sometimes overwhelms. You have to fight to develop it, and it burns your legs and lungs. Athletics is a great avenue for character education because it teaches us something important about becoming a virtuous person—the embodied reality that "practicing the virtues" is difficult.

Virtue and Knowledge

In a post-Enlightenment age, we often assume that knowledge alone is transformative. There are two senses in which this statement might be true:

(1) The first is to conceive of virtue in the way Plato's Socrates does—as a kind of knowledge. For Socrates, we never do wrong willingly because if we knew—*really* knew—what our good was, we would certainly act in terms of it.[38] On this account, there is no separation between 'what we know' and 'who we are,' so acquiring knowledge of the good would indeed be transformative.

Many philosophers do not share Plato's view of virtue. For example, Aristotle describes weakness of will—knowing what the good is and failing to do it (*akrasia*) and knowing what the good is and forcing yourself to do it, not because you want to (*enkrateia*).

An example of *akrasia* is that I know I should stretch before running. I have read a lot of articles about this. But I still can't get myself to do it. Often, I remind myself that I stretched one time about ten years ago, and—insofar as ten years ago is prior to today—I suppose I did stretch before this run. You will notice here that my reasoning faculties are intact, and I am still not practicing the good. My reason is misaligned with my desires and actions.

An example of *enkrateia* is that, often when I congratulate competitors after races who have beaten me, I do so begrudgingly rather than from a sincere delight in their performance. I act in terms of celebrating my competitors because I know it is what I ought to do, but it certainly is not easy for me. In this case, my reason is aligned with my actions, just not with my desires. I still lack virtue.

In Chapter 2, "Practicing Courage in My Sneakers," I describe the phenomenology of virtue, or what it might feel like to be a person for whom reason, desires, and actions are aligned. Virtue feels different than *akrasia* and *enkrateia*. For Aristotle, virtue is not described as the performance of arduous goods. You take pleasure in good actions, and it is natural and unforced.

(2) A second way in which it may be true to say that knowledge transforms us is to restrict this claim to only include transformative knowledge. People often speak about religious knowledge as having this quality, such that knowing a person (such as a god or God) is by itself transformative. There are other, nonreligious kinds of relational knowing that are likewise described as transformative. For example, we often speak of the significant people in our lives in this way, making claims such as "Knowing you has changed me." But it seems that when we say this, we do not mean *mere* knowing, but the kind of knowing that invites action. Relational knowledge often transforms us by inviting or provoking us to action.

In general—unless one were to conceive of virtue in the Socratic way, as *knowledge*—it seems what we *do*, rather than what we merely *know*, is what transforms us. We have to take up the knowledge bodily. In the same way that reading books about running does not increase my leg speed, increasing knowledge of virtue does not make me a better person. I have to act on the knowledge I gain.

Consider the study by American philosopher Eric Schwitzgebel. In 2007, he examined the moral lives of professional ethicists—those (like me) who specialize in teaching and researching moral philosophy. For every measure he included—voting in public elections, calling their moms, eating meat, donating to charity, responding to student emails, and so forth—Schwitzgebel found that there was no significant difference between how the ethicists behaved and how the general population did. However, the ethicists held stronger moral norms. They had a clearer sense of right and wrong for each action.[39] Schwitzgebel refers to this phenomenon as the "cheeseburger ethicist"—the kind of person convinced that eating meat is wrong, while also continuing to eat meat.

You may have assumed that ethicists, of all people, would be morally good. After all, they have chosen a life dedicated to pursuing questions of goodness. They own, and even write, books about ethics. They are exposed to the best arguments about morality and are trained to reason well about good, bad, right, and wrong. Indeed, this mature knowledge is reflected in the fact that they possess stronger moral norms. However, there is a sizeable (Texas-sized) gap between knowing and acting, as evinced by the fact that the ethicists behaved no differently from anyone else.

So, yes, perhaps knowledge can be valuable in positioning a person to act well, but it is not sufficient for acting well. We also need to act in light of that knowledge. An example is knowing that I am lazy or that I have biases against certain people. Knowing these things is a valuable form of self-honesty. But I also need to reckon with these things, or act on this knowledge, if I would like to change my character.

What is special about athletics is that it takes seriously our embodiment and the fact that we are formed by physical practices. It also provides structure, difficulty, and quiet opportunities—like my team had on dark mornings at the track—to be edified in one another's company. In sports, you do grow in *knowledge*. You learn about your strengths and weaknesses. But you do not *merely* know these things; you address them every day in practice.

To that end, this is not just a book intended to increase your knowledge about virtue and vice; I hope you act on it, and that it enriches the way you practice your sport.

Two Clarifications

Embrace the gawky phase. Acquiring virtue can initially be an awkward process. Consider this: In elementary school, I signed up to play the violin in my school's orchestra. While my parents were gracious with me through the process of learning how to play, there was a *very* short period (about ten years), when listening to me practice was not a delightful, melodious experience. Eventually, I became marginally better, but there was that *very* short decade of time when I was not good, which we had to get through for me to become passably competent.

One of the first things I tell my athletes about developing virtues is that getting started—while theoretically simple (To get started, you just get started)—is awkward. It is like learning how to play the violin, or acquiring skills in other domains.[40] In the beginning, you feel uncoordinated as you stumble through performing virtuous actions. But over time, you develop a kind of mastery. It becomes more natural and enjoyable for everyone involved. This is because, in acquiring a virtue, you act in terms of a trait you do not yet possess. Again, Aristotle writes, "For the things we have to learn before we can do them, we learn by doing them, e.g., men become builders by building and lyre players by playing the lyre; so too we become just by doing just acts."[41]

A similar idea is expressed by Canadian author (and distance running enthusiast) Malcolm Gladwell. In his 2008 book, *Outliers*, Gladwell describes a 10,000-hour rule, drawing on the work of psychologist K. Anders Ericsson.[42] He writes that you can become world class at just about anything if you put in 10,000 hours of deliberate practice.[43] This is equal to about 5.5 hours per day for five years, or 2.75 hours per day for a decade.[44]

Gladwell's claim in *Outliers* is overstated. (Ericsson notes that his study only examined the lifetime practice of *experts*, not the general population. It does not follow that *anyone* can become an expert upon practicing a craft for 10,000 hours.[45]) But the more modest claim—that 10,000 hours of deliberate practice is required for the experts of various domains to become experts—is still astounding. That is a long time to perfect a craft, and it is a long time to be *not* great and possibly awkward. If moral development is anything like acquiring mastery, we should expect a long process. We should embrace the gawkiness of it all.

We often forget to talk about this—the awkwardness of building good habits of thinking, feeling, and acting. But insofar as we are habitual beings who likely already have habits in place when we try to develop new ones, the process of dishabituating bad habits and replacing them with new ones can feel uncomfortable.

Surely, this idea resonates with a runner. Oftentimes, the process of training is best explained as acting like the athlete you want to be until it ceases to be acting. You lift weights that are a bit heavier than you did last season. You run efforts that press you slightly further than are comfortable now. Training is the process of *leaning* in the direction of the athlete you would like to be tomorrow. This way, you take steps to close the gap between the athlete you currently are and the good athlete you would like to become.[46]

As a coach, I tell my athletes this because I do not want them to become discouraged the first time they attempt to be patient in a race and execute their patience poorly, or try to be a more supportive teammate and bumble through their encouragements. I tell them to embrace the gawky virtue stage and proceed with their practice, knowing that acting in terms of the virtues will not always feel awkward, and it will be worth it long term.

Practice is not merely external. A second clarification about virtue practice is that it involves actions, but not only our actions. In practicing virtue, we also need to develop the appropriate motivations for our good behavior.

A common intuition of virtue is that not all virtue-tracking actions are virtuous if done for the wrong reasons. For example, imagine a wealthy donor who gives a large sum of money to a children's library. If we subsequently discover that he did so because of raging narcissism, rather than from a genuine concern for children's literacy, we might cease to think he is generous. Or, imagine an outstanding runner who just performed the greatest display of determination you have ever observed in track and field. If the athlete later reveals that he dug deep in order to garner more "likes" on social media, this vainglorious motivation undercuts the admirability of the action. This is because part of what is admirable in a virtuous action is the internal state that generates the action—the motivation.

Why this matters in sport is that, in practicing good traits—such as perseverance or courage—we should make sure that we self-examine regarding what drives us. Otherwise, we develop ourselves into a Potemkin village of sorts—a façade, or something that looks good on the outside but is rotten on the inside. We might act in virtue-tracking ways but do so for unvirtuous reasons.

Again, I do not think this is an unfamiliar idea for runners. Runners often discuss "knowing their why." It means making sure that the motivations sustaining your training and racing are good, solid ones. In Chapter 2, I describe virtue-conducive motivations in greater detail.

The Remainder of the Book

In elementary school, my pride ran-eth me into a shed. Since then, I have continued to be formed, in good and bad ways, by my daily practice of running. This chapter offered a brief introduction to Aristotelian-informed virtue to provide a framework for the discussions that follow. It also defended the value of placing these ideas in conversation with distance running. Over the remainder of the book, I probe these ideas in greater depth. The chapters proceed as follows.

Chapter 2

Distance running is a laboratory for virtue. This chapter explores the specifics of virtue development in the context of sport. It includes a helpful metaphor from Aristotle. We are warped boards, which need to be pulled in the direction that opposes our natural warp to progress toward virtue. I talk about what this means for hill repeats and character development.

Chapter 3

Comparison is *not* the "thief of joy."[47] In this chapter, we examine emotions relevant to competition and teamwork. These include envy, admiration, gratitude, and awe. We also explore what emotions are and their relevance to both virtue and running.

Chapter 4

Exemplars are role models who demonstrate what a good character looks like. In this chapter, we examine four kinds of exemplars. We explore the process of becoming like the people we admire and discuss the ways admiration might go awry, such as in the case of a bad coach.

Chapter 5

Certain virtues are not only constitutive features of a good life but also performance-enhancing. They can help us run faster. In this chapter, we explore five performance-enhancing virtues—joy, resilience, patience, perseverance, and humor.

Chapter 6

Performance-enhancing vices are defects of character that assist us to be better performers in running. These vices result from a misalignment between a good life and a good run, and they are a difficult set of vices to root out because of their constructive impact on performance. To commit to having a good character can have a performance cost. This puts athletes and coaches in an odd position. In this chapter we examine four—selfishness, intransigence, pride, and envy. We investigate whether high-level athletes should be excused from virtue in these respects.

Chapter 7

There are three dominant models of happiness, two of which are faulty. In this chapter, I explore all three and their limitations, and I commit to the *eudaimonic* account, which is Aristotle's view. This chapter raises the question "What are people for?" It investigates the ways athletics might contribute to, or undermine, a good life.

Chapter 8

Maybe the "limitless" rhetoric we often employ in sport is misguided. This chapter places limitlessness in conversation with considerations of nature and community. It examines Faustian bargains with our health and the dangers of overstepping our natural limits in sport. It also critiques how suffering is often regarded in distance running, such as with the lionizing of physical damages that follows from phrases like "No pain, no gain" and "Pain is weakness leaving the body."

So are you ready? Runners, take your mark. Get set. Let's go.

2

Practicing Courage in My Sneakers

Virtue and Development

"Girl, I like your boot," announced a woman wearing a neck brace. She sat down next to me and gestured toward my stress fracture boot.

"Thank you. Nothing else goes with this outfit," I told her. "I like your necklace."

I was sitting in the physical therapist's office, and an elderly woman in a neck brace befriended me. Sure, we were strangers, but we were *injured* strangers, and this offered a unique kind of camaraderie. The woman and I were also comrades in repair. Realizing we could not fix ourselves, we reached out to a physical therapist to guide us through the arduous process of rebuilding our bodies. We were resilient. We were broken ladies intending to be whole again. There are events that only strike you in retrospect as defining moments in your life. For me, this was one of those moments. This was my athletic nadir—waiting in the physical therapist's office, broken, with a foot pain that radiated up my leg, humiliated to know that I was responsible for putting myself in that situation, and bonding with a stranger. But, in that office, I made a commitment to return to form. This was a commitment that would ask a lot of me physically, in terms of retraining muscles, regaining strength, and dishabituating unproductive movement patterns. It would ask a lot of me in terms of my character, too, as a relatively independent person who, historically, has not enjoyed asking for help. Becoming an athlete again would not be a purely physical process. It couldn't be.

In fact, it makes sense to speak of physicality and character as separable, in the same manner that we speak of convex and concave as distinct to highlight different things.[1] Still, in practice, we know that convexity and concavity are inseparable, as flip sides of the same curve. Likewise, when I speak of physical development, this is rhetorically clarifying, as I raise certain questions and highlight different issues than I would if I spoke about character development. However, my physical development is not, in practice, separable from forming virtue or vice. And when I change my character, this informs how my physical body moves through the world. In rebuilding myself as an athlete—a painstaking process of physical drudgery, occasional fun, and difficult habit formation—both my body and my character would be transformed.

In this chapter, I consider distance running as a laboratory for virtue. (1) I first defend why we should care about virtue development. (2) Then I provide a developmental assessment of two sorts—evaluating how we acquire virtues and how we grow in agency, such that we can choose well and self-govern effectively, in the context of sport. (3) Finally, I address several critiques of employing athletics in this way, including a concern with character asymmetry, and the limitations of using sport toward the end of character education.

The Case for Character

My return from injury to competition was onerous. It was full of nontrivial (but seemingly inconsequential[2]) tiny exercises alongside my friend in the neck brace, and the time post-fracture was characterized by a long stretch of mediocrity with little visible progress. It was a difficult time for me—a slow, intentional process of development—but when I eventually returned to high-level competition, I was grateful for all of it. I had grown physically, developing greater core stability and ancillary muscle support through my recovery, which would serve me in my attempts to run hard across difficult terrain. I had also matured in my character.

My setback and recommitment to training made me more resilient—better able to rebound from hard moments. It made me more perseverant—better able to stay in place through difficulty without feeling like I needed to (or wanted to) flit off to do something else. It also made me more grateful for the opportunity to compete. These were dispositions reinforced through training that supported my objectives in the mountains.

When faced with the question of why we should care about our moral characters, the simple answer is that doing so is a practical necessity. We are not cicada shells. We are living, breathing, thinking, feeling beings moving through the world. As I described earlier, my physical development, while theoretically distinguishable from my character development, is not separable in practice from the formation of virtue and vice. What I do informs who I am, and who I am informs what I do. So when I tie my shoelaces and set off to ascend a series of mountains, it is not just my physical body that participates. My character informs whether and how I do so.

This has a performance bearing, of course—that my patterns of thinking, feeling, and acting are inseparable from my athleticism. But my character also informs who I am when I am home, among family members and neighbors. It informs how I act as a citizen, how well I steward the natural environment, and whether I position myself to live a rich, long life outside of sport, oriented toward good ends. These are not insubstantial considerations. This is why character matters.

Why Care about Character in Sport Specifically?

Some might concede that character matters in general but argue that part of what we enjoy about athletics is vice. Pride, vainglory, and selfishness make sports riveting. We love bravado and backbiting among players. Rudeness appalls us, and we cannot look away. Impulsivity makes headlines. Since athletics is about entertainment, as much as it is about physical practice, we should permit vice or, at the very least, not extinguish its presence in high-level sport. A concern with character would detract from what we love about sport.

I have three responses to this argument. First, most practitioners of sport are not marketing agents but amateurs. Generally, the entertainment we offer is to a handful of spectators who show up to support local 5-kilometer races, most of whom attend because of familial obligations or . . . free bananas. I am not actually sure why people attend local 5-kilometer races. Thus, in amateur sport, the idea that vice is more entertaining for fans is of little relevance. A more salient consideration is how the sport shapes our characters in ways that are constructive for, or detract from, the rest of our lives.

Second, the claim that vices are the only traits that make sport entertaining is dubious at best, especially in distance running. Consider the following. At the New York City Marathon in 2022, the victors were Kenyan runners, Sharon Lokedi, perhaps best known for her 10-kilometer National Collegiate Athletic Association (NCAA) Division I title while competing for the Kansas University Jayhawks, and Evans Chebet, who also won the Boston Marathon earlier in 2022. After the race, World Athletics tweeted the following:

> Sharon Lokedi displayed remarkable discipline to win the @ nycmarathon on her debut at the distance, while Evans Chebet's patience paid off to win the men's contest in the Big Apple.[3]

Their victories were attributed to discipline and patience, respectively. Of course, these traits are not complete explanations for why Lokedi and Chebet performed well. Training systems, genetics, shoe technology, and a confluence of other factors also contributed.

But certainly, these virtues are salient for how one performs. On balance, the patient athlete is likely to perform better than the impatient one. She will be able to accelerate when it is the appropriate time to do so, not because she lacks the internal resolve to wait.

There are many virtues like this—perseverance, courage, grit, and prudence—that facilitate good performance in the athletic arena. Insofar as these virtues raise the level of performance, they make the sport more entertaining. So vices are not the only traits that add entertainment value to athletics. Virtues do, too.

But given the possibility that there are *some* vices, such as pride and envy, that make sport entertaining, the idea that allowances should be made for these vices in the highest levels of the sport is problematic for at least four reasons.

1. Whether or not they intend to be, professional athletes are often exemplars,[4] or role models, for others. If they exhibit vices of pride, vainglory, or otherwise, they set a standard of action that others are likely to emulate. Therefore, professional athletes' actions, however entertaining, have social repercussions beyond sport.

2. As I described in the case for virtue formation in general, virtues are constitutive features of a good life. Insofar as athletes do not have them, this positions them poorly to flourish, perhaps in the moment and certainly in the long term. Moreover, insofar as athletes do not exist in a vacuum, the happiness of their communities is compromised by their vices as well.

For example, we may be inclined to delight in an athlete's pride and outsized confidence on the field, but there is a secret we harbor privately, which is that godlike pretensions and inordinate self-importance are not good-making features of people in general. When we leave the arena, these are qualities we hope not to discover in a child, a neighbor, or a friend. Moreover, the athlete, however admired and ascendant in the field of play, *is* someone's child, neighbor, and friend and, on balance, his hubris may detract from his ability to lead a happy life. His pride may make him vulnerable to pressing his physical limits in ways that are costly for his wellness in the long term. He may decide to play while injured rather than relinquish his playing time to a teammate, and he may attempt reckless maneuvers in the arena because his pride makes the dictates of practical reason harder to hear. Off the field or court, the athlete's pride might also imperil his relationships and condition him to respond to correction in anger. Pride can make him less teachable. So, in the same way that we ought not wish injury on an athlete out of human decency, we should not wish vice on him either.

Of course, in situations in which an athlete's bad character imperils his own happiness, other people are likely to be impacted as well. For example, there is empirical support for there being a higher incidence of domestic violence among players of certain sports than others. Reporter Lindsay Giovannone notes, "Intimate partner violence accounts for 15% of all violent crimes in the United States. For NFL players, domestic violence is the highest criminal charge at 55% of total arrests made."[5] This is a nontrivial difference and certainly supports the idea that we ought to take the character impacts of sport seriously, for the sake of public safety. Other sports have reported similar abuse trends to the NFL, such that Major League Baseball and the NBA now have policies in place regarding how to address occurrences of domestic, sexual, and child abuse. They have counseling and other services available for their athletes as well.[6]

It can be difficult to ascertain whether these findings are correlational. For example, it seems likely that those who are naturally more aggressive tend to participate in higher levels in contact sports than those with more amiable dispositions. Anecdotally, meek children seem less likely to register enthusiastically for football because the sport runs against the grain of their natural dispositions. But it also seems likely that having a daily practice in acting on aggression—in a sport that not only tolerates but rewards impulsivity, physical forcefulness, and hostility—might reinforce these dispositions.

There is evidence that this may be the case. In the past, a folk assumption was that acting on anger and aggression was a means of catharsis to avoid emotional outbursts elsewhere. Just let kids hit each other so they get it out of their system! Viewed in light of this assumption, contact sports could be understood as a productive outlet for misplaced emotions. Now there is empirical support for the opposing position—that acting on aggression breeds, rather than diffuses, future aggression.[7] It reinforces these dispositions. If this is true, then we should worry about how daily practice in aggression increases these tendencies and subsequently impacts life outside of the athletic arena.

The focus of this book is distance running. Hostility and aggression—while by no means absent in this sport—are less broadly characteristic of participants. Even so, there are plenty of vices commonly reinforced in distance running, such as envy and certain forms of intemperance. These vices may aid our performances but have negative personal and community repercussions as well. I discuss these issues in Chapter 6—"Bad Competition: Performance-Enhancing Vices."

3. Sports require a certain amount of integrity among participants to sustain the competition itself. Without this integrity, the audience loses confidence in the game, and the terms of success in the competition are subverted.

For example, consider the vice of dishonesty. Any time an athlete tests positive for performance-enhancing drugs, this erodes the confidence the public has in the sport. People begin to assert that likely all high-level athletes are doping. These claims make it difficult to appreciate the efforts of clean athletes or to take anything at face value, and the sport seems less aspirational and inspiring. Of course, the athletes *seem* superhuman. Their performances artificially exceed what is humanly possible. Since sports, at their core, are about nature rather than artifice—or about what we can make our human bodies do, rather than about what we can accomplish through contrivance or technology—performance-enhancing drugs damage the spirit of the activity. And while it may be interesting for some to watch a bunch of presumed-to-be enhanced athletes perform technology-assisted actions, this ceases to be sport.[8]

In situations when the players of a game lack integrity, the game itself is denatured by violating the terms of success. So, at the very least, we should say that certain virtues, such as honesty, are needed to sustain the integrity of the activity. In the same way that many vices erode community and society, many vices also erode sports.

4. Many virtues are performance- enhancing.

In Chapter 5, I argue that certain virtues—such as joy, resilience, patience, perseverance, and humor—are good-making features of a flourishing life, which also have performance benefits commensurate to, or greater than, the performance enhancement offered by other tools, like carbon-plated racing flats or well-timed beet juice. Our moral characters are important for how we perform.

This is perhaps a less noble reason to support virtue development than caring about the quality of lives of athletes or the integrity of the sport. Still, if what we are concerned about is performance, this is a reason to invest our attention in considerations of character.

Developing Character

Growing in Freedom

I am standing on the start line of a race. It is my second year at the event, and it is pouring rain. Many of my competitors and I are dressed in trash bags—the big black ones, with holes cut out for our arms and heads. We are dressed this way, not for style reasons but because, while it is cold, it is not cold enough to run in raincoats.

Trash bags are light and fast, and we can crumple them up and stash them in our pockets if the rain stops. Plus, trash bags are one-size-fits-all and effective at keeping a runner dry, legs and all. So we runners stand there in our trash bags, lined up, side by side, like it is trash pickup day in the suburbs, waiting for the starting gun.

The gun sounds, followed by a sustained, massive swish of our trash bags as we advance off the line together and into the darkness. The race is on.

The start line is where I rehearse my goals before the race. It is where I stand with poise and elegance in my trash bag and remind myself about my intentions. For this race, I have three goals:

- a time goal (under fifteen hours for 100 miles),
- a virtue goal (run with greater courage than I have in the past), and
- a completion goal (to the extent that it is within my control to do so, I will finish the race).

Knowing the difficulty of the task before me, the most important goal is always the third one—completion. There is dignity in completion. And finishing is not something that can ever be taken for granted over the course of a 100-mile run. Reasons to quit always present themselves throughout the day, and these reasons grow, if not more *logically* compelling, certainly louder when we are tired.

Being able to resist these reasons and finish the race is important for the sake of my integrity as an athlete. It also offers practice in being the kind of person I want to be outside of sport—someone who holds fast to the commitments in my life that really matter, even when doing so is challenging. This capacity, to act in terms of one's commitments, is a big part of what it means to be a free person and a foundational consideration in the development of a good character.[9]

Free Will

Earlier, I said I would provide a developmental assessment of two sorts—both evaluating growth in agency and how we acquire specific virtues in the context of sport.

By growth in *agency*, I mean the capacity to reason clearly and choose well for oneself. In part, this capacity depends on someone's ability to make decisions without being misdirected by their own ill-fitting or heightened emotions.[10] The ability to downregulate heightened emotions is an asset in distance running. For example, impulsivity and rage are likely to impede performance in a sport that benefits from an even temperament and the ability to keep rogue emotions in check. If a runner leans too far into passing emotions—happy, sad, scared, or anxious—these emotions can be an energy cost when energy demands are already high.

Having practice in downregulating emotions—such as pausing before acting impulsively, modulating responses when excited or angry, and exercising self-control when emotions are heightened—can be an asset for character outside of sport, too. For example, driving in heavy traffic, shopping before the holidays, and talking about politics at the holiday dinner table are situations in which emotions are often high. The ability to think clearly and act well in these situations can save a person from speaking or acting in ways they later regret.

There are sports that seem to reinforce impulsivity and emotional excess—such as contact sports in which athletes are rewarded for spiritedness and explosive moves—but distance running is not among them. Running provides the space to practice emotional control, since we need to mete out our efforts evenly over a great distance. To quote reigning Olympic 1500-meter champion Jakob Ingebrigtsen, "Feelings are not going to make you run fast. If you feel too much, then it's just an obstacle."[11]

By growth in agency, I also mean the development of freedom with respect to ourselves, or the ability to self-govern effectively. We may be inclined to assume freedom is merely something granted, rather than acquired. Some freedoms—as in, allowances to do one thing, rather than another—are granted, but our ability to navigate choices well (or to exercise free choice[12]) is developed. Thankfully, distance running provides the occasion to practice freedom of this sort.

Internal and External Impediments

In popular discourse, "free" is often regarded as synonymous with unimpeded or uncoerced. This language concerns *external impediments* to freedom—the things that stand in the way of doing what we want. For example, if a friend asks whether you are "free" to run on the weekend, but you have a big work deadline approaching, you may need to answer no. There is a barrier to your free action.

Often, external impediments are put in place for our benefit. For instance, if you would like ice cream for dinner as a child and your parents say no, they stand in the way, as an external impediment, to your free action. But they impede you, not for the sake of limiting freedom itself, but for your good, since, as children, we are often unable to see what our good is for ourselves. When there are traffic restrictions, such as a speed limit, this restricts our freedom to drive whatever pace we would like, to keep us safe. And when coaches limit training volume during the offseason, they restrict our choosing, but they do so to promote rest, to protect our in-season objectives. In these situations, our choices are limited, but not for the sake of restricting freedom *simpliciter*, but to position us for goods perceived as better or higher, over the long term.

In contemporary political discourse, the removal of external impediments is often how we frame discussions about freedom. Civil liberties—like freedom of religion and the right to privacy— are examples of freedoms from external constraints. Another example is having the right to peacefully assemble. There are no legal barriers to doing so.

However, there is a second kind of constraint on free action, which is often neglected in our current conversations about freedom. These are *internal impediments*. Internal impediments are features of ourselves that constrain free action. They restrict our ability to self-govern effectively.

Examples of internal constraints on free action for runners can include runaway and outsized emotions. They can include vices, such as laziness, intemperance, distractibility, and irresolution. These are defects of character that prevent us from becoming what we ought to become, or from achieving what we aim to achieve. They also prevent us from seeing our commitments through to completion.

If I am free from external impediments, then this means that nothing outside of myself constrains my actions. But if I am free from internal impediments, this means I won't get in my own way.

I can choose well and remain in my commitments without succumbing to fickle emotions, impulses, or roving appetites, wherever they lead me. I can start a paper and finish it, without being distracted or turned aside by other things. I can commit to a career goal and put in the work that it takes to achieve it. I can sign up for a race and then discipline myself well enough in the process of training such that I am well-prepared to finish it. I can start a mountain race and see it through to completion.

Puzzles of Freedom
In the history of philosophy, there is a long-standing puzzle about the development of freedom referred to as the Paradox of Moral Education. The paradox is that moral education involves the external imposition of desires, attitudes, and actions in a learner, which undermines attempts to develop her own powers of critical reflection. Stated differently, we might wonder how a person becomes free—or able to choose well for herself—if forming one's

freedom occurs by being acted upon. Freedom is formed through a process that seems decidedly *un*free. This is a worry because we are held accountable for our moral characters. As stated in Chapter 1, virtues are considered a kind of achievement, or *up to us*, to a considerable extent.

Earlier, I described how external impediments to our freedom are often put in place for the sake of our own good, or for our perceived good. One such good is our long-term character development. A parent restricts a child's access to ice cream at dinner because the child cannot recognize her own good (presumably health and longevity), and she does not yet love the right things (presumably what is being served for dinner). Now imagine the same family years from now, such that the child has grown into a forty-five-year-old adult. It would be odd if the parent were still limiting this person's access to desserts. Usually, adults—as mature thinkers with reasonably well-ordered desires—can choose well for themselves.

Plainly, the objective of parenting is not to remain permanently between a child's desires and the objects of these desires, intervening to redirect her choices. The objective is to show a child what is good and choice-worthy such that she can choose well for herself. Thus, the puzzle for moral educators is how we actively form a learner's freedom to move them from Point (A)—the external imposition of desires and limitations on a child—to Point (B)—where the child can self-govern effectively and make good choices for herself.

As a general puzzle of character education, I do not undertake to resolve the Paradox of Character Education, other than to recommend—as others have also recommended—that a learner's agency needs to be actively matured. Learners need to be invited to participate in the development of their own freedom as they grow, step by step, by making more of their own choices. But as a paradox specific to distance running, it seems clear how to move an athlete from Point (A)—the external imposition of rules and instructions—to Point (B)—self-governance. Developing freedom is a natural progression that occurs within one's training, in part guided by a coach.

As we mature in the sport, we build a broader foundation of endurance, but this is not merely (or even primarily) an external development. It involves an internal practice in learning how to manage oneself well. We develop the ability to commit to good ends, to remain with difficult tasks, and to persevere through loud or misplaced emotions. To improve in the sport also demands we learn how to self-govern well outside of running itself—making better sleep and nutrition choices, managing schoolwork responsibilities prudently to be able to attend practice, and learning how to perform ancillary work, such as stretching and lifting. To not do these things—that is, to fail to grow in self-governance—is to impede our own progress. A sincere commitment to performance requires growth in freedom.

Early on in this process, coaches more or less direct these activities, such as by imposing disciplines and cultivating an athlete's affections for certain activities. Then as athletes mature, they take greater ownership for the process of training. (In my case, a physical therapist imposed certain restrictions and disciplines on me, which I took increasing initiative for over time.) As they grow, athletes learn how to read their own bodies and are equipped to think critically about training principles. They hold themselves personally accountable for good and bad decisions.

As athletes grow in the sport, the relationship between coach and athlete becomes less vertical (or hierarchical) and more horizontal (a relationship between relative equals). The athlete continues to answer to the coach and profits from the guidance the coach offers but is positioned to make decisions for herself. These decisions may even oppose what the coach recommends, as the athlete learns how to read her body for herself. This is natural, and it follows the same logic of good parenting. In the same way that a forty-five-year-old is not ordered about like a child, but is afforded the space to choose for herself, a mature athlete grows into the freedom to navigate decisions on her own.

A note of caution here: a good coach–athlete relationship is never one that should involve uncritical obedience or blind dependency, at any stage of coaching. There should always be checks in place to protect vulnerable athletes from misuses of power and from other questionable actions, such as recommendations of doping, on the part of the coach.[13] But this relationship is also one that should grow in autonomy as the athlete matures, rather than encouraging an odd, protracted adolescence that is asymmetrical to the maturation occurring in other areas of life.

Surely, there are variations in the personalities and needs of particular athletes and coaches. For example, some athletes desire less insight about the technical aspects of training than others do. But, as a general rule, coaching should be hospitable to an athlete's growth. It should invite the athlete to understand her training and racing and should involve (for lack of a better description) the planned obsolescence of the coach.

Ultimately, distance running provides ample opportunities to grow in freedom. This growth, however paradoxical, seems less a practical puzzle in distance running and more an inevitable progression for the committed athlete.

Exercising Free Will

On Mondays in high school, my track team used to run 400-meter repeats after school. We did a lot of repetitions with minimal recovery, increasing the number of repetitions as the season progressed, and the workout hurt. As an underclassman, I would spend every Monday morning fretting about this workout, fearing the difficulty ahead, and not wanting to be so uncomfortable. Then, when I arrived at the track, I would inevitably pace things poorly. I would complete the first set of 400s too quickly, rendering myself incapable of hitting the paces in the second half of the workout.

In short, I did not self-govern well. I lacked restraint in my pacing and did not respect my limits.[14] I allowed my nerves to drive me, rather than self-governing appropriately. These deficits impeded my performance. Over time, I grew better at managing my effort and my nerves. I realized that if I could hit the prescribed paces—forcing myself to run easier at the beginning when I felt good—then I could accomplish the entire workout as written. I also realized that there is a difference between *feeling bad* and *feeling bad for myself*, and I am the only one who gets to decide how I respond to a hard workout.

Running is instructive because it is demanding. It asks a lot of us. Accordingly, we have to turn inward and take stock of certain defects of our character—like imprudence, impatience, and the inability to self-govern—since these are internal impediments to our performing well. They prevent us from being free to choose certain ends, such as successfully completing workouts. In running, we learn to show up when we do not feel like doing so and try our best anyway. We learn to see our commitments through to completion. This is a crucial part of our education in freedom because maybe no one is making you do anything, but can you make yourself do something? If not, you are not a free person.

In Plato's *Laws*, the Athenian Stranger describes this type of training in self-governance as necessary. He warns that, otherwise, we will not be able to "stand firm" and will be "enslaved" by our own desires and pleasures.[15]

And if you do not believe me (or Plato), take it from Eliud Kipchoge, the world-record holder in the marathon. He was recently quoted as saying this: "Only the disciplined ones in life are free. If you are undisciplined, you are a slave to your moods and your passions."[16]

Virtue Development

What would it look like to use distance running as a laboratory for virtue development? How can we use training to become more patient, prudent, and all-around excellent people?

In Chapter 1, we defined virtues as *acquired* excellences of our person. To call them acquired means they are a kind of achievement. They are not a consequence of a person's biology or qualities that have been manipulated or developed in a person apart from the participation of his or her will. They are traits "possessed by someone who has cooperated in [their] formation."[17]

We described two kinds of virtues—intellectual virtues, or excellences of reason motivated by securing and retaining intellectual goods; and moral virtues, or excellent dispositions of thinking, feeling, and acting. Intellectual virtues are acquired through teaching and experience, whereas moral virtues come about as a result of repetition, "whence also its name *ethike* is one that is formed by a slight variation from the word *ethos* (habit)."[18] Moral virtues develop as habits do, by repeated practice.

In distance running, there are relevant intellectual virtues. One is *sophia*, or wisdom. Wisdom helps us to align ourselves with worthy ends and to recognize what is of value. For example, we may be inclined to register for a big race that will require a lot of energy, preparation, and attention. Maybe this is a good investment. But if the investment comes at the cost of spending time with a friend in need, or with one's children or spouse during an important season of life, it may not be what we ought to do. A wise runner can navigate competing responsibilities and identify what is of value.

Moreover, all moral virtues have a dependence relationship on the intellectual virtue of *phronesis*, or practical wisdom.

Practical Wisdom
In early high school, I had dubious race tactics. For cross-country meets, I would sprint off the start line and run as fast as I possibly could for the first mile. Then I would hang on and try to neither lose the race nor die for the final 2.1 miles. Brilliant.

I ran this way because I felt uneasy waiting in the pack, biding my time for a late-race duel. I was afraid to wait. I wanted to decide the results of my races immediately—to effectively put away the competition as soon as I could so that I could breathe again, having secured the victory whenever doing so was feasible. But this was not a great way to mete out my efforts, and my strategy was costly, both in terms of race times and my enjoyment of the experience. It took me a couple of years of high school before I learned how to compete at a level commensurate with my fitness. To compete well, I needed to grow in courage and in practical wisdom.[19]

Practical wisdom is the excellence of acting well in various circumstances.[20] In my case, its absence resulted in poor tactics and an inability to act for my own good in racing situations. A second example of its importance is that a distance runner may benefit from developing the moral virtue of patience, but what patience requires in a fast-paced race, versus in a sit-and-kick race, versus in the offseason far removed from racing, will look different. To be virtuously patient requires that we can act well in terms of the virtue across these different situations. This demands practical wisdom. All moral virtues depend on practical wisdom.

So, if practical wisdom is so important—for running and otherwise—how can we secure it? (And why don't they sell it at my local running store?)

The good news is that practical wisdom is free. We can all acquire it. The bad news is that it can take a while to develop. According to Aristotle, we grow in practical wisdom through teaching and experience.[21] In distance running, this can mean the following.

The first way we grow in practical wisdom is by running more. There is a steep learning curve in distance running. Upon entering the sport, athletes learn how to structure training and to manage body work, such as active stretching and weightlifting. They learn what certain efforts (recovery runs versus tempo efforts versus interval training) should feel like. They learn how to eat well, rest, and recover. Runners also learn how to compete well—something I clearly lacked in early high school. Often savvy racers win over those who have better fitness because experience matters in helping runners to *see* the race, to understand when surges are happening, and to know when to respond.

The second way runners can develop practical wisdom is through teaching. This can be through active research and reading about performance tactics. This can also look like associating with, and learning from, more experienced athletes. Training with veteran athletes can help a novice to acquire practical insights about training and racing without needing to proceed through a protracted process of trial and error across many seasons. The better an athlete knows the sport, the better she will be positioned to make good choices with respect to different moral virtues—to act virtuously patient, courageous, and perseverant in the athletic context.

Developing Moral Virtues

Prior to and during my time in graduate school, I taught and coached distance running at a small school in Texas. It was a school that considered character education a curricular priority—a priority that extended beyond classroom instruction and into the athletic department. The school also provided opportunities for students to serve the city as a community, and the older students sometimes mentored younger students, too.

At the same time, I was steeped in the history of philosophy in graduate school, studying the classical tradition, and acquiring a vocabulary of virtue, vice, suffering, flourishing, exemplarism, and considerations about limits and the boundaries of nature. Learning these things enriched my running, as they helped me to understand myself as an athlete. Learning these things also chastised me in certain ways.

They helped me ask good questions about my training—about whether pain is an unqualified good (it's not) and about whether the "limitless" rhetoric in sports is sometimes unwarranted (it is).[22] I was prompted to reconsider how well I was stewarding my body in ultrarunning (likely not well), whether having a good character was a sincere objective in my own participation in sport (less sincere than I would have imagined), and how well my preoccupation with running supported my theoretical commitments to serve the community and to be fully present with others (it detracted from these commitments, without qualification). Being presented with the opportunity to teach and coach with the goal of character education in mind, while I personally wrestled with questions of what it meant to be an athlete of good character in classrooms, during physical therapy sessions, and while ascending mountain passes, was a tremendous gift. It was also a riddle and a challenge as a coach.

In-Class Learning

In the classroom, my students received character education lessons. There was a fifteen-minute block each day when we discussed a virtue (or vice[23]) in focus. We talked through definitions, read stories of people who exemplified these traits, reflected on how to act in terms of a virtue in their own personal contexts, and sometimes read newspaper articles looking for instances of virtue and vice. The discussions my students had were often rich, and it was a valuable time together. It also provided our community with a shared vocabulary for discussing community values and expectations.

In the same way that studying a discipline such as environmental science can help a person to better navigate the natural environment, being equipped with a vocabulary of virtue and vice can help us to better navigate community—ourselves, friends, authority figures, heroes, and cultural norms. Learning these concepts helped my students to better see themselves—their excellences, their deficiencies, and their agency with respect to developing these traits.

However, the objective of character education is not to learn about virtues in a detached way, or to hold them at arm's length, but to grow in good character. This is why the school emphasized virtuous practice, too, and incorporated virtue education into athletics.

In-Practice Learning

As we explored in Chapter 1, acquiring knowledge about virtues is not a sufficient condition for developing them. In fact, it may not be a necessary condition either. For example, we may know an admirable athlete—someone who consistently performs with honesty and integrity and is gracious toward competitors. This athlete may be unable to define honesty. However, insofar as she acts honestly, consistently, and from fitting motivations across situations, many would be inclined to call her honest. Her inability to provide a definition almost seems beside the point.

Some philosophers argue that being taught explicitly about virtue and vice can facilitate virtue acquisition.[24] I have made this kind of claim here. In acquiring a moral vocabulary and learning to discuss motivations for, and consequences of, certain actions, learners become more mature moral reasoners, sensitive to good and bad actions. There is a sense in which maturing moral reason supports the active work of virtue formation. For example, as a coach, the fact that my athletes were fluent in virtue and vice concepts and were eager to have conversations about them facilitated the process of incorporating virtue education at cross-country practice. Growth in virtue was a shared project—something we talked about and something I did *with* them, rather than *to* them. We grew more joyful, courageous, and perseverant together.

Regardless, having the opportunity to *practice* virtues (rather than just talk about them) is of central importance for acquiring virtues. Although, in aiming to acquire virtues, we should probably ask, with greater specificity, what a virtue actually *is*. (We are going to *briefly* pass through some theoretical weeds. So wear high socks and be prepared to slow down, as you would with weeds on a hiking trail.)

Thus far, we have said that a virtue is an acquired excellence that makes something a good instance of its kind. But a virtue may be one of several different kinds of things. It may be a normative[25] trait, or a set of dispositions that define our characters in a stable way.[26] For example, introversion is a trait; it characterizes a person in a stable way over time as part of their personality. Maybe a virtue is a trait alongside introversion. It might be a habit or something habit-like (like brushing one's teeth),[27] or a skill or something skill-like (like riding a bike).[28] A virtue might be a cognitive-affective unit, or a trait consisting of cognitive-affective units, that is situation-sensitive,[29] or it may be something else entirely.

For some virtue theorists, virtues are a kind of knowledge.[30] For others, they centrally feature reason.[31] For others still, reason is not very important in the possession of virtues at all.[32] Some accounts of virtue are ordered by considerations of flourishing, defined in different ways.[33] Others are ordered toward good consequences.[34] On other accounts, virtues are agent-based, or are qualities derived from, or identified with reference to, admirable people.[35] A virtue may constitute a kind of social intelligence.[36] Achieving virtue may be exceedingly rare and require we meet a high threshold of good action,[37] or it may be appropriate to attribute virtues to children. On some accounts, virtues are stage- and ability-specific, such that we possess them if we act well based on our present maturity levels.[38] So, while it is likely that you can list a number of virtues by thinking about your favorite athlete—bravery, conscientiousness, or grit—defining "virtue" is more difficult.

There are many varieties among virtue accounts, and these are not just theoretical distinctions that have no bearing on practice. They inform how one might go about acquiring a virtue. Interestingly, in the *Nicomachean Ethics*, Aristotle *first* asks the question of how a virtue comes to be, before answering the question of what a virtue is. This seems to indicate that how virtues develop offers important insights about definitional considerations. For example, if virtues are acquired in much the same way that traits are, we may be inclined to classify them as traits. If virtues develop in ways similar to how we acquire new skills, we might define them as skills. So, perhaps surprisingly, while we can learn about virtues in a classroom, by focusing on their *development*, we grow in clarity about what virtues are.

In what follows, I align with those who regard virtues as dispositional traits, which is the dominant view. But I provided this background for two reasons. The first is to note that, for the philosophically inclined reader, there is a rich literature to enjoy on the metaphysics of virtues. Second, for all readers, the descriptions of virtue development that follows might vary, given a different conception of virtue.

(All right, we are out of the theoretical weeds! We can pick up the pace again.)

In my own coaching, virtue development occurred in primarily four ways: (1) practicing virtue, (2) exemplar exposure, (3) goal-setting, and (4) modeling well-ordered loves.

Practice
Twice per week early during cross-country season and once per week during track season, my athletes ran hill repeats. For cross-country, hills were a practical necessity. Many of the courses we competed on were hilly, so the runners needed to develop the stamina and confidence to ascend quickly. During track season, we ran hills not because we would encounter them in races but because hills are speed work in disguise. They build strength. Strong runners can maintain their form and hold fast paces at the end of races through mounting fatigue.

The hill was formidable, and many of the runners (and I, in all honesty) were nervous before these workouts. Over time, we started to frame the objective of the workout in terms of fortitude, or the development of courage. I gave my athletes two objectives: a pace goal and a virtue goal, the goal of running courageously.

Prescribing a virtue as a workout objective is interesting for two reasons. The first is that moral virtues are not acquired through actions alone. In Chapter 1, I described how virtues require that we act from suitable motivations. For example, if someone displays great patience to demonstrate her superiority to her peers, we would be unlikely to attribute to her the moral excellence of patience. As a coach, I had no access to the reasons my athletes trained and raced as they did. But we did have conversations about fitting motivations—such as supporting their teammates, stewarding their abilities well, and self-improvement. These conversations occurred quite naturally among my athletes, since runners often talk about their "why." It is important to know and rehearse our reasons for running hard because, otherwise, it is easy to succumb to the temptation to quit.

Regardless, participating in athletics is not the final word on character education. It is likely that athletes did have unfitting or immature reasons for their actions. Even so, having the opportunity to build good habits, even purely actional habits, toward virtue is valuable. My athletes had the time and space to orient themselves toward good ends after track practice.

Prescribing a virtue as a workout objective is also interesting because people err in different ways. Some of my athletes were inclined toward rashness, experiencing too little reservation in the face of risk. They were inclined to rush off the start line and lead the group in a reckless way, only to self-destruct halfway through the workout. Other athletes had a more tepid approach. Their fear was too great for the challenge at hand. They were inclined to underperform, to avoid feeling the discomfort of running a pace that felt unsustainable or uncomfortable. Aristotle describes these opposing tendencies, and suggests how to correct toward virtue, in the following way:

> But one must examine what we ourselves readily incline toward, for some of us naturally incline toward some things, others to other things. . . . And we must drag ourselves away from it toward its contrary; for by leading ourselves far from error, we will arrive at the middle term, which is in fact what those who straighten warped lumber do.[39]

Developing a virtue is like straightening warped lumber. You challenge yourself in the direction that opposes your natural warp, to correct yourself in the direction of the mean. In the case of developing courage in my runners, this meant I could not offer a uniform directive to the team about pressing harder at the beginning of the workout. This instruction would profit the cowardly and imperil the reckless. I had to direct my athletes on an individual basis. This way, they were inclined to practice dispositions suitable for them.

There were other things I learned about virtue development from coaching. The first was the interrelation of different virtues, and of different vices. For example, earlier I described practical wisdom as an intellectual excellence that supports moral virtues. In developing my athletes' fortitude, I noticed that when they struggled to manage fear, their failings were often both in terms of too much or too little fear *and* in their inability to act prudently in light of their fear. They lacked the practical wisdom to ascend the hill in ways that were less (or more) risky. Part of learning to manage their fear was acquiring enough experience so they could make prudent choices about their ascents.

A second example is that *pride* often provoked my runners to take greater risks than they ought to have taken. *Impatience* was also sometimes the result of pride, prompting runners to act with unwarranted confidence in their abilities. Sometimes impatience resulted from *recklessness*, or from taking too little fear of the consequences of running too quickly to sustain. *Envy* and pride were entangled. Also, *laziness* and *apathy* often came to track practice together. Here is a coaching tip. They often hid together behind the football stadium rather than completing the full warmup. When debriefing with athletes after a run, we would try to disentangle what had gone awry, and often there was more than one faulty disposition at play.

In the classroom, we name virtues and vices as isolated concepts, but in practice, they rarely appear in isolation. Virtues support virtues. And, as I discovered at track practice, many vices seem also to support other vices. This lends credence to theoretical positions such as the one I introduced earlier—that there is a single master virtue, rather than many individual virtues. This position makes more sense when you consider how entangled seemingly discrete aspects of character are.

These kinds of considerations are often classified as a "unity of virtues" position, which holds that virtues are interconnected in some way. A strong version of this view is the "identity of the virtues" thesis, which holds that all virtues are really just manifestations of one overarching virtue.[40] This view seems implausible to many, since it implies that one moral defect means you lack *all* excellence. I have already noted that, as a coach, I noticed the reliance of certain virtues on other virtues. However, it seemed to me that some of my athletes really were excellent in some respects, even if not in others. It was helpful to name distinct virtues and vices to pinpoint excellences and defects, rather than assuming a monolith of virtue. A weaker claim, which I have suggested here, is the reciprocity thesis. On this view, only certain virtues are bound together.[41] For example, it would be difficult to find a runner excellent in endurance who is not also excellent in patience. These virtues are so tightly connected, that they are linked as a single concept in Greek. The term *hupomoné* means "patient endurance." It involves steadfastness or remaining under a burden.

Even so, it is difficult to determine the nature of this connection. For example, we notice that two virtues regularly appear together. This may be because there is some substantial, metaphysical connection between the virtues, such that (1) they have a relationship of identity, being part of the same virtue, or (2) there is a third subsidiary virtue that grounds both virtues. (3) An additional possibility is that their relationship is purely incidental, as the result of developmental happenstance. For example, it would be difficult to try to develop endurance and patience in isolation from one another, in the context of distance running. Maybe these are distinct virtues in terms of essential characteristics and grounding, but they appear together because of the practical impossibility of developing one without the other.

As coaches and athletes, we do not need to resolve this question. It is not something that is addressed at athletic department meetings. (If philosophers were athletic directors, then this would be high priority on meeting agendas.) But it is helpful to note that it is difficult to target a single virtue for formation, or a single vice for extinction. They are often entangled, so it can be confusing to figure out what has gone well and what has gone awry.

As a coach, I also learned that practicing virtue is an awkward process, in the way that acquiring skills often is. So, if a coach sincerely desires to prioritize growth in character, it is important to embrace the gawky stages of virtue acquisition,[42] rather than expecting perfection from her athletes.

For me, this meant making allowances for, and commending, athletes in practice whose early attempts at courage amounted to running too rashly or too conservatively. While in general, practicing virtue can be uncomfortable, in the athletic context, it can also have a performance cost. One example is trying to practice patience in racing situations and mistakenly waiting too long to make a move. This can negatively impact one's performance. A second example is attempting to be a more caring teammate by showing increased interest in teammates' performances. In attempting to acquire this virtue, one can ask too many questions and stress the teammate out before her race. Ultimately, being a patient person or one who supports those around her are excellences that will profit the athlete and her community, but while she *acquires* these virtues, there may be failures and frustrations.

This gawky character of virtue development is all the more reason to practice virtues in the context of athletics. While we care deeply about running and want to perform well, for most people, it is still a hobby. In other areas of life, such as careers and relationships, it can be costly to make the inevitable errors of virtue acquisition. In athletics, the costs are minimal.

For example, imagine that I am a boss of a small company. I would like to develop my courage by initiating difficult conversations, rather than avoiding them. To become more courageous in this way is an asset in a boss, both for the sake of my own character and for the overall health of the company. However, as I strive to become more courageous in the workplace, the gawky phase of development can be a social liability. I might initiate too many difficult conversations, or do so too harshly, lacking in grace. I am leaning in the right direction, warping my character toward virtue, and, ultimately, I may develop suitably courageous dispositions. But my virtuous practice may cause undue harm.

Conversely, distance running is a less vulnerable space to work on our character. The costs of poorly executed courage—such as starting a race too quickly or trying to maintain a pace in practice that is beyond my capabilities—are uncomfortable but have minimal cost to myself and others, in the domain of a hobby. Distance running is a useful laboratory for developing virtues.

Exemplar Exposure

In Plato's *Republic*, Socrates laments the qualities of the Homeric heroes. Achilles, for example, is insubordinate and ruled by his anger. He is irreverent toward the gods, impatient, and intemperate in his passions. Even after death, Achilles is a poor exemplar. The ghost of Achilles laments that he would rather be a serf in the land of the living than a king of all the dead.[43] The consequence of this statement—from their famed war hero—is that the soldiers start to fear dying. He is not a great role model for them, yet the stories of Achilles are compelling! They make Achilles seem charismatic and attractive. People admire him. And this is why Socrates, in his City in Speech, expresses concerns: We are imitative beings, motivated to emulate those we admire. As such, exemplars who model the wrong qualities are a liability.

As much as bad exemplars can be a liability, good exemplars can be an asset, and perhaps a stronger tool for character education than any kind of direct moral instruction on offer. It is one thing to be told that an action is good. It is another thing to see someone we admire perform this action, and to be shown that the action is choice-worthy. The first case is often met with resistance, or willful obedience, at best. The second is met with admiring feelings and strikes us as an invitation to do likewise.

Having someone we admire before us can provide a vision of what it looks like to be excellent. They can model good deeds, set the culture, and demonstrate practical considerations of how to do well in a particular context. Moreover, the fact that we *admire* them carries with it a kind of motivational force to do and be likewise.

Among the professional ranks of athletics, and especially in distance running, there are many exemplars who might influence young athletes in productive ways. In Chapter 4, I name several of these athletes. I also describe potential liabilities of learning from role models in sport. Despite these liabilities, as a coach, I often used exemplars to help motivate my runners toward virtue. Notably, I was more inclined to use athletes from our team as exemplars than professional athletes. I did this for two reasons.

The first was that, even though progress has been made recently in this respect, there is still a substantial disconnect between recreational and youth athletes and the professional running scene.[44] Whereas coaches of other youth sports, such as basketball, soccer, or football, can likely point to excellent players as models of certain excellences, running coaches cannot rely on the same name recognition. I could have pointed out excellent athletes, but I am not sure many, if any, athletes on my team would have known who they were.

Second, I drew on my team for exemplars for an empirical reason. We tend to be more motivated by relatable, attainable exemplars than by those whom we perceive as too far off from us, or too morally perfect.[45] Teammates would be relatable. If I could give a platform to the athletes of good character in their midst, this would be an effective strategy for character education. So that was what I did, through team management and the selection of team captains.

For students who had cultural capital among their peers or were natural leaders, I did not ignore their cultural capital. Instead, I often invited these more charismatic team members into conversations about taking ownership for team culture and supporting younger students. This way, athletes who were already inclined to lead would take their leadership positions more seriously and would be invested in building something positive.

Second, prior to selecting team captains, we talked about what our team values were for the season. We talked about how the best captain was not necessarily the fastest athlete on the team but the person who would lead by example in integrity, perseverance, and community focus. This way, athletes were primed to select someone who represented these things. Captains were given a platform—meaning, they became models or exemplars for the team—and other athletes were inclined to take cues from these people.

Goal-Setting

At the beginning of the season, our team gathered around picnic tables and wrote down personal goals. I asked them to write two or three performance goals, such as placing at districts and time goals they hoped to hit by mid-season and by post-season. I also asked them to write down virtue goals, such as "race more courageously" or "manage my schoolwork more prudently so I can attend practices." They discussed their goals among themselves. We also talked about what virtue goal we wanted to have as a team. For example, one season we focused on joy—a kind of buoyancy or internal fixity on one's good purpose.[46]

Throughout the season, we rehearsed our goals to each other, marked progress, and held each other accountable. At the post-season celebration dinner, I gave out typical performance-relevant awards—such as Most Valuable and Most Improved. I also gave out a Virtue Award to those who best exemplified our season's virtue in focus. Performance goals are important—both for considerations of *character*, since being committed to a goal is a great way to develop self-governance, and for considerations of the *sport*— because excellence is an objective of any craft we undertake with any seriousness.

Furthermore, the fact that we both integrated the virtue into practice and celebrated progress in that respect at the end of the season made the project of character education a sincere objective of our season, rather than a pantomime or hollow gesture toward character goals.

Modeling Well-Ordered Loves

During one of my first seasons of coaching, our women's team was seeded to perform very well at the state championships, so we set the goal of finishing in the top three. Deep into the race, we were positioned to do so until everything went awry. A girl from a different team fell as she approached the finishing chute. One of my athletes saw her fall. Rather than run past, she stopped to assist the girl to her feet and then helped her to slowly proceed down the final straightaway. While this happened, streams of runners passed my athlete to the finish, such that she was no longer a scoring member of our team. In the official results, her name did not appear at all. She was officially disqualified for assisting the other girl, due to an anti–Good Samaritan rule. Unfortunately, we did not place at the state championship that year.

This was an interesting situation as a coach. Often, the character goals we set in distance running support good performance. For example, perseverance is an excellence of our persons, which is also an asset on the cross-country course. But this was a situation in which performance goals and character goals were opposed. Being a good person was detrimental to placing well.

In the moments that followed, I had to check my heart. I did want my athletes to see and respond to the needs of others, and I was proud of my runner. Still, we (and I) wanted to perform well as a team. Our team debriefed after the race. I registered disappoint-ment in the outcome—a disappointment we all shared—but also celebrated the integrity my athlete showed in her race. On balance, this was more important than winning a race. If this had not been more important, then I probably should not have been a youth ath-letics coach.

Modeling well-ordered priorities as a coach is important. It was important at the State Championship that day—to cele-brate what I professed to value. But it was also important in small ways throughout the season preceding the race. I modeled cares through my own habits of attention, what I congratulated and what I prioritized. For example, when a runner finishes a race, I should not only comment on his paces and race outcomes. I should also note whether he grew in patience or persevered better than last time. It was important that I *acted* in terms of a genuine concern for character, rather than just spoke about it.

Ideally, this would come easily to me. What I professed and what I *truly* desired would be aligned. This is what it means to be virtuous.

What Is It Like to Be Virtuous?

A couple of weeks ago, I ran down my driveway, then up a hill to enter my favorite road loop. It was a bitterly cold December day, still dark, and sleeting, and I tightened the hood of my raincoat so that only my eyes were exposed to the conditions. It was enjoy-able, though. Rainy runs are only uncomfortable while you are still getting wet. Once you are wet, they remain the same level of bad, at least for a while, such that you cease to think about the conditions. Afterward, a friend who drove past me that morning told me, "You are the reason why people say runners are crazy." For good or ill, I had not considered staying home.

Willpower

It seems like any time I talk to a nonathlete about training, there is a disconnect between how I envision my daily schedule and how they envision it. They say something about how I must have great willpower to get myself out the door every morning, to eat well, and to do weight training, but I am not, for the most part, exercising willpower at all. There are some exceptions to this: On particularly egregious weather mornings and on days when I have a lot of work, I do sometimes linger on the possibility of staying indoors. Other times, deep into an ultramarathon, I see my family at aid stations and wonder what it would feel like to step off the course and drive far, far away from my racing ambitions to start a new, comfort-driven life, surrounded by pillows. In those moments, I will myself forward. But, in general, I do not struggle to motivate myself to run. I act from habits and affections, not from arduous choice or force of will.[47]

This is a key characteristic of virtue ethics, as opposed to other normative systems. The vision of a virtue and the good life is not one dominated by the exertion of one's will and motivated by duty alone, or by careful calculations about consequences. It involves a kind of ease and pleasure around good choices—the kind of ease that accompanies good habits, or well-ordered dispositions. For Aristotle, the virtuous person has a correct *conception* of the good, is *motivated* to perform these good actions, and does indeed *perform* them. And, while the process of *becoming* such a person can involve competing desires, internal conflicts, and concerted efforts to perform good actions (the kinds of gawkiness and difficulty I described as characterizing virtue development at track practice), these conflicted feelings are often described as being found primarily upstream of virtue, in its development; they are less descriptive of virtue itself.[48]

There are exceptions, of course. Sometimes doing a good action requires that we slow down and consider whether and how we ought to act, such as in novel or difficult circumstances, in the same way that we might pause to examine how best to approach training or racing in a certain situation. But as a general rule, the virtuous person moves with the kind of ease and preparation that bespeaks his or her practice in thinking, feeling, and acting excellently.

So what is it like to be virtuous? From the way Aristotle describes it, it seems more like having good habits in place than forcing one-self to do good actions. For a runner, this kind of ease and auto-maticity around actions and decisions should be a familiar feeling because it is how we sustain our training—by forming good habits. The goal is to do so with moral virtues, too—virtues such as justice, patience, perseverance, and kindness.

Track and Fielding Objections

A reader might have two objections to thinking of distance running in this way—as a tool for character growth. The first is that doing so will result in an asymmetrical character, with only some virtues represented and others ignored. Second, character education is pa-ternal. We should not intrude upon someone's freedom in this way.

The Asymmetry Concern

Someone might argue that only certain aspects of character are formed through sport. Other moral virtues, such as gentleness and charity, and intellectual virtues, such as fairmindedness and in-tellectual honesty, are not reinforced in sport. This asymmetry is a problem because athletics will shape learners to be imbalanced, lacking such excellences.

The asymmetry concern is a good objection. Both Plato and Aristotle raise a version of this worry.[49] Gymnastics hardens a person, but humans need to be softened, too, lest they become like dogs. This is why Plato, Aristotle, and the classical tradition that succeeds them include poetry as a humanizing complement to gymnastics—because gymnastics alone would form young citizens to be brutes.

A similar concern was raised in medieval Europe's feudal system. Bravery and excellences of war were reinforced in the knights, such that they developed asymmetrical characters. The knights became dangerous to those they were ostensively protecting and lacked gentleness, humility, and other virtues of civility. In response, chivalric codes were instated to encourage the knights to be both meek in the hall and ferocious in battle. C. S. Lewis clarifies that this combination meant "not a compromise or happy mean between ferocity and meekness; he is fierce to the nth and meek to the nth."[50] He is both.

My response to the asymmetry concern is similar to that of Plato, Aristotle, and the churches of feudal England: Physical practice should not be conceived of as a stand-alone tool in the formation of humans. It is clear that certain excellences are not reinforced in athletic contexts, so if this were the only practice used to form a person's character, that would be a problem. As it is, a student has a broader social context beyond sport, including formal education, the arts, religious or spiritual practices, and parenting, that also play a role in shaping a learner. All of these domains play a part in forming a learner's character.

The Paternalism Concern

Someone might contend that character education is paternal, or an overstep of authority. To educate for character is to intrude upon someone's freedom.

This is a common objection in contemporary culture. For example, many public schools today consider themselves out of the business of character education. They see their role as the neutral deliverer of facts, treating students as information receptacles who can passively receive content. In many cases, the only moral treatment permitted in public schools is what is called Values Clarification—a process of helping students to clarify the values they already possess. The idea is that to direct students' loves is to show preference for certain ideas and values, which is at odds with a pluralistic society.

This objection is well-placed, in that it correctly recognizes that character education *does* limit our freedom to do and to be whatever we want in the moment. Character education involves discipline—self-imposed or other-imposed. It involves the formation of one's affections and the turning of a student toward certain goods, goods that they did not already recognize as such or have the discipline to pursue. This is because character education assumes that learners, as they are, are not already excellent. The word *character* even implies such things. In Greek, it means "etching" or "engraving," capturing a kind of external impression. The learner is formed, or acted upon, to develop virtue.

I have two responses to the idea of character education as paternalistic. The first is that, even in a pluralistic society, there is broad consensus that a number of virtues are good-making features of persons. For example, most people would not protest if their children were encouraged to be kind, patient, or disciplined. These qualities make classrooms and teams functional and are generally welcome qualities in society. There are certain schools and associated athletic departments that have thicker mission statements— religious schools, military academies, and schools with explicit commitments to citizenship education. In these settings, a broader range of virtues, such as theological virtues, may be actively educated. Character education will look different in these settings. However, even in public education, there are many traits that it would be uncontroversial to instill. It would be valuable to educate for such virtues.

A second response is that, to a certain extent, character education is unavoidable. As I described earlier, how we think, act, and move through the world shapes—and is shaped by—our characters. Therefore, there is no option for a retreat from character formation. There is only the decision to feign a withdrawal from character education, which amounts to the decision to form character without any intention or plan. This seems like a perilous choice in a society that is already struck by addictions, social justice concerns, mental health crises, unscrupulous leaders, and citizens struggling to care about the natural world and one another. Good character seems a social imperative.

As far as the intrusion upon an athlete's freedom goes, earlier in this chapter I discussed a puzzle of freedom. Our freedom is, paradoxically, formed through the imposition of disciplines. To become free people, able to govern our own desires and choose well for ourselves, virtue education is an important tool in maturing our agency. So, yes, freedoms are restricted, but it is for the sake of being free in a fuller, long-term sense.

3

Feeling *Good*

Running on Emotions

In first grade, I was one half of a great rivalry. Once a week in gym class, we ran a perimeter loop around the softball fields in front of my school. The first ten students to finish the loop won baseball cards—not the greatest incentive for a seven-year-old girl. But unofficially, the first student to finish the loop also got bragging rights on the playground, and this was incentive enough for me.

The problem was my foe, Matthew.[1] He was very fast, and our victories were split. It was an edifying rivalry, to be sure, and he made me a lot better, since I almost had to de-combust to beat him. But Matthew was a sore loser. (It takes one to know one.) On the days when it was clear I would secure the victory, he would suddenly stop running and say, "Today, I'll let you win." And he would walk it in.

I'll let you win.

Decades later, this still makes me angry, so I guess I need to work on my forgiveness. While I was not exactly a gracious loser myself (understatement of the millennium), at least I could admit defeat. Matthew's response was such that, if he did not win, I could not win either. He deprived me of my victories.[2]

One of the perennial questions in athletics—and a question I regularly receive because of my two vocations—is whether there is such a thing as virtuous competition. Can we compete well and aim to win without compromising our characters? My answer is that we can, but that it is a challenge to do so.

In part, our ability to compete well depends on which emotions mediate our relationships to competitors—envy, admiration, or something else. In this chapter, (1) I first define emotions and describe their relevance for virtue. (2) Then, I introduce a set of emotions especially important for discussions of competition. (3) Finally, I describe ways in which we might diffuse the presence of envy in our sport.

Emotions

In September 2022, Kenyan marathoner Eliud Kipchoge broke the world record in the marathon in Berlin for the second time, running 2:01:09.[3] A lot of things were remarkable about this accomplishment. At thirty-seven years old, Kipchoge, a father of three, ran faster than any marathoner in history, and the record he broke was his own. It looked effortless, too, except for his smile in the later segments of the race.

Based on his own admission, we know that Kipchoge smiles to allay discomfort.[4] Positioning his face into a grin signals to the rest of his body that he is happy. Paradoxically, Kipchoge's smile is often the only indication to viewers that he is struggling.

Kipchoge's strategy is backed by research in support of what has been dubbed the Facial Feedback Hypothesis. This hypothesis states that facial actions trigger subjective experiences.[5] For example, in one study, researchers placed pens in participants' mouths such that their faces were unwittingly positioned into grins. The participants watched cartoons. The ones with pens in their mouths reported more intense humor responses than those without pens in their mouths.[6] Maybe the next time you run a marathon or are attending a family function you are not excited about, you should swing by Office Depot and grab some writing utensils for your mouth.

Our emotional lives are strange. Emotions can cause our bodies to move in certain ways, such as when we are angry and slam doors. Most people are familiar with this phenomenon. But our bodies also move our emotions. This is especially relevant for runners, albeit not particularly surprising. Apart from Kipchoge's masterly demonstration of facial feedback, runners often speak of how motivation follows action. The idea is that you may not be eager to run, but if you set your body into motion, the motivation will follow. Our feelings play a causal role in how our bodies move, and our bodies play a causal role in how we feel.

Emotions are physiological and affective states; they are bodily phenomena. But as I discuss in the following section, they are not only, or even centrally, characterized in these ways.

Why should a runner care about the emotions? You should care because, if there is anything that is going to derail a race, apart from low-quality training, it is your emotions. We have a lot of control over our emotional lives. So let's figure out what they are and how to manage them so that, on race day, your efforts are not thwarted by mysterious entities.

Defining Emotions

In general, there are five components used to characterize the emotions. Different accounts of the emotions emphasize different ones. Here we will explore all five with emphasis on one component in particular: their evaluative character.

Emotions Involve Subjective Experiences
I stand on a start line, afraid to compete. My subjective experience is a feeling of apprehension.

By "subjective experiences" I mean the kinds of feelings that typify an emotion. For example, sadness involves an unhappy or dispirited feeling. Anticipation involves future-directed expectancy or apprehension.

This is the most familiar feature of emotions. Often when we are aware of an emotion, it is because of these feelings. However, it is important to note that, while emotions dispose a person to experience certain feelings—and despite the fact that we often use these words interchangeably in casual discourse—emotions and feelings are not the same thing.[7] Someone can be characterized in terms of an emotion, without any accompanying sensations or feelings. We discuss this idea later in this section.

Emotions Involve Bodily Phenomena

Because I am afraid of my competition, certain bodily phenomena may result from my emotion. My chest tightens, and adrenaline is released.

This is the physiological side of emotions. One example is Kipchoge's smile trick, eliciting feelings of happiness. A second example is the experience of becoming angry and having your heart rate increase. The same is true here, as of subjective experiences. We can be characterized in terms of an emotion without the accompanying physiological changes.

Emotions Involve Behavioral Components

My fear prepares me for fight-or-flight mode. I sprint off the start line, perhaps more quickly than I ought to, entering the race with my adrenaline high.

By behavioral components, I mean that emotions can incline us to perform certain actions. This follows from the previous component—that emotions involve bodily phenomena. The physiological changes are, under another description, preparation for action.[8] I am angry, so my heart rate increases. These physiological changes play a causal role in how I behave. I shake my fists and slam a door. Alternatively, I am happy. This increases my parasympathetic nervous system activity.[9] In this parasympathetic state, I smile and give a high five.

Emotions Can Be Expressive

As I stand on the start line, my eyes are big, and my mouth is ajar. My fear is communicated by how I carry myself and the way I position my face.

We are social creatures, and our emotions are, in part, expressive. They communicate how we feel to others. Maybe if I were a savvier racer, I would wear some sunglasses to disguise my worried face. Or maybe I could disguise my fear behind a confident façade to mislead my competitors about my actual state.

Emotions Are Evaluative

In experiencing fear, I perceive my situation as meriting apprehension. Whether I am correct or incorrect to do so, I see the race as a fearful situation.

To say that emotions are evaluative is to indicate that they are a source of information, appraised as being a certain way. A second example is that, when I am angry at a friend, I see that friend as worthy of my ire.

In this book, we are examining virtue largely within an Aristotelian framework. Central to this framework is this final feature: the idea of emotions as evaluative kinds of perception.[10] This means that emotions are a source of information about the world.[11] Moreover, that emotions are evaluative means they do not receive information neutrally; they appraise or process the information received. So my emotions do not just report that I am standing on a start line next to talented runners. Whether correctly or incorrectly, they also evaluate this as a worrisome predicament.

An example of an evaluative model is Robert Roberts's view that emotions are concern-based construals.[12] By "construals," Roberts means to 'see something *as* something,' or to recognize it as such. This is a kind of perception, which also involves acts of the imagination and thought.[13] By "concern-based," Roberts means we have an interest or concern implicated in what is seen. When I am afraid on the start line, I *construe* the situation as threatening, and my *concern* is my own well-being, which I understand as being under threat.[14] When I love someone, I *construe* them as loveable, and my *concern* is whatever or whoever is the object of my affection.

A second version of this view is to understand emotions as construals that either entail or consist of judgments.[15] This is Robert Solomon's view. For example, to be angry at another is, under another description, to judge him or her as blameworthy in some way. To be fearful is to judge a situation as unsafe.

This evaluative character of the emotions is important in conversations about virtue development. Often the evaluations of our emotions are wrong. We may be fearful at the wrong times, in the wrong ways, and with the wrong intensities. We may be angry in situations that, upon reflection, do not merit it. An important part of developing a good character is emotional training.[16] And the great news is that this can benefit our running as well.

Training the Emotions

I once had a cross-country team lose a race because of too much excitement. It was an important race—and local—so the school surprised our team by sending a bus full of students to support them. They had friends across the course, cheering everywhere. It was very kind! But when I saw how quickly my runners came through the first mile, I thought, "Oh, dear." Their excitement rendered them incapable of executing their race plans. They came undone by mile two when the shock of that first quick mile settled into their legs. Thereafter, I watched them jog to the finish like their legs were encased in a Jell-O mold as their peers looked on, clapping.

There is an expression in the running world: "Emotions can cook your food or set your kitchen on fire." The idea is that the emotions you experience in a race—irritation, frustration, joy, gratitude, offense, boredom, and otherwise—can be a great source of strength if rightly directed, but can cause your undoing if not.

For example, you may become frustrated by a miscommunication with your race crew. Perhaps they mismanage their time and fail to appear at an aid station, leaving you alone to refill your own hydration pack at a critical point in the race. In the heat of the moment, this can be upsetting. You may start to dwell on the situation and grow angry. Strictly speaking, you may not be wrong to feel this way. But doing so can be a distraction and an energy cost. If you let it go, or—even better—redirect your frustrations into your effort, this can be a source of strength.

Positive emotions can also derail a runner. Excitement can make you feel bulletproof and energized, but if you do not manage your excitement well, you can figuratively "set your kitchen on fire" by starting the race too quickly. A substantial part of racing well is learning how to superintend emotions.

Through racing, I have learned a lot about emotion management. I have learned that, if you feel particularly bad or particularly good, just wait a few miles; emotions generally regress to the mean. I have learned that emotions shout at you when you are tired. And I have learned that there is a difference between 'feeling bad' and 'feeling bad for yourself.' The latter imperils more races than the former.[17]

Thankfully, ill-fitting and poorly managed emotions are not something we are stuck with. An important part of our growth in virtue is maturing the emotions, such as by refining their evaluative character. We receive some guidance about what this means from Aristotle.

Emotions and Virtues

Athens, Greece is the site of Pheidippides's mythical marathon run,[18] which, if it truly occurred, took place in about 490 BCE.[19] Athens is also the site of the first modern-day marathon, which was held as part of the 1896 Olympic Games. Surely it is not a coincidence that the most storied site in history for the marathon was also the home of Aristotle, who wrote some insightful things about emotions. Nothing makes a person question their emotional maturity quite like a long run.

Aristotle sees the emotions as centrally featuring in a good life. For instance, moral virtues are defined with respect to emotional domains. For example, courage is an excellence with respect to *fear*. Temperance is an excellence with respect to *pleasure*. Wittiness is an excellence with respect to how much *enjoyment* one finds in a joke.

For Aristotle, the good life involves a kind of psychic unity, involving the emotions. The virtuous person is integrated—having a correct conception of the good, being motivated to perform actions that are indeed good, and performing these good actions.[20] There are some emotions that are not constructive for one's growth in virtue; examples include spite and envy.[21] But, for the most part, the objective is not to suppress or do away with our emotions. To do so would be to lose an important means of seeing, knowing, and experiencing the world. Instead, the goal is to train our emotions, as we train our bodies, so that our emotions are well-ordered and contribute to a good life. But what does this look like?

Emotional Training

In Chapter 2, we examined the process of acquiring moral virtues. We examined the gawky stage of developing courage during hill repeats, practicing taking suitable risks. We said that experiencing too little or too much fear of a hill can impede our running. Some runners incline to be reckless, experiencing too little fear of consequences relevant to the task at hand. They run too quickly and implode before the workout is over. Others tend to be cowardly, experiencing too much fear of discomfort, so they hold back and fail to run the workout they are capable of.

Both cases miss the mark of courage. In advising athletes to adjust their strategy, their emotions are submitted to reason—in this case, *my* reason, as their coach. I know what they are capable of, and I know how steep the hill is. I give them a plan in terms of this knowledge, and they act in terms of it, repeatedly. They practice acting in line with reason. What is interesting about this process of development is that their actions—their willingness to act in terms of suitable fear—precede having a fitting emotion. Having an appropriate construal, or seeing the hill as fittingly fearful, follows from their experiencing it as such.

This process seems odd. Earlier, we discussed how moral virtues are developed by practice: "[M]en become builders by building and lyre players by playing the lyre; so too we become just by doing just acts, temperate by doing temperate acts, brave by doing brave acts."[22] This sounds reasonable as stated, that virtues form through doing. But if moral virtues are constituted in part by fitting emotions, this means that emotions are also educated through doing. I run more quickly up a hill and realize it warrants less fear than I imagined. A second example is that I pay more attention to the people at a table than the meal itself, and, in so doing, I start to take proper pleasure in food and drink. To train our emotions, we train. We *act* well in accordance with reason (our own reason, or the reason of a trustworthy coach), and our emotions follow.

Interestingly, while *actions change emotions* is a tried and tested process we encounter through sport, this is not the only version of the developmental sequence of virtue development. Consider the following. In his book *The Character Gap*, philosopher Christian Miller evaluates how we might increase helping behavior, citing psychological studies on the question. He writes, "If people are made to feel empathy, they are more likely to help. Not just a little bit, and not just doing easy tasks. They are also more likely to help with very inconvenient tasks, in a time-consuming way."[23] If we pause to reflect on how someone feels, we are more likely to extend aid. This demonstrates the opposite sequence: *emotions change actions*.

As a reminder, doing a good deed once is not enough to acquire a virtue. If I tell the truth once, this does not make me an honest person. If I help once, this does not make me helpful. We have to do them repeatedly until they define us, and we are inclined to do them without prompting. So it is not simply the case that an emotion (empathy) causes a virtue. However, certain emotions can get us started. They can incline us toward performing virtuous actions, such that they initiate the process of virtuous practice.

Empathy is not the only emotion that has the power to provoke good actions. Another one, which we will examine in near the end of this chapter, is admiration.

Countercultural Implications

Let me make two additional clarifications about emotions and virtue, before we turn to the emotions relevant to competition.

Your Emotions Are Not beyond Reproach

The first should be obvious, but it is important enough to be stated directly: In accepting that many emotions are educable, this means that many emotions, as they currently are, may be uneducated.[24]

Consider anger. One day, I become angry (and perhaps a bit envious) when I see two running friends meet up for lunch. They did not invite me! So I retaliate. During a race the following weekend, I refuse to share my nutritional gel packet when one of these running friends starts to bonk.[25]

First of all, the emotion of anger is ordered to *injustice*. Its evaluative content or construal is that something is unjust. The fact that my friends met up for lunch without me is disappointing for sure, but it is not unjust. I am wrong about that. I need to direct my anger at its proper object—an instance of injustice. Second, the action my misplaced anger elicits as recompense is outsized when compared to the slight of lunching alone. Lunch is an hour long; race results are forever.[26] To accept that our emotions are educable means reconciling ourselves to the fact that our emotions may be amiss.

I point this out because there is a strong cultural current of understanding our emotions as inviolable experiences, or as beyond reproach—that if something *feels* right, then it must *be* right. However, just because I feel something does not mean my feelings are fitting or adequately represent reality. For example, the feeling of *schadenfreude*—taking pleasure in the misfortune of another—is almost never appropriate because it is at odds with charity. And perhaps I feel good about deceiving a friend. Even so, it may not be something I ought to do.

This perspective—that one's subjective experience is their truth—is a form of moral relativism called *subjectivism*. On this view, 'goodness' and 'badness' depend entirely on our individual experiences, and there is no independent grounding for morality apart from what we feel. While subjectivism is a contemporary phenomenon, the perspective is nothing new. Subjectivism was first famously expressed by the ancient Greek Sophist Protagoras of Abdera, who wrote, "Of all things the measure is man: of those that are, that they are; and of those that are not, that they are not."[27]

Subjectivism's appeal is that it seems tolerant or open-minded to think in this way—to withhold judgment regarding the subjective experiences of others. But there are serious problems with this view. The first is that, if man is indeed the measure of all things, then we are above reproach.[28] Anything that someone happens to prefer—including stealing or brutality—is *fine* for them, and we have no grounds to critique them. They are just living their own truth. We often speak this way. But considering we have international tribunals to hold leaders accountable for war crimes, and there are some actions we do not tolerate (such as oppression or random torture), surely not all feelings are equally fitting or permissible.

Additionally, in the process of parenting and the socialization of young children, we do not act as though emotions are inviolable. Part of one's growth in maturity is learning to experience emotions when we ought, in the ways we ought, and our emotions are not naturally directed at the right ends. Consider a toddler, throwing tantrums that defy reason. "Are you mad that I won't let you eat any marbles? I am sorry you feel that way." These emotions are correctable, and this process of correction does not end in the toddler years.

An example in running that illustrates how we often misunderstand the educability of emotions is how people often conceive of perseverance. Many athletes claim that they are just not wired for endurance. It is not in their nature to persevere. Sure, there is a genetic component involved in facilitating an athlete's success in this respect. Natural limitations may impede their ability to reach the highest levels of the sport. However, the vast majority of runners can improve their perseverance, relative to themselves, through practice. That captures the objective of character education—to progress toward excellence, whatever that means relative to one's abilities. What is usually at issue is *desire*, rather than any failure of natural capacity. Athletes do not *want* to persevere toward the end in question. This is an emotional impediment, not a physical one.

Students often make the same error. They claim that their attention spans are short, and that this is just the way it is. However, a short attention span—that is, a lack of intellectual perseverance—is not fixed. Students can practice "staying in place" with their work and cultivate a greater desire to learn. As we explored in the previous section, performing the *action* of staying can transform the relevant *desire*.

Happy Feelings Are Not the Goal of Emotion Education

A second clarification about the emotions and virtue is perhaps equally as obvious. It is that the goal of emotional development is not to just have happy feelings. It is to have veridical emotions—emotions that correspond to reality.

For example, imagine losing a close friend. The suitable emotion in this situation is sadness. It would be wrong *not* to be sad.

It would mean we were not seeing the world, and what has value, clearly. A second example involves anger. Imagine learning that a successful competitor, who won a number of major races, subsequently tested positive for performance-enhancing drugs. Seeing how many victories and how much prize money she stole from clean athletes, the suitable response is to feel angry. Sure, sadness and anger are not enjoyable feelings, but they are part of a rich human life, and they are fitting responses on these occasions.

At the moment, a pervasive view of the good life in the Western world is a hedonic view of happiness—the idea that a happy life is one that consists of more positive subjective states than negative ones. We examine this view in Chapter 7. I call this the "good vibes only" mistake. In holding this view of the good life—even without recognizing that we do—we may suppress negative feelings and pursue positive ones, whatever the cost. And there are high costs. Some of the most significant experiences in life, like climbing mountains, having children, and working toward difficult goals, involve a fair amount of discomfort. Furthermore, all meaningful relationships involve difficulty, hard conversations, and sharing another's burdens. The hedonic view of happiness robs us of rich relationships and arduous goods.

So what does this mean for our racing? In part, it means that the negative emotional states we experience while running, like frustration or loneliness, should not be viewed as inherently problematic. Rather, they are an important means by which we see and respond to the world in the ways that we ought.

For example, loneliness is an emotion I used to struggle with in the middle of long races. I would be out on the trail by myself, wondering what my friends were doing, and wanting to join them. But, at some point, it occurred to me that if I were not running 100 miles alone in a forest, most likely I would be working alone in my study cubicle. So, yes, I felt lonely on the run, but I would also feel lonely if I were not running. Loneliness is an unfortunate feeling, but it is not a reason to quit a race. Now when I experience loneliness, I remind myself about the kinds of life choices I have made—ultramarathoning and academics—that make loneliness a reality for me. I remind myself that I mostly enjoy independent pursuits. I interrogate my loneliness, refining its construal.

One caution is that, while negative-valence emotions like sadness and anger are important in a good life, it can sometimes be helpful to constrain them on the run and to revisit them later. For example, one study found that, when we are sad, we perceive hills to be steeper.[29] Sadness intrudes upon our spatial perceptions, misinforming us about topography in a way that has consequences for our running. The sadness may be suitable and well-ordered, but it also may not be helpful while running. A second example is anger. If a competitor impedes your progress, this can make you mad, rightfully so. That is a veridical emotion. However, the physical dispositions of anger (high heart rate, tight fists) can have negative performance costs. For both anger and sadness, redirecting our attention away from an emotion, however suitable that emotion is, can be valuable for performance reasons.

Emotions and Competition

I opened this chapter with a description of a rivalry I had with my first-grade classmate, Matthew. I described how he resigned in the middle of races he was losing, rather than admit defeat. If he could not win, then he preferred that I could not win either. Many of us have been there, in how we regard our competitors, and there is an emotion to describe this feeling: envy. In this section, I examine envy in competitive settings, and I introduce a set of emotions that are good alternatives to it. They are called the "other-praising emotions."

Envy

"Comparison is the thief of joy"[30] is a popular refrain these days. I have said this. It has been said to me. But it is unclear why. Why is comparison the thief of joy when we have so much to learn from one another?

The sentiment behind the quotation is something like this: A person's life should stand on its own because if we live with integrity and do our best, then there is nothing else left for us to do. Life is not an Oreo-stacking competition, and it does not matter how many achievements we stack up compared to another person. It does not matter how fast someone else runs if we run our fastest. And it does not matter what accolades someone else collects if we performed our best. The successes of others do not detract from our own.

Practically speaking, comparing one's own life to another's life is often unproductive, since we all have our own situations, responsibilities, strengths, and weaknesses. Regardless, the designation of comparison as a "thief of joy" seems not to be a problem with comparison *in general*. There are many constructive, prosocial forms of comparison. Admiration, emulation, edification, and awe are examples. As imitative creatures, a great deal of social learning comes by way of comparison. It is how we identify moral and conventional norms and possibilities for excellence, and it is often how our athletic imaginations are formed. We see someone perform a great feat, and we bring it to bear on ourselves. We think, "I wonder if I can do that, too."

Comparison helps us to dig deeper so we can get more out of ourselves than we otherwise could if we were alone. This bears out in the scientific literature. The presence of others—dubbed "social motivation"—reportedly increases one's drive toward accomplishing goals, improves effort, and increases learning.[31] The competitive presence of others is also correlated with improved academic performance.[32] In athletic settings, we find that the presence of another person increases physical effort, in both short[33] and long efforts.[34] Furthermore, in economics, competitive environments tend to see more innovation.[35] Comparison is productive. It seems that the problem is not with comparison *simpliciter*. The problem seems to be with a particular type of comparison: envy. Envy is the thief of joy.

There are several emotions which may be elicited when we encounter an excellent other. Envy is one of them. It is defined as the vice of "feeling bitter when others have it better."[36] Envy is common in competitive running, where there is a very real sense in which another person's gain is one's own loss. Only one person can win a race, so we may be inclined to regard a competitor's victory with bitterness, as an impediment to our own success. But envy is a response that imperils relationships, reduces what "success" in the sport means to finish placement alone, and has a heavy emotional cost. Envy is also a kind of theft. It robs one's competitor of the satisfaction of victory, as Matthew did to me all those years ago.

In Chapter 6, I examine envy as a performance-enhancing vice, explaining why responding with sorrow to another person's successes is not constructive for our own happiness, our future performances, or the running community more broadly. I also explain how it compares, in terms of competitive advantage, to the emotion of admiration.

Other-Praising Emotions

In lieu of envy, there are several emotions we might cultivate in response to excellent others instead. These emotions are classified as "other-praising emotions," or emotions arising from others' exemplary actions.[37] Here we will explore three: (1) gratitude, (2) awe, and (3) admiration, which will have varying impacts on our running.

Gratitude

Here is a running tip: You can't feel grateful and bad for yourself at the same time. Gratitude decreases negative affect.[38] So when races are challenging, you can reflect on what you are grateful for. These feelings will crowd out self-pity and help you to stay positive.

Gratitude is a response to another's goodness. It involves the perception that one has benefitted from another[39]—a benefit "not necessarily deserved or earned."[40] Gratitude is a social emotion with a positive valence, and it recognizes the acts of generosity or thoughtfulness of others.[41] It is an emotion correlated with higher rates of life satisfaction.[42]

Furthermore, gratitude is prosocial, in that it elicits socially constructive actions. When we feel grateful for another person, we are inclined to be helpful and emotionally supportive in return.[43] As such, gratitude is a productive emotion to cultivate in a team setting. For example, while the envious runner perceives the victories of a teammate as undermining her own successes, the grateful runner is thankful she has such a talented teammate to drag her along to better performances than she could accomplish alone. This grateful runner may look for ways to support the talented teammate, such as by leading repetitions in workouts or offering emotional support. These actions facilitate the future growth of both runners.

We can lament when a teammate exceeds our own abilities, or we can be grateful to this person for calling us to a higher standard and work to return the favor. This makes gratitude a fruitful emotion for sustaining hard work and promoting friendships among runners on a team. Friendships are valuable in themselves; they also increase the likelihood that runners will find joy in the process and perform well over the long-term.

Awe

On September 17, 2018, the running world erupted when Eliud Kipchoge broke the men's marathon world record for the first time at the Berlin Marathon. Mastery in any domain is mesmerizing, and this certainly was. Kipchoge ran 2:01:39, or a staggering 4:38 per mile. If you are like me, you have never run a single mile that fast. If you are like me, then by comparison, Kipchoge runs like a cheetah, and you run like a lion. A sea lion.

Kipchoge has a stunning reputation for long-standing mastery of the sport and for doing so, as far as we can tell, above reproach. He is the consummate exemplar for distance running—talented, humble, eloquent, affable, perseverant, and brave. I could learn a lot from him.[44]

But after Kipchoge's performance, my temptation was to be amazed, of course, but then to put him on a pedestal or to set him aside as an outlier, without ever bringing his achievement to bear on my own (comparatively meager) athleticism. I wanted to chock his performance up to rare natural ability, far beyond my own. Since by natural province Kipchoge is exceptional, then I do not have to feel bad about how unremarkable I am in contrast. Friedrich Nietzsche describes such a response in this way: With respect to the excellent person, "only if we think of him as being very remote from us, as a *miraculum*, does he not aggrieve us."[45]

What I experienced toward Kipchoge was awe. Awe is a complex emotion, notable for the mixed affect it generates—positive feelings, such as contentment and pleasure, mixed with negative feelings, such as fear or diminution.[46] It is an appreciative emotion, connected to humility, and it is often characterized in terms of veneration and respect.

Additionally, while we have said that gratitude elicits action (generally returning a favor), awe is often stunned to passivity. The person struck with awe "sometimes construes himself as lacking personal adequacy to 'deal with' the object of awe—to understand or otherwise get control of it."[47]

There are certainly times when awe is appropriate. In religious contexts, for example, worship is often described in these terms. For example, in the Judeo-Christian tradition, people encounter God and drop to their knees in veneration; they are arrested from movement, and this facilitates worship. But in the athletic context—even regarding someone as ascendant as Kipchoge—awe is often an inappropriate emotion. This is because, while Kipchoge greatly exceeds us talent-wise, we have much more in common with him than not.

Like Kipchoge, we are all runners. We participate in the same activity and set out daily to improve, whatever that means for us. Moreover, like Kipchoge, certain excellences are "open to us"— excellences such as courage, perseverance, and humility. These are virtues that we can acquire for ourselves, regardless of how fast we run. So while we may never run as fast as Kipchoge does (no one in history ever has), we can improve with respect to the same excellences he displays. For this reason, an emotion that provokes passivity, as awe does, is usually the wrong response. What we want is to cultivate an emotion that elicits imitative action, so that we profit from the excellences of a superior other. A good candidate is the emotion of admiration.

Admiration

To admire is to appreciably perceive the excellences of others.[48] Admiration is an emotion with an overall positive affective valence,[49] and it is often described in opposition to envy. Søren Kierkegaard characterizes the difference between these two emotions in this way: "Admiration is happy self-surrender; envy is unhappy self-assertion."[50] While envy is pained by a superior other, admiration rejoices in the good perceived, even if this good is not one's own.

Additionally, admiration inclines us to act in several constructive ways, broadly construed as "promot[ing] the value that is judged to be present in the object of admiration."[51] Sometimes we are moved to praise the admired person to others.[52] This can be helpful because it socially reinforces certain excellences by giving the exemplar a bigger platform. Alternatively, our admiration might dispose us to do another good act, different from the one we observed the admired person perform.[53] Maybe we notice an admired runner's patience on display in a big race, and this motivates us to be more courageous in our own running.

Most characteristically, admiration inclines us to emulate the good action observed in the admired person. For example, I notice the conscientious way an older teammate stretches after practice, and I am motivated to do the same. This is valuable for character development because—as we described in the Chapter 2—virtues are acquired by practice. We repeatedly do good actions until they define us in a stable way. Admiration affords us this practice.

The admiration of excellent others is important both because it provides us with a vision of what is good and choice-worthy, modeling what it looks like to have a good character in sport, and because we are motivated to put on these excellences ourselves. This makes it a valuable emotion for character development, and athletic development more generally; we often learn how to throw, shoot, pass, and sprint by observing these skills modeled by others. We also learn how to be courageous, honest, perseverant, and prudent, from observing these virtues modeled by others. That said, we are not always inclined to admire the right people or to imitate the right qualities in the right people. In Chapter 4, we examine exemplars, or the people we admire. We assess how doing so can benefit us, and we explore some pitfalls of admiration.

Diffusing Envy

The word *compete* means "strive together" or "strive in common."[54] It is a concept that is more collaborative than antagonistic, but this is not the sense we get when the word is used today. In general, when I am asked whether I am competitive, people do not intend to ask whether I strive with others; they want to know whether I am, to put it plainly, envious. Am I undone by the successes of others? Do I need to win? Am I willing to compromise the goods of friendship because of this need? Today, envy is so entwined in our cultural imagination of competition that we have a difficult time conceiving of competition apart from it.

So how might we take back competition from envy and employ one of the other-praising emotions instead? Here are three suggestions:

You Can Expand What It Means to Win

Envy perceives victory as a limited good, and in the narrow sense of winning the race, it is. Only one person can cross the line first. However, there are so many other ways to measure a victory. Other measurables—like improvements on a course, running courageously, practicing patience, or doing a better job meting out your effort on a hilly course—can be reframed as victories. None of these are limited goods. Everyone can win at patience. Everyone can do their best at the same time, and that makes the competition even stronger so you can get the best out of yourself. Ultimately, it is a more valuable thing to get buried in an honest field than be victorious in a weak one.

Practice Your Gratitude

It is hard to be grateful and envious at the same time. Try it.

I really do mean *practice* gratitude, in the same way that we practice other aspects of the sport—like downhill descents and remaining calm at threshold pace. Often in this sport, we work hard to fine-tune minor aspects of our physical performance, and then we throw up our hands regarding our character. We need to practice that, too. We do not develop good characters by accident.

Make Other People's Successes Your Own Delight, and You'll Never Run Out of Reasons to Celebrate

I used to teach this to my middle- and high-school track athletes, and I was always impressed by the ways in which they encouraged each other and were each other's cheerleaders. Sometimes you can't race well. Other times you are unable to race altogether, but there is always someone out there doing something worth celebrating. Seek out the successes of others and cheer them on. Doing so means a lot to others and takes nothing away from your own successes.

Track and Fielding Objections

I anticipate at least two objections to the idea of emotional education.

The "It's Too Late for Me!" Objection

Often, when adults hear about educating their emotions or changing the way they feel, they respond that they are too old for that. Their emotions are as they are! It is too late to change.

This is a good objection. Actually, Aristotle shares this sentiment. In Book II of the *Nicomachean Ethics*, he writes, "It makes no small difference, then, whether we form habits of one kind or of another from our very youth; it makes a very great difference, or rather all the difference."[55] The idea is that forming virtue is for the youth, rather than adults. Changing the affections of children is easy. They are like canoes, easy to move around. Adults already have habits and affections in place. They are like barges, slow to move.

I will say this: Aristotle was not a track coach. I do not share his cynicism about transforming the character of older people because I have seen distance running do the work of turning barges. Running helps people to grow in discipline. It makes them aware of how they are treating their bodies, so they make better choices regarding sleep, eating, and health. It gives them space to introspect so they can think about what is important. It also gives them a new social context—friends who are likewise reflecting, learning to manage their emotions, and trying to improve in a (mostly) constructive activity. This work can and does transform our emotions.

To be clear, distance running is not a panacea for all our ills. It is not, as we will examine in Chapter 6, an unqualified good. There are vices not only present in the sport but also reinforced by it. Even so, running can play a constructive role in transforming one's affections and desires. It follows the developmental sequence of *actions changing desires* we examined earlier.

The "Why Shouldn't I Be a Stoic Instead?" Objection

This objection makes me angry and sad (Stoic joke). There were several Stoics in the classical period, so there are a range of positions that characterize their views. I will not distinguish among them here. Briefly, one common idea among Stoics is that emotions like anger, disappointment, sadness, and regret are unhealthy for us. They are the result of bad reasoning or misjudgments about both the good life and what we have control over. An example given by Seneca is that, when you do someone a favor, you should never expect to receive anything in return because you have no control over what anyone else does.[56] To experience disappointment in these situations is to be wrong about what is within your power.

On these grounds, the 'Why Shouldn't I Be a Stoic Instead' objection would capture something like this: We should not feel anger or disappointment at all. They are not *eupatheiai*, or good emotions. Do away with them entirely! Lately, popular interest in Stoicism is growing, and it is easy to see why. In a time of pandemic and social and political unrest, there is appeal in a position that erects fences around the things that are outside of our control. We do not have to deal with the hard things that happen to us against our will. We can focus on virtue and manage whatever is within our power. This perspective appeals to distance runners, too, for obvious reasons. A lot can happen to us over a long run—rain, mud, hills, and aid station mishaps. Controlling what we can control is ultimately all we *can* do, and we should not get upset on account of what is out of our hands.[57] Even so, there are good reasons not to become a Stoic.

Many objections have been raised against the Stoic view of the emotions. Some thinkers have argued that the overly rational approach to agency misunderstands human action. Others have questioned whether Stoics have a satisfactory understanding of happiness. For example, Augustine argued that the Stoics lacked an adequate vision of the human end.[58]

On empirical grounds, someone might argue that genuine *apatheia*, or equanimity—the prescribed state of mind in which one is indifferent or not moved by emotion—is implausible. For example, those with impaired emotional processing are often marked by indecision.[59] They struggle to mobilize their reasons into action. Furthermore, neuroscientist Antonio Damasio points out that "reduction in *emotion*[60] may constitute an . . . important source of irrational behavior" and that "the powers of reason and the experience of emotion decline together."[61] In conceiving of ourselves as rational agents, it would be a mistake to neglect the substantial role the emotions play in our choosing. Stoics may commit this error.

My own response to the Stoicism objection is to note that there is an asymmetry in the sorts of emotions that are considered healthy by Stoics and those that are not. And, oddly, this asymmetry tracks a mistake we see in the world of track and field.

Often in distance running, we tend to celebrate victories ("I persevered!" or "My courage won me that race") and explain away our defeats ("There was heavy wind!" or "It was very hot out," or "I ate some bad chicken last night"). We draw on *agential* reasons for our successes and *circumstantial* reasons for our losses. Really, if we are going to claim our successes, then we should also claim our losses, and, if neither, then neither. Luck factors into both situations. Character factors into both situations. The worry is that dividing good and bad emotions on the basis of what is "in our control" sets us up for this kind of attributional bias.

Lastly, just to be clear, you do not need to become a Stoic to constrain your emotions temporarily during races to compete well. We discussed this earlier. We can delay reflecting on these difficult emotions until after crossing the finish line. This is not Stoicism; it's prudence.

Final Thoughts

After first grade, Matthew switched school districts, so I did not see him for years. A decade later, I encountered him at a regional Brain Bee (a neuroscience competition structured like a spelling bee). Again, we were competitors, and we recognized each other immediately. My first thought was, "My foe!" I felt all the old resentment and wanted to invite him outside for a footrace across the parking lot. By contrast, Matthew greeted me with warmth and kindness, as an old friend. His memories of the rivalry were positive, and—as it turns out—he is really a lovely person.

Neither of us was a good competitor in first grade. If I am being honest, we were both guilty of envy. Years later, it is still not always easy to celebrate the victories of my competitors, but I am going to keep practicing. It is freeing to not have my identity tied up in the performances of other people, and it is a whole lot more fun to celebrate than to crumble when my competitors do well.

Postscript

I beat Matthew in the Brain Bee.
He did not let me win.

4

The Runners I Look Up To

One of my greatest memories in the sport was competing at the 2018 Trail World Championships in Spain. The athletes stayed at the Hotel Intur Orange Benicasim, and it was an Olympic village of sorts, with forty-nine nations represented. The days preceding the race were filled with team meetings, gear and health checks, shakeout jogs, course previews, and naps.

We shared rooms with our teammates, and we ate together in a dining hall. If you are wondering what 500 of the strongest trail runners in the world eat, the answer is everything. We were hungry. With my own eyes, I watched a man stack multiple chicken breasts as a vertical pile onto his plate. It was a Tower of Babel, stretching to the heavens, made of chicken. There were stacks of toast, eggs of all forms, fruits, vegetables, rice, meats, and sweets. You had to arrive to the cafeteria early if you wanted beets because beets are de rigueur in the endurance community right now. Beets reportedly improve one's cardiorespiratory endurance if you eat them before running. I also ate beets, not because I was acquainted with their salubrious qualities at the time but because of the force of the *ad populum* fallacy.

Here is a note of interest. At just shy of 5′5,″ I was among the tallest trail runners. I walked around like LeBron James, towering above other runners. In a basketball world consisting of trail runners, I could be a power forward. With my brown hair, I felt like Hagrid from *Harry Potter*.

So, when I say I looked up to many of these people, you should know I mean this figuratively. I was surrounded by my heroes—runners I had only read about in magazines. I was mesmerized by their training and racing, and in awe of their storied careers. That week, as I prepared for my race, I continuously had to remind myself: Do not put these people on a pedestal. They are only humans. You can admire them and emulate their excellences, sure. But awe—the kind of posture that stuns you to passivity—is the wrong emotion to be feeling as you line up shoulder to shoulder to compete among your heroes.

Exemplars are role models. They are the people we admire. For me, many of the runners I competed against at the World Championships were among them, and the proximity I had to these people was a great opportunity to learn and grow, if I managed my responses to them suitably.

In this chapter, we examine how to learn from excellent others in the context of sport. First, we examine exemplars, the people we admire. We inquire about the ways in which admiration of them can go awry, in general and in the athletic context. Next, we name several exemplars in distance running whose character merits our admiration. Then, we conclude by exploring how to proceed from admiration to exhibiting these excellences ourselves.

Exemplarism

Back in 2012, I was a young ultrarunner with a lot of enthusiasm but a lack of guidance for how to succeed in the sport. I did what anyone in my position would do. I imitated what my role models were doing.

I admired a runner named Sophie. She took rest days and targeted workouts, rather than running hard every day, so that was what I did. I admired a runner named Nikki, who was a gracious, humble champion and who thanked volunteers at every aid station. I aimed to do the same. And I admired a runner named Connie. I read an interview in which Connie said American women needed to break 150 miles in the twenty-four-hour run to be competitive on the global stage. I made that my goal. Because Connie spoke so confidently about the eventuality of the feat, it didn't even occur to me that it was not a reasonable thing to do. I cloaked myself in Connie's courage: If she could do it, I could, too. These women were my exemplars—walking embodiments of the excellences I desired for myself—and emulating them made me better.

What is an exemplar? How do we choose them? How does it benefit us to do so?

Definitions

Exemplars are the people we admire, or are inclined to appreciably perceive and imitate. Much of our social and moral learning happens by way of their demonstration. For example, I learn table manners from observing my parents (social learning). While my parents may use explicit instruction to guide me in how to hold a fork, watching them do so is as beneficial, or more so, in helping me to form good dining habits. Moral instruction is similar. Someone may tell me to be charitable toward others in need, but it is more instructive and motivating to observe someone I admire act generously toward the poor. I am inclined to do likewise, and to see value in doing so, more so than I would when the good action is presented as an opportunity to obey an ethical command.

These two functions are known as an exemplar's *epistemic* and *motivational* roles. By *epistemic* is meant that exemplars are a source of knowledge. They are a means by which we learn moral norms. Exemplars demonstrate what actions one ought and ought not perform. In the childhood context, an example is when parents are kind to restaurant workers or other people in service positions. They do not have to say anything to the child about it, or demand that a child does likewise. Yet, in watching their parents, a child learns that this is the right thing to do.

In the athletic context, observing veteran athletes is how runners learn the norms of performance. For example, an exemplar might demonstrate how to pass on the outside of the lane and only cut in ahead of the runner being passed when the passer is a full stride-length ahead.

Ideally, the kinds of information acquired by way of exemplars is good information, and amenable to growth in virtue. But if you are already wondering about the kinds of unhelpful lessons exemplars might supply, you are right to be. That epistemic concern is raised later.

The *motivational* role of exemplars is just as it sounds. We are social creatures, and other people's actions—particularly those of whom we admire—set a precedent that we are likely to follow. It is more motivating to see someone act excellently than to be told to be excellent. For example, I might be told that to be a good runner, I should lift weights, stretch, and run a set number of hours each week. However, if I see a runner whom I admire perform these actions, I see them as choice-worthy. I act from a desire to become what I admire, rather than from obedience.

Four Exemplar Types

There are at least four kinds of moral exemplars:[1]

1. *Sages* are exemplary in wisdom, or more broadly, in intellectual ability. There are very few sages in contemporary Western culture, where wisdom is a forgotten currency. We Google instead of wonder about things, and we often fail to examine what is of value. The loss of wisdom has a tremendous social cost, as we bumble about, working at a frenetic pace to secure bad ends or pursue goods that will never satisfy us.

The sage is a category of exemplar that is not very present in athletics, since athletics is not ordered toward securing intellectual goods. Even so, it would be valuable to have an athletic hero who could model well-ordered aspirations in the sport and to demonstrate the proper place athletics can have in a flourishing life. Wise runners give running its proper place. They are disinclined to pursue goals that compromise objects of greater value—be that family, one's long-term health, or something else.

2. *Saints* are known for their loves. The word *saint* often carries a religious connotation. For example, Christianity, Islam, and Hindu have figures they hold in high regard for their holiness or friendship with the gods or God. As a category of exemplars, "saint" extends to all of those who love others well, regardless of theological affiliations. There may be saints in running.

For example, one of my early track coaches was marked by his loves. He wrote our team encouraging notes and was intentional about affirming us, regardless of how we performed. He loved everybody, from the state contenders to the back-of-the-pack folks. This coach was not exemplary in every way (or even most), but he certainly modeled how to love others well through sport.

3. *Heroes* are marked by their great deeds or courage. This term is applied widely—to action figures, firefighters, military leaders, and literary figures. For example, Beowulf, Dante, and one of the greatest literary endurance adventurers of all time—Odysseus—are all called heroes. "Hero" is also a term we apply to those we admire in the athletic context. Athletes perform great feats. We see them as beautiful and transcendent in certain ways. We want to be like them.

4. The final category of exemplars includes those we admire who do not fit neatly into any of the first three categories. I call this final category *mundane exemplars*. Most exemplars are characterizable as such. Coaches, caretakers, peers, older

teammates, and teachers—anyone we admire—can fit into this category. Of course, it is the "anyone we admire" line that should concern us, since admiration can, and often does, lead us astray. Certainly, not all of those we admire are deserving of our admiration. I discuss this in the following section.

Thus far, we have examined positive exemplars—those we admire and are drawn to emulate. There are also *negative exemplars*, or people who demonstrate what we do not want to be like.

An example is a professional runner who lauds her own abilities with such frequency that, in conversations, there is little space to talk about anything or anyone else. I do not think this runner does so consciously or maliciously. Furthermore, she is so talented that her abilities merit celebration. Still, her conceit crowds out her love for others, and she demonstrates, by example, what I do not want to be like. Paradoxically, she motivates growth in humility.

There are two worries about negative exemplars. The first is that a young or naïve athlete may not recognize that an excellent runner is not exemplary in other respects. He or she may take cues from this bad athlete, practicing the wrong qualities or mistakenly treating a negative exemplar as a hero, saint, or sage. I discuss this issue later in this chapter. I refer to it as the "Alcibiades concern," named after a war hero exceptional in his military prowess and odious in his character.

A second worry is that, even in recognizing that a notable athlete is a negative exemplar, this athlete can still play a role in culture-setting. Consider the proud athlete who brags consistently. Surely, many people recognize this tendency as untoward. However, we can become accustomed to her pride, and when we notice it in others, be inclined to grant these tendencies permission as part of the culture of sport. Whereas moral exemplars are like buoys, lifting everyone else up around them, negative exemplars are like anchors; they drag others down.

We ought not *admire* negative exemplars. That is not the suitable emotion here. We ought not imitate them either. But they can serve the role of sharpening our vision about what a good character looks like and motivate us to do better.

Admiration Gone Awry

In Plato's *Symposium*, the odd relationships that Socrates has with his students are on full display. Socrates considers himself not a teacher, or someone who imparts knowledge. Even so, the young men of Athens regard him as such. They hold Socrates in high esteem, demonstrate affiliative behavior, and follow him uncritically, a situated complicated by the Greek convention of pederasty.[2] An example of this uncritical allegiance to Socrates is seen in the *Symposium*. Socrates invites a young man, Aristodemus, to join him at a dinner party that Aristodemus has not been invited to. Aristodemus responds, "I'll do whatever you say."[3]

To be clear, it is productive to regard the excellent people in our lives with some amount of deference, since this makes us teachable. It is also a gift when the people we admire are accessible to us so we can see and learn from them in person. But the responses Aristodemus and others have to Socrates often demonstrate uncritical, affiliative behavior. This is not productive for growth in virtue and might even place Aristodemus in a vulnerable position—a position in which his values are compromised. Admiration of this sort is not constructive.

Admiring others in problematic ways is an ancient problem that still afflicts us today. From Socrates and his fawning student, Aristodemus, we can learn some important lessons that will benefit us, particularly in athlete–coach relationships. For starters, "I'll do whatever you say"[4] is not a constructive posture to have toward your coach.

In this section, I address four ways our admiration for others in the sport can go awry, starting with (1) Aristodemus's brand of affiliative behavior. I also address (2) admiring the wrong people, (3) admiring the wrong qualities in the right people, and (4) character asymmetry concerns in athletes.

Uncritical Alignment or Affiliative Behavior

During the Track and Field World Championships held in Doha in 2019, a famed distance running coach from Oregon was banned from the sport for indiscretions related to performance enhancement. He appealed the ban. It was upheld. Subsequently, an additional ban was added—a Safe Sport ban for sexual and emotional misconduct. He is now permanently prohibited from coaching and participating in Olympic and Paralympic sport.[5]

Prior to these bans, there were indications of this disgraced coach's micromanagement of athletes and controlling ways. For example, he was, by one of his athletes' admissions, "obsessed with athletes' weight . . . [and] every aspect of their training, even suggesting that [an athlete] cut her hair to reduce drag."[6] Moreover, many of his athletes spoke of this coach as a father figure.[7] This is not a good posture to have toward a coach because that kind of relationship—a parental relationship—would be less critical or circumspect than one's relationship with a coach ought to be.

Like Aristodemus, these athletes demonstrated affiliative behavior toward their coach, a kind of fondness and trust that was likely the result of having grown up in the sport under his care. Maybe the coach was fatherly and supportive and treated them well. Still, I wonder whether they were less awake to his transgressions because of their affinity for him as a person.

Uncritical alignment, or affiliative behavior, toward an admired person is the first way admiration can go awry in distance running. It can make us vulnerable to the character deficiencies of powerful people, and it can place us in positions of submission that compromise our own safety and values. Since young athletes are the most vulnerable to abuse and are the least aware of what types of behaviors may be problematic, accountability structures should be put into place to protect them.

I have two clarifications about these alignment concerns. First, there is often a great deal of ambiguity in coach–athlete relationships because we are humans and are likely to have layers of relationships with our coaches. For example, some athletes are married to their coaches. Other athletes have friendships with them. Even so, it is important to retain a sense of personal agency when it comes to training, to keep oneself safe and to make good decisions that reflect the kind of people we want to be.

Second, the tendency to say—as Aristodemus did—"I'll do whatever you say" is often confused as admirable itself, as a form of teachability or obedience to an authority figure. It is not. Rather, this demonstrates a self-effacing diminution of oneself that is im-proper in the athletic context. Athletes should retain some degree of agency and power so they are not pressed into decisions, such as doping, that do not reflect their values.

I should also mention that athletes are accountable to coaches, but they are also accountable to the World Anti-Doping Agency (WADA) and to their families, friends, and communities. These other accountability relationships should have some bearing on how much authority is given to a coach. For example, WADA, in-sofar as it regulates the integrity of the sport for both coaches and athletes, is a higher allegiance for athletes than the coach–athlete relationship. It is important to consider which accountability relationships are the most important. Otherwise, we are likely to submit to whichever person in authority is the loudest or has the greatest emotional power over us.

The takeaway is that, regardless of how much we admire figures such as our coaches, there are unconstructive (and potentially un-safe) postures we might adopt toward them. One is the noncritical, affiliative stance we explored here. The goal is to emulate good actions, rather than to forfeit our agency toward admirable figures.

Admiring the Wrong People

Whether or not it should be, coolness is important. We are inclined to admire athletes and others in the sport who bear this sparkling quality—call it charisma, popularity, or something else—more so than we might be inclined to imitate a less cool person.[8]

Moreover, this is not a novel concern. "Cool" has always been a confounding feature for virtue. Socrates, in Plato's *Republic*, and Aristotle, in his *Poetics*, both worried about the kind of people being set up as heroes. The Homeric tales that dominated ancient Greek culture gave some figures with questionable scruples— such as Alcibiades, an insubordinate, anger-driven war hero—a platform. They were made to seem beautiful. Plato's Socrates and Aristotle feared that these people would have an outsized influence on the city. The young men would hold these heroes in high esteem and emulate their qualities.

Considering we cannot cast out certain heroes or diminish their presence in the public square, it can be helpful to nudge young athletes toward noticing truly excellent people in the sport and what makes them exemplary—their perseverance, integrity, or courage. We can also remind ourselves that charisma and moral character are not the same things.

Where this can become confusing in our current cultural context is that appearance and charisma are qualities that tend to produce large social media followings. If we use 'follower counts' as a proxy for 'admirability', we may set ourselves up to be shaped by people who model traits and actions that, upon reflection, we may not desire for ourselves.

Admiring the Wrong Qualities in the Right People

When American runner Anton Krupicka burst onto the trail and ultrarunning scene around 2007, he became an ascendant figure. He experienced immediate success in key races such as the Leadville Trail 100-mile, Miwok 100K, Rocky Raccoon 100-mile, and others, and everyone was talking about him. Soon after, there began a curious phenomenon of young men training and racing in minimalist running shoes, with long hair, shirtless, and wearing small shorts—adopting Anton's characteristic aesthetic. They admired Anton, so they dressed like him.

This is not a phenomenon unique to running. Football and basketball franchises make a gold mine selling player merchandise, such as jerseys with favorite players' numbers on the back. Young players get haircuts modeled by their favorite athletes. They wear the same sneakers. This phenomenon is a significant part of sports fandom. Furthermore, nothing is inherently problematic about mimicking an admired athlete in this way. It is a nice gesture of support.

However, viewed from the perspective of character education, it is not productive for us to emulate the accidental features of a person, such as haircuts or clothing. We become no more excellent or like the athlete, in ways that actually matter. It is much more productive to emulate the substantial features that make an athlete admirable in the first place.

For Anton, we might emulate his perseverance or preparation. We might imitate his reportedly peaceable demeanor, his reflective nature, or his minimalist approach to possessions in an otherwise consumer-based culture. No amount of merchandise or clothing changes can help us to adopt these excellences. We have to practice these traits to acquire them.

So this is the third error we often make toward those we admire: We imitate accidental features of their person, when it would profit us much more to reflect on what makes them exceptional and to emulate those qualities instead.

Character Asymmetry Concerns

A final way admiration may go awry is to assume that an athlete we admire for some observed excellence is above reproach in *every* way. We tend to think of humans as caricatures of humans, all good or all bad—heroes or villains. This is odd since, upon introspection, we tend to find a mixture of good, somewhat good, bad, and somewhat bad thoughts, motivations, and actions in ourselves.[9] While there are some exceptions—people who are broadly morally virtuous—this is rare. Even those who are broadly morally virtuous, insofar as they are human, they are not morally perfect and will make mistakes. Thus, our admiration should always be circumspect and neither fawning nor naïve.

Furthermore, in general, athletic heroes seem to exhibit a particular kind of character asymmetry. They tend to be excellent in terms of the virtues reinforced in their sport—virtues such as courage, grit, resilience, and perseverance—and less so for virtues of civility, such as gentleness, or for intellectual virtues, such as fairmindedness.

For example, not only is gentleness *not* an excellence in sport, it is sometimes a deficiency of an athlete. Gentleness can prevent athletes from meeting performance objectives. Imagine the gentle lineman or the gentle cross-country runner. A gentle lineman may be disinclined to block opponents effectively. A gentle cross-country runner might lack the rawness and aggression required to tackle the mud and hills. Even so, this trait is often an asset in life outside of sport. Gentleness helps us to respond to conflict with restraint and mildness. It is a good quality to have; it is just not one that we often see modeled by our athletic heroes.

This is something we should be aware of. In admiring an athlete—or in admiring anyone excellent in a specific domain—certain virtues are excluded. This is a coverage reliability issue. Athletes may indeed demonstrate excellence, but it may be excellence of a narrow, or asymmetrical, sort. For this reason, it can be valuable to admire people across different domains, rather than to place our attention on only one person or one kind of person (such as distance runners). This way, a range of good qualities are modeled for us.

Second, we should be cautious about whether and how the people we admire influence us *outside* of their domain of excellence. For example, we would not look to a dentist for weight-lifting advice because this is outside of their area of expertise, nor should we look to a musical celebrity to tell us how to brush our teeth. Likewise, it may not be helpful for us to look to an athletic hero for guidance in how to prioritize family, who to vote for, or how to pursue intellectual goods. They may happen to be excellent in these respects, but whether or not they are is irrelevant to their area of expertise.

Generalizing a person's admirability is a mistake we make in many fields. For example, there is a fallacy we often commit called *ad verecundium*. This fallacy concerns inappropriate authority, or an appeal to an authority outside of the authority's area of expertise. In admiring an athletic hero, we should be aware that, while this person is a valuable model of certain virtues, this does not make them an expert in affairs that extend beyond sport. It is not wise to regard them as such.

Have I made you concerned? Great! Now you are equipped to admire the excellent people in our sport—not uncritically as though they have no faults, not without forfeiting agency, not emulating accidental features of their person, and not acquiescing to their authority in areas outside of their expertise. We are ready to emulate the greats—to learn from them and to become excellent ourselves.

A Sport Full of Exemplars

In January 2021, my teammate, Jim Walmsley, attempted to break the 100-kilometer (62.14-mile) world record, running laps around a marked course in Arizona. I spectated the event from my home computer, impressed, as Jim methodically clicked off the miles. The entire event was a seemingly inhuman spectacle, the way his stride appeared unchanged as the miles passed, and I was certain he would do it. But in the final stretch of the race, Jim started to flag. Viewers watching from home screamed at their computers as Jim willed himself through the finish line.

That day, Jim ran 100 kilometers in 6 hours, 9 minutes, and 26 seconds, or 5:57 pace per mile.[10] He obliterated the American record but fell a painful 12 seconds short of his goal—the world record. I felt a lot of things—proud of Jim, deeply impressed, and in disbelief at what a great athlete he is. I was full of admiration. I shut my computer and returned to my schoolwork. I carried on with my day.

There is a tendency, described by Danish philosopher Soren Kierkegaard, to be *mere admirers* instead of imitators. We see someone excellent and appreciably perceive him but remain unaffected. We carry on unchanged. In contrast, an *imitator* is compelled by the excellent other and acts on what he appreciably perceives.[11] Kierkegaard writes, "An imitator is or strives to be what he admires, and an admirer keeps himself personally detached [and] does not discover that what is admired involves a claim upon him to be or at least to strive to be what is admired."[12]

I am reminded of this distinction as I shut my computer and carry on with my day. I can let my admiration of Jim Walmsley remain inert, as a pleasant feeling that fills me up and then evaporates as soon as I turn my attention to something else. Or I can be an imitator. I can strive to be what is admired.

We are in a sport full of admirable people. I have already introduced Jim Walmsley, who prepares so well for races that he achieves or threatens the greatest records in the sport every time he steps on a starting line, but there are many others as well. In what follows, I provide a few examples.

Courtney Dauwalter

To know her is to love her. Courtney is a former Nordic skier, turned trail and ultrarunner. Her mega talents are exceeded only by her great humility and humor. Among the races Courtney has won are the Hardrock 100 (course record holder), Ultra-Trail du

Mont-Blanc (two-time champion and course record holder), and the famed Western States 100-Mile, one of the most prestigious trail races in the world (course record holder). She is so tough that she once won the Run Rabbit Run 100-mile while battling temporary blindness in the final miles due to some combination of high altitude and contact lens complications, and in 2017, she won a 238-mile race outright by nearly ten hours.

There is much to admire Courtney for athletically. We can imitate her training methods to become faster. But our focus here is on her character, and there is much to emulate in this regard. Furthermore, while physical capability and durability seem to be partly genetic (and may not be entirely imitable on that basis), virtues are open to us. We can improve in these respects.

As I have already mentioned, Courtney is marked by humility. She resists talking about her accomplishments and praises her support team, instead of herself. Humility is a virtue we can practice. She is also marked by humor. Courtney is renowned for her easy-going demeanor and for the dad jokes she tells during races. Having this kind of levity and delight in the activity of training and racing is something we can learn from Courtney and practice ourselves.

Clare Gallagher

Clare is a trail runner from the suburbs outside of Denver, Colorado. She ran cross-country and track at Princeton University, where she also studied ecology and evolutionary biology.

There are two kinds of people in the world—people who enter a room like "Here I am!" and people who enter a room like "There you are!" Clare is the latter. Clare is a supremely talented athlete with incredible leg speed, who has won big races like the Leadville 100-mile and Western States 100-mile. But the first time I met her, I was mostly startled by how present she was in conversation and how she made the room about other people. Her presence is hospitable, or welcoming. This is an excellence we can emulate in Clare.

Also of note about Clare is that, when not running, she invests her energy and attention into advocating for and caring about the natural environment. Take this cue from Clare. If we want to run across and enjoy natural spaces, we should take care of them as well.

Dylan Bowman

Dylan is a trail running champion. Following a collegiate career playing lacrosse at Colorado State University, he transitioned to trail and ultrarunning in his early twenties.

Like Courtney and Clare, Dylan has his fair share of victories. They include the Miwok 100K and Ultra Trail Mount Fuji, with podium finishes at Western States 100, Hardrock 100, and Transgrancanaria 128K. And—like Courtney and Clare—his natural talent greatly exceeds most of ours. But something special about Dylan is how he uses his platform as an athlete.

Dylan works tirelessly to introduce the sport to a broader audience and to share people's stories, through the media company he created. He works to raise the profiles of rising athletes. He is an advocate for the sport, facilitating its growth so that it has a stronger financial future for those who wish to pursue it as a career. Dylan's efforts demonstrate generosity of time and attention. We can't be Dylan Bowman, but we can become more like him in this respect.

Another admirable trait in Dylan is his willingness to rest. Many athletes struggle to take time away from the sport to allow their bodies to recover following long seasons, but Dylan speaks happily about rest seasons. In this way, he models good stewardship of his body. We can emulate him in this respect.

Sara Hall

There is so much to admire about Sara Hall. She is a champion in every sense of the word. Sara is a mother of four adopted daughters from Ethiopia, and she and her husband, Ryan, founded a nonprofit called the Steps Foundation to fight global poverty.[13] She is also one of the greatest road and track runners in American history.

Sara has been competing at the highest levels of the sport since high school, when she won the Footlocker National Cross Country title. Since then, she has competed professionally in every distance event from 1,500 meters to the marathon. Between 2020 and 2022 alone, Sara ran the second fastest marathon in American history, broke the American record in the half marathon, and placed fifth at the World Championships in the marathon. She competes with integrity and courage, often pressing the pace from the gun, and she has stewarded her body so well over the years that her victories span across decades.

We may not be able to emulate Sara's natural ability—her oxygen uptake or raw leg speed—but we can certainly emulate her charity, or love. It is clear from the choices she makes off the track that she prioritizes the people in her life, and that her world is bigger and more service-oriented than running sometimes inclines us. It is really easy to prioritize oneself in distance running, and Sara's example is one of pouring yourself back out, to see and love others, through her parenting and foundation.

The Others

All of the runners I listed here are professional athletes, but there are admirable runners well beyond the elite ranks. Here are a few other runners and people who shape my running:

- There is a runner I admire in Virginia, named Sophie. She is a leader in the trail running community, who encourages people to join in. Sophie also loves her family well and balances ultrarunning with her career. She demonstrates how to order priorities well.
- I admire the elderly man I regularly see out jogging in my neighborhood. I do not know him, but he smiles and waves as I pass. He does a great job remaining consistent and enjoying the process, even after his fastest days are behind him. I admire him for that.
- I admire my dad. He used to be a runner, prior to and during my childhood. I remember how, when we went camping, he would try to slip out of our camper to run before we kids woke up. I would wake up and want to spend time with him or join him on my bicycle, and he never begrudged me. I never realized what a special thing this was—the fact that he received me with love, in his one window of time to go running—until I became a parent. I try to emulate my dad in this way. I would rather be a loving mom than an unavailable yet speedy mom.
- I admire my husband.[14] He is a runner, but that is not the reason I admire him. The reason I admire him is that he has integrity in big and small ways—in teaching, parenting, finances, and the way he answers emails. Also, he always gives me the better of two baked goods, thinking I do not notice. I always notice. My running can profit from the emulation of a person like my husband, who I admire on nonathletic grounds. I can have integrity in my training and racing, and I can show preference to others through sport. Furthermore, life is a lot bigger than sport. Running aside, it is good to emulate excellent people and aim to live likewise.

Admiration to Excellence

I began this section with Kierkegaard's distinction between *mere admiration* and *imitation*. It would be a mistake to merely admire these excellent people and leave unchanged. They demonstrate what a good character looks like, and I want to acquire these excellences myself. So how do I proceed from admiration to possessing virtues myself?

Select a Good Exemplar

The exemplars I named are a great start. But distance running is full of wonderful people. Our sport affords athletes a great deal of time alone in their sneakers with ample time to reflect, while being humbled by big mountains, long runs, and bad weather. These challenges can refine our character in certain ways.[15] It seems that the number of admirable people per capita in distance running is high. Of course, I am biased.

In selecting an exemplar, feelings of admiration can be our guide, but we should critically reflect on the objects of our admiration. As discussed in the previous section, we often admire the wrong people, such as charismatic figures with otherwise bad characters. French and Raven call this "referent power," a kind of authority rooted in a person's likeability.[16] Maybe it is unwarranted, but we are more influenced by people who are likeable or popular. For example, think of the popular kids in your middle school whom everyone took social cues from and wanted to dress like. Just because a person is magnetic or powerful does not mean that he or she is worthy of emulation.

Furthermore, there is empirical support for the idea that we are more likely to imitate exemplars who are relatable to us.[17] What this means is that you do not need to admire the best runner in the world to profit from the emulation of exemplars. Choose someone you find excellent and share something in common with. I used to admire those who squeezed out every ounce of themselves in races, ran high mileage, and put training first in their lives. These days, I tend to admire running moms who compete well but also live well-ordered lives, prioritizing time with their families. Running moms seem accessible to me, and therefore more imitable than those whose lives are distant from my own. In the past, I would have found mothers unrelatable, and it would not have been beneficial for me to set them up as exemplars.

Name the Excellence in Question

It can be helpful to name what is great about your exemplar. Young children imitate without doing so, but the ability to name excellences and defects in those we look to for guidance can make us more circumspect admirers. It can help us distinguish which traits are truly excellent from confounding features like popularity or charisma.

Naming excellences can also help us to figure out which of an exemplar's good qualities are imitable. For example, physiological idiosyncrasies may aid an athlete's performances, such as great height in basketball players and long Achilles' tendons in high jumpers. I may never be able to emulate the long, loping stride of Jim Walmsley or achieve the aerobic efficiency of an Olympian in the 5,000-meter track event. These traits are not "open to me" because of physiological constraints. But I can emulate these athletes in their perseverance, humility, humor, and courage. These qualities are imitable, or available. I can improve in these respects.

In virtue theory, there is a debate about what is called the "articulacy requirement" of moral virtue. It concerns whether someone must be able to name an excellence in order to acquire that excellence. For some virtue theorists, such a requirement ensures that a person's acting in terms of a virtue is truly free—that their action is unmanipulated and involves their own volition. Many theorists find that virtue articulation is too high of a requirement for virtue and argue instead that recognizing a good quality as such, regardless of whether you can explain why, is sufficient to qualify a virtuous action as free.

Regardless of where someone lands in this debate, it can still be valuable to be able to name what is excellent in those we admire. This helps us to guard against confounding factors of personality like popularity, as we have said. It also helps our imitation of excellent people to become more focused. For example, if I can recognize that *resilience* is the quality I admire in a certain mountain runner, this sets me up to practice resilience in particular, rather than to admire this athlete in an amorphous, unspecific way that does not lend well to acquiring the virtue myself.

Furthermore, there is a difference in the role of language in one's admiration, based on maturity level. Children are often shaped by the people they admire in a somewhat naïve way. They imitate largely without resistance, both because they are less discerning than adults and because they have fewer habits already in place.[18] Thus, actions and affections are more "catchy" to them. Children are more likely to be shaped in substantial ways by exemplars because of the immediacy of their imitation.

Conversely, teenagers and adults are more resistant imitators. This is because they already have habits and affections in place. The significance of this is two-fold. First, because young children are less discerning and more strongly impacted by exemplars, it can be valuable for caretakers and coaches to help direct children toward those worthy of emulation, to help them admire excellent people, to the extent that they are able to do so. Second, while young children may not need to name excellences and commit to a plan for how to appropriate these excellences, teenagers and adults generally benefit from using language to do so. Emulation is something that requires more willful action as we mature. Willful actions, insofar as they are characteristically rational, often involve language.

For example, imagine setting a New Year's resolution or a big racing goal. In both cases, speaking one's intention makes the goal more real. There is a kind of accountability that comes from speech. It is easier to explain away a goal when committing to it becomes challenging if you never said it out loud.

Yes, it is unlikely that articulation is necessary for the acquisition of virtue. But it can be beneficial to speak about one's intention to emulate an excellence. Doing so functions as a success condition because of the accountability it offers.

Practice the Excellence

As Kierkegaard observed, it is one thing to notice an excellent quality in an admirable person. It is something else entirely to act in terms of that trait, or to imitate the actions of an exemplar. Imitation means someone's excellence makes a claim on us to do likewise. At this stage, one moves from a mere admirer to an imitator.

Here is an example. I admire the perseverance of an athlete, so I set out to practice this trait alongside the other athletic skills I am developing in my training. I might do so by sustaining an effort for longer than I would be inclined to usually, or I might try to persevere in the focus I have during runs. I practice perseverance in my own context, performing it myself in contexts relevant to me, and I become excellent like the person I admire.

There are three reminders about this process. First, in the same way that we do not run hill repeats once to become competent in mountain running, it is not sufficient to imitate an excellence one time to acquire it. For example, I cannot become a courageous runner by taking a risk once. I need to make a habit of it, practicing a virtue until it becomes my second nature and defines me in a stable way.

Second, we do not want to merely appropriate the same action, mimicking it verbatim. We want to take ownership of the excellence in our unique context. Courage might require different things from me in my situation than for the athlete I admire. First, if I do precisely as the athlete does, I am not the sole author of this action. I am still indexing my actions to another person.

Also, if I am only imitating actions verbatim, I am limited to only performing traits in the ways I have observed them being performed. Consider a comparison to the process of learning how to paint. A novice may become excellent at imitating the pictures someone else has painted. But an *artist* can paint with greater freedom. She can apply the conventions of painting on her own canvas, in her own way. The artist takes ownership for these skills. The virtuous person does the same. She can persevere across various situations, in various ways, rather than only mimicking the way an exemplar perseveres at the end of a race, for example.

A final reminder is that virtue practice is not merely performed by our bodies. We also need to develop fitting motivations for good actions. Philosopher Linda Zagzebski points out that, often when we admire a person, we emulate both a person's *actions* and what we perceive as the *motivation* for the action, too. This is because "part of what [we] admire in the person is the motive."[19]

For example, I admire a young runner on my team who makes a courageous move in the championship meet. I admire the move itself, but I also admire that this teammate rose to the challenge of an important day and fought hard *for her team*. This motivation is part of what is admirable in the courageous action.

I could be wrong in identifying my teammate's motivation, of course. Maybe my teammate was courageous for a bad reason, like trying to win a bet or to make a competitor sad. Even if I am wrong about what actually motivated the action, when I emulate my teammate, I also emulate the perceived motive for that good action. This affords me practice, not just in the mechanics of the good action itself but also in bearing the good sentiment that motivates the action.

Track and Fielding Objections

There are at least two critiques likely to be leveled against moral learning by way of exemplars: (1) the misanthropic rebuttal and (2) the sports are no place for admiration rebuttal.

The Misanthropic Rebuttal

The misanthropic rebuttal goes something like this. If there is anything we should have learned in recent history, it is that humans are untrustworthy and unscrupulous. We should teach our young people not to admire, but to be wary! The world is full of people who will let them down.

My response is first to concede that people are often disappointing. (I can introspect and figure this out right away.) If we examine even the most exemplary person's life closely enough, we are apt to find blemishes. Even so, it is important to take emulation seriously and employ it as a tool for character development. This is for two reasons.

The first is the inevitability of imitation. Aristotle points out that, by nature, we imitate.[20] We find pleasure in doing so, and imitation is a significant means by which social and moral learning occur from an early age. Since imitation is inevitable, doing so with greater self-awareness—and shepherding young athletes toward emulating those who truly merit their admiration—is the most reasonable course of action.

Second, moral infallibility is too high of a requirement for the people we admire. We can learn a great deal from people who are not above reproach in every way, and we should assume that they are not. We have already said that our admiration should be circumspect, rather than naïve; it should be informed by the reasonable expectation that people fall short of being infallible moral guides.

Sports Are No Place for Admiration Rebuttal

Someone might argue that sports are no place for admiration. Sports are for tough people and competitive mindsets, and admiration softens athleticism in unwelcome ways.

This is an interesting rebuttal. Athletics does appear to be an inhospitable place for certain "softer," prosocial emotions and dispositions, such as admiration, patience, and caring. Instead, we perceive sport as an adversarial space, where envy and anger are dominant emotions. But this is more of a caricature than a reality. Many soft emotions sustain relationships among teammates and help us to enjoy the richness of sports. For example, when I care about my friend, a sprinter, and she becomes injured, I deeply empathize. I feel sad with her. This is what it means to be a good teammate. And when she rebuilds herself and returns to her winning ways, I admire her and learn from her resilience.

Often, we speak of our emotions in purely physical terms, but emotions are intentional states, too. They are "about" something or someone. Emotions can be defined as concern-based construals, or representations of the world that see certain objects as valuable.[21] For example, love sees someone or something as loveable. Anger unhappily perceives an injustice.[22] Admiration appreciably perceives an excellent person. In making sports hospitable to a broad range of prosocial emotions (including "soft" ones), our experiences in sport become richer because we can see one another, ourselves, and the world more clearly and perceive what is of value. This helps us to have more well-ordered relationships to the people we compete with and against. Admiration has its place among the emotions that enrich the relational side of sports. And as we described, it can also help us to become better athletes and people ourselves.

5

Good and Fast

Performance-Enhancing Virtues

In early October 2016, I broke the navicular bone in my foot three weeks out from the Trail World Championships. I broke it through a combination of an imbalance, which had developed in my stride, and by running too many miles on hard surfaces. Having had little experience with broken bones, I did not detect a growing pain that should have been a cause for alarm, so I caught the injury after it was too late to recuperate with a few days of rest. The body is resilient if given the space to recover. I did not give it the space.

This was a pitiable occurrence, so close to the Trail World Championships, and I was embarrassed to report my withdrawal from the team. I buried my sorrows in physical therapy appointments, where I went through the arduous process of rebuilding my body back to strength. It was a frustrating season of life.

If you have ever been to a physical therapist, you know what I mean by arduous. The difficulty is not in daring deeds or impressive feats of strength. It is in subjecting oneself to seemingly trivial movements and trusting that they matter. At physical therapy appointments, I was assigned a series of tiny exercises— frustratingly tiny—to perform over a long period of time. I performed ankle rotations and single-leg work. I corrected my stride asymmetry with hamstring curls and clam shells using large rubber bands, and I repeatedly launched off the ground in a simulated running movement, with the physical therapist pulling me backwards using a sling contraption he held onto for resistance. I did these movements repeatedly for weeks on end, restarting upon finishing, and I confess that I had a hard time imagining Sisyphus happy.[1]

By December, I was running again. By February, I had won another national title. It was ugly, but I did it. For the rest of the year, I continued racing a lot—and poorly. Close to a decade of consistent training ended abruptly with my broken foot. Speed came back quickly, but my strength did not because strength is earned over multiple seasons. I needed to put in the time and to recover patiently. And, while I did not always see progress from week to week, I trusted that the investments I made were not in vain, and that I would be strong again. This was true. It took about a year, but I eventually returned to full form.

In my year of return from injury, I learned a lot about resilience— the virtue of recovery. I learned that small exercises make a big difference, and that bouncing back is a considered choice. I learned that recovery, like all forms of training, is a hopeful act. This is unsurprising, since philosopher Nancy Snow writes about resilience's intimate connection to hope.[2] Substantial hopes provide us with mental resolve, help us not to lose heart, and enable us to "maintain effective agency in the face of fluctuations in evidence."[3] Maintaining agency is important. It means we continue to *choose* and to *act* in light of the possibility of renewal, even if we lack visible evidence of progress.

In my injury recovery, I also learned that patience wears sneakers, not slippers. If I could just stay patient—*actively* patient, the kind of patience that would diligently perform the exercises I was prescribed by my doctor—I might become the athlete I was before the injury. I might become an even better athlete. The resilience I gained in my process of renewal would make me a stronger, more adaptable athlete, and this would pay off—both in the process of training and within competitions.

Performance-Enhancing Virtues

A perennial topic in athletics is the maximization of performance. Athletes wonder how they can get the most out of themselves to compete well when it really counts. There are many legitimate ways to go about doing so. Runners can emulate the best athletes in the sport, mimicking their workouts and training routines. This is an effective way to get faster, if we do so sensibly.[4] For example, we should emulate with sensitivity to our own life situations and to our current stages of athletic development. A young runner may not benefit from imitating the training of a runner with years of mileage and experience in the sport. He or she would lack the physical callousing and aerobic base to absorb as much training as a seasoned runner. Also, a runner with a full-time job and all of the stresses that come with employment would lack the time and space to recover properly from workouts, as compared to a full-time professional athlete. For the runner with the full-time job, exact replication of a professional runner's training schedule may result in injury. However, if the runner were to emulate the basic structure of an advanced athlete's training, such as how this athlete periodizes workload across a season, or the traits that sustain the advanced athlete's performances, such as patience or grit, then he or she is positioned to benefit from emulation. Emulation can offer performance benefits because it calls the immature athlete to a higher standard, allowing him or her to "put on" the conditions of the advanced athlete's success.

Athletes can also improve performances by tapering down mileage before an event so that they are well-rested.[5] They can fine-tune their speed work and mimic the topography of the race course in key training runs. Athletes can make improvements to the quality and timing of nutrition and hydration. For example, they can eat beets before races for the cardiovascular benefits that beets purportedly offer.[6] Athletes can buy the best gear, featuring the newest technology. They can wear special carbon-plated shoes and aerodynamic kits, within the legal parameters of our governing body's technology guidelines. Some athletes have even been known to get haircuts prior to important competitions to reduce wind resistance.[7] All of these examples are suitable and effective means of improving athletic performance.

Of course, there are also unscrupulous means by which people maximize performances. Some athletes take performance-enhancing drugs or illicit supplements. They cut courses or find alternative ways to gain a comparative advantage at the cost of their own, and the competition's, integrity. Some athletes tear down course markings midrace so that the athletes behind them are directed off course, as someone once did to me. This was unethical, even though there were no rules in the race manual that explicitly said so. The athlete's performance benefitted from undermining his competition. Thankfully, unscrupulous means of performance enhancement seem to be the exception, rather than the rule, in distance running.

To summarize, there are many ways, legitimate and otherwise, by which athletes maximize performance. For the invested athlete and for dedicated coaches, often no stone is left unturned in training, and no expense is spared to find an edge. Yet, oddly, I have never heard anyone describe moral character in performance-enhancing terms, and character makes a significant difference in how we perform. For example, Athlete X has a competitive advantage because of her unsquelchable joy in the face of difficulty. Athlete Y is thankful. Her gratitude for friends and competitors crowds out agitation in stressful situations. Gratitude provides her with the motivation to continue when conditions are challenging. On balance, gratitude makes her a much more successful athlete than she would be otherwise. It gives her an edge over the competition.

Surely there are other virtues, or acquired excellences of our persons, that improve a runner's performance. Possibilities include resilience (a virtue near and dear to my heart, which was an asset in my own recovery) and humor. These are the carbon-plated shoes of the soul. We cannot buy them, but we can all develop them. They enable us to perform better in running, and they also help us to live fuller, richer lives of good character outside of it. These are called performance-enhancing virtues.

Virtues—A Conceptual Review

Chances are, you can already name several virtues. In fact, if asked to name the qualities you admire in a best friend or in a favorite teacher, you would probably list a few examples of virtues—honest, trustworthy, humorous, or wise. If I asked you to name the traits you admire in an athlete, you might name determination, patience, or courage. These are all examples of virtues.

As a reminder from Chapters 1 and 2, a virtue is a kind-specific excellence. The Greek word for virtue, *aretē*, is best translated as "excellence." By 'kind-specific,' I mean that there are certain excellences proper to different things. A good cat is fluffy, for example. A good tree is not fluffy, since this quality is not relevant to what makes trees excellent. The philosopher Aristotle investigates the virtues of a thing by asking what something's *ergon*, or function, is. This is called Aristotle's Function Argument, and it offers a helpful way to figure out which virtues are relevant to different things. For example, the function of a knife is to cut well. The qualities that permit it to fulfill that function (or to be a good knife) include a sharp blade and a sturdy handle. These are two of the knife's virtues.

Consider a second example: a school bus. The function of a good school bus is to transport students from home to school, safely and on time. Thus, the virtues of a school bus include a sturdy engine and safe seating, among other things. Virtues are kind-specific because not all excellences are relevant to the good in question. It would be odd if the good qualities one sought in a pet cat, for example, included a sharp blade or a sturdy engine. These are not excellences suited to that thing.

When Aristotle speaks of virtues as being suited to something's *function*, he means its characteristic or essential function. For example, a knife can be used as a paperweight, but that is not what a knife is *for*. An essential function concerns something's *nature*—its "principle or cause of being moved and of being at rest in that to which it belongs primarily, in virtue of itself, and not accidentally."[8]

As we discuss in Chapter 7, when it comes to humans, questions of nature and function are more challenging. In part, this is because human life is rich and varied, so it is difficult to identify humanity's essential function. This is also because people have competing beliefs about what a human is *for*. How we answer this question is informed by empirical insights about what a human being is, as distinct from other, nonhuman animals. It is also informed by the various philosophical and theological commitments we individually and collectively hold.[9] For Aristotle, what humans are *for* is to pursue our greatest good, and our greatest good is *eudaimonia*—a rich kind of happiness, or flourishing, suited to our rational natures.[10]

Performance-Enhancing Virtues

Setting aside broad considerations of human nature, Aristotle's Function Argument can be helpful for discerning which virtues support narrower objectives—such as specific goals or vocations. It can also be helpful for identifying performance-enhancing virtues proper to a given craft. By performance-enhancing virtues, I mean the set of character excellences which enable us to perform better in a given role. For running, this means the set of virtues, or character excellences, that offer a constructive impact on an athlete's ability to run far, over those who lack the virtue. How much constructive impact they offer is an empirical question, and the impact is likely variable (from person to person and from virtue to virtue), just like other sources of performance enhancement.

A second way to identify performance-enhancing virtues is to conceive of virtues as excellences of a given practice, as philosopher Alasdair MacIntyre does.[11] Unlike many voices in the virtue ethics tradition, MacIntyre does not identify virtues with respect to the human *as such*. Rather, he identifies virtues in a piecemeal way, deriving them from one's participation in social practices. MacIntyre describes how every human practice—or "socially established cooperative human activity"—has certain standards of excellence.[12] For MacIntyre, we define virtues with respect to meeting these standards of excellence. Virtues are qualities which "[tend] to enable us to achieve those goods which are internal to practices and the lack of which effectively [prevent] us from achieving any such goods."[13] For example, cunning and self-awareness are qualities conducive to success in chess, so these are virtues of chess. Courage and patience are qualities that support the ends of distance running, so these are virtues of distance running. They improve one's ability to run well. They are performance-enhancing.

There are at least two reasons why we should care about performance-enhancing virtues. The first is that, while moral character is frequently overlooked as a means of improving athletic performance, I will argue that certain virtues have performance impacts commensurate to, or greater than, the performance enhancement offered by other tools, like carbon-plated racing flats or well-timed beet juice. Our moral characters are important for how we perform. Moreover, considering that virtue acquisition is open to everyone,[14] at no financial cost, we should take advantage of the improvement they offer.[15]

Second, many of the virtues that are performance-enhancing in distance running are also traits that support a happy life outside of it. Stated differently, many virtues that support successful performance as distance runners also support our *essential function* as humans, the kind of flourishing life *eudaimonists* describe. Joy, resilience, patience, and humor are all virtues that have a measurable benefit on how we perform in sport, and they also position us to meet many of the challenges of daily life. These virtues are traits that we would desire in a friend, a citizen, or a colleague, and they contribute to a happy life overall. By working on developing these virtues, we are also building better characters and richer lives, athletics aside.

So what are some examples of performance-enhancing virtues? For a distance runner, the objective is to run far or (sometimes) to run far *quickly*. There are many virtues that support this end, and most will be unsurprising. For example, perseverance, the virtue of "persisting long in something good until it is accomplished,"[16] is a foundational virtue of distance running, without which we are left unable to do the very thing our sport is about—endurance. If we cannot persevere, it does not matter how aerodynamic our running clothes are or how well we time our pre-race nutrition because we will not be able to finish the run. There are other virtues that support running that may be less obvious. They include joy, humor, and resilience. In what follows, I will introduce each of these four virtues,[17] making the case for their classification as performance-enhancing virtues. Then I will explain why we should develop them.

Resilience

As mentioned earlier, in 2016, I broke the navicular bone in my foot three weeks out from the Trail World Championships, and this break, and the protracted recovery that ensued, occasioned my development of the virtue of resilience. I should confess that resilience is a virtue you never *really* want the occasion to develop. This is because having the opportunity to develop resilience means that something has gone wrong, or you are broken in some way and in need of repair. It means you enter an uneasy space, having to figure out if you are indeed fixable. Not all broken things are. Ask Humpty Dumpty.

Resilience is the virtue of recovery. Philosopher Nancy Snow defines resilience as an excellence relevant to how we cope with or overcome adversity.[18] To be excellent in this respect depends on the *means* of expression. For example, if a runner overcomes the sadness of an injury by wounding a competitor, we would be disinclined to attribute to her the virtue of resilience. Rather, constructive choices, such as weight training and rest, are suitable expressions of the virtue. Second, the virtue of resilience depends on *practical wisdom*. A resilient runner makes prudent choices in the face of adversity. If, in attempting to rebound from a broken foot, a runner just continues to run on it, this would not make her resilient. It would make her imprudent.

Lastly, possession of the virtue depends on the *motivation* for resilient actions.[19] For example, if someone overcomes trials in order to exact revenge, or to return to a life of crime, these faulty motivations would disqualify the person from having the virtue, in the same way that we would be disinclined to attribute the virtue of generosity to a wealthy donor who gives money to satisfy a narcissistic hero complex. The motivation is a central part of the expression of the virtue, and it is also an important part of what we admire in the virtuous person. An example of a suitable motivation for resilience is a desire for restored well-being. Another example is wanting to be happy and whole.[20]

Snow also points out that resilience is often spoken of using faulty metaphors. We speak of *bending*, rather than breaking, or springing back after being hit. These images are problematic because "people are not pieces of foam rubber that simply spring back into shape after being hit by a hard object. We carry the marks of adversity with us ... [and] often we do not regain our original shape."[21] In the case of my own injury recovery, this was a good thing.

Had I regained my original shape, I would have regained my stride inefficiencies and the physical constitution that disposed me to break in the first place. I would have recreated vulnerabilities instead of taking the opportunity to rebuild myself in a stronger way. This was true physically—that my body changed. Internally, I was not the same either. I had grown more aware of the way my body moved through space. I paid more attention to it, valued it, and was on guard against future brokenness.

Additionally, in my injury recovery, I became gritty in the face of difficulties. This was true both across seasons and within races. When I had setbacks in training, I knew how, practically speaking, to rebound, and I was confident that I would. Within races, I could rally back from disappointments. A resilient runner is one who meets disappointment with thoughtful actions and rebounds from defeat. Considering how many setbacks there are in running, this virtue is invaluable, and it is certainly performance-enhancing. It is tough to beat a runner who never gives up.

Joy

Often when I run, I am a theater of passing sensations. I feel happy and bad, elated and sad, in turn, repeatedly all day long. I pass a runner and feel excited. I fall behind on my nutrition and feel dispirited. I get lost and feel sad. The sun shines in my eyes and I feel frustrated. But these are just feelings. They are transient.

To be clear, feelings[22] offer important feedback about external conditions and about what is going well or poorly, such as when we need a snack or whether we have encountered something threatening, and we should do our best not to ignore them. But feelings often have no substantial bearing on how we are actually doing,[23] and they need not define us in the long term. When we run, it can be difficult to remember this because our heart rate is high, and our emotions are heightened. When we run, our feelings shout instead of whisper.

So what is joy? It is another feeling competing for limelight in the theater of passing sensations. Not quite. But it is not entirely separate from the theater either. Joy informs how the actors in the theater perform. It restrains sad feelings from overtaking us, preventing us from falling easily into despair. It also bolsters the spirit. Joy is like a buoy. When pressed, it resists sinking.

Depending on who you ask, joy is defined in different ways. And Thomas Aquinas defines it as an "act or consequence of love," rather than a separate virtue of its own.[24] One thing that seems consistent among contemporary treatments of joy is that it is regarded as something steadier and deeper than passing happy sensations, like happiness. Joy is popularly regarded as a kind of buoyancy or equanimity in the face of discomforts. It involves dispositions to be largely secure from ups and downs—dispositions which are not merely, or even necessarily, emotional in character. By one definition, joy involves emotional dispositions, as well as dispositions to *think* and *act* in terms of what matters most.[25] By this definition, joy is a kind of happy alignment with one's good purpose that offers internal stability.

Furthermore, while feelings are caused by exterior conditions, such as things that please us, surprise us, or cause us harm, joy is sustained by *interior* goods.[26] Joy can arise from a personal sense of accomplishment. Twentieth-century Dominican Servais-Théodore Pinckaers describes how joy "proceeds from a personal act, a choice that we make, a decision we have reached, an action undertaken that conforms to our sense of truth and of the good and to which we give consent in spite of the effort or the needed sacrifice."[27] Joy can be experienced through struggle and sacrifice.[28] It is a kind of purposefulness that sustains us through peaks and valleys.

Joy is a performance-enhancing virtue because there are many peaks and valleys, literal and metaphorical, in mountain running. Having this kind of buoyant fixity on our purpose, or an internal anchor, can keep us afloat through really difficult times. Joy is a carbon-plated shoe of the soul, offering extra cushion and bounce when we really need it. Realistically, joy has carried me many more miles than fitness has.

Perseverance
When I coached a middle school track and field team, I ran alongside athletes in practice. When I noticed they were struggling,

I would say something to the effect of "Perseverance means to remain under a burden. I am not asking you to do anything different from what you are already doing. I am just asking you to *stay*."

Perseverance is a virtue that is conceptually simple. All you have to do is stay where you are, or to keep doing what you are already doing, in working toward some good end. But "conceptually simple" is not the same thing as "easy." It does not feel good to persevere in many cases. We feel it in our lungs and in our legs, and we can be tempted to quit—or to do anything else other than to *stay*.

Aquinas defines perseverance as "persist[ing] long in something good until it is accomplished."[29] It is the virtue of endurance or staying in place, and it is an auxiliary excellence of the principal virtue of fortitude. Unlike constancy, which is the disposition to stand firm against external difficulties, perseverance's object is internal to its task, and its difficulty "arises from the very continuance of the act."[30] Stated differently, continuing to do the same thing is hard, regardless of any obstacles that come our way. This is something we tend to know as endurance athletes. Doing the same thing for a long time is difficult, and it requires commitment and training. If there is one virtue that belongs to the sport of distance running, it is perseverance. And if there is one virtue that is performance-enhancing in our sport beyond all the others, it is also perseverance. However, perseverance is a virtue that is easy to get wrong, and there are two main ways that we do so: irresolution and intransigence.

In the classical tradition, moral virtues are often described as being positioned between two vices—a vice of excess and a vice of deficiency. For perseverance, the vice of deficiency is a kind of softness, or an inability to persist.[31] When considering perseverance as an intellectual virtue, philosopher Nathan King applies the term 'irresolution' to this vice, and he describes how it is often connected to sloth. As an example, he names "the high school student who abandons his geometry homework after five minutes because he finds it difficult."[32] In running, we may be inclined to do the same thing—to quit as soon as our task becomes challenging.

Irresolution is a helpful word for runners, since, if we are not resolute, or steadfast, in our commitment to reach the finish line, it is unlikely we will make it. We need to be trees deeply rooted in our purpose, in the same way that we characterized joy. Reasons to quit always present themselves over the course of a long run, and these reasons grow, if not more *logically* compelling, certainly louder when we are tired. Being able to resist these reasons, through the virtue of perseverance, positions us to be much more successful athletes. That ability is performance-enhancing.

However, perseverance has a vice of excess, too, and it is called pertinacity. It involves bullheadedness or "hold[ing] on imprudently."[33] King uses the word *intransigence*, describing a stubborn persistence to a goal that is no longer worthwhile.[34] This vice, while likely less common than irresolution among the general population, describes a disposition not uncommon among distance runners. The phrase "death before DNF"[35] is indicative of it. Distance runners are characteristically recalcitrant.

Persisting through difficulty is generally helpful. Indeed, it is one of the best things we can learn to do. It is an asset to our running—a performance-enhancing virtue—and a disposition that makes us more successful in many spheres of life. It involves a kind of self-mastery or the ability to self-govern in order to commit to an end, rather than flit off or quit in the face of difficulty. What could be more valuable than that? But it would be a mistake not to mention the possibility of intransigence, particularly among those who are inclined to push themselves too far.

Persistence itself is not an unqualified good. It does not always constitute the virtue of perseverance. Sometimes we should rest, call it a day, or reconsider our commitments. It all depends on the good we are committed to (whether it is indeed good) and how that good squares with the rest of our lives. For example, we would not want to press through serious injury to finish a race, even if we were capable of getting ourselves to *stay*. The virtue rests on practical wisdom regarding which goods are worth sticking to.

Humor

In the summer of 2019, I competed in a 50-mile race in the cow fields and trails of western New York. Before sunrise, a group of us gathered by the start line, and we had the kind of conversations in which you say hello while looking at your feet lest your headlamp blind your interlocutor as you introduce yourself. There is no eye contact with headlamps. You meet one another by voice only and then re-meet each other as the sun comes up. The whistle blew, and we were on our way.

The race was hard. In the weeks preceding, I had been feeling somewhat overextended in training after a long season, and, while this feeling often abates for me once the gun goes off, that day it didn't. I felt slow and stale in the humidity. After the first of four loops, at 12.5 miles each, I knew it was going to be a long day. I was also probably taking myself too seriously. I ran through the fields, ankle-deep in cow manure (this is not a metaphor), thinking, "Look at your life! Look at your choices." Then it started to rain.

This was not a summer sprinkle. It was a deluge so great the course flooded, and sheets of rain restricted my vision such that I felt like I was running through plexiglass. Rain was the best thing that could have happened to me. Alone in the fields, I started laughing. And I ran hard.

What saved my race in the cow fields that day was humor, or the blithe recognition of the comically incongruous in my situation. It was a performance-enhancing virtue, without which I might have despaired.[36]

If any of the virtues listed is a surprising candidate for a performance-enhancing virtue, it is probably humor. First, it may be unclear why laughter is an *asset* for athletic performance. Someone might wonder whether the presence of humor is actually indicative of a problem—that the athlete is not taking her craft seriously enough. Second, many people fail to consider humor as a virtue at all because there are so many malicious forms of the quality.

For example, often people use humor as an expression of superiority, or as a means of disparaging their peers.[37] There are racist and sexist forms of humor. Other people take inappropriate or outsized pleasure in jokes, such that they act like buffoons.[38] Still others use laughter to expose problems in society. Aristophanes did this in ancient Athens and political satirists do this now, and, if received well by their hearers, this can be a constructive use of humor in a democratic society that relies on frank speech. However, in other cases, the kind of response political satirists provoke in their hearers is disdain for the state of things, rather than the motivation to effect change. When humor is used to this effect—provoking disdain— it may be unconstructive. There are many questions to ask about humor—its forms, motivations, and consequences—and there are certainly many suspect, if not outright harmful, forms of humor.

The kind of humor that I am referring to here as a moral virtue— and a performance-enhancing one at that—is a special kind of humor. It was first described by Søren Kierkegaard and later refined by philosopher Robert Roberts. Roberts defines it as a kind of "blithe humility," or a humor about oneself that is morally excellent.[39] Humor is a happy perception of the comically incongruous. It involves the ability to see the contradictions in ourselves, and in the world around us, and to respond with levity. Examples of contradictions include not living up to the expectations we have set for ourselves and failing to meet our objectives, as well as the little incongruities that define us as humans—imperfect, messy, irrational, contradictory *humans*. To see clearly the contradictions in oneself is considered an important part of wisdom.[40]

The virtue of humor is indispensable in races. Things rarely, if ever, go perfectly, especially as race distances grow longer. Sometimes we get lost on course, fall behind on hydration and nutrition, or fail to compete as we intended to or think we should be capable of. And considering we are often alone with our thoughts for long stretches of time during races, frustrations can fester.

Admittedly, humor has probably saved more of my races than I can count. It is valuable to be able to laugh at yourself. Performance-wise, it is profitable to perceive the comically incongruous in your situation, to meet it with a smile, and to keep moving forward. A racer who laughs is more effective than one who wallows.

Additionally, humor is performance-enhancing when it comes to preparations as well. This is because it positions us for personal growth. Blithe humility allows us to rightly perceive our deficits, or the space between the people we *currently are* and the people we *should become*.[41] Moreover, we perceive these deficits happily, or as a nonthreatening ground for improvement. This posture makes us teachable and positions us to continue growing over time, inching closer to our objectives. It is a mindset helpful for the athlete, who needs to maximize her potential over the course of her athletic career.

Don't Miss the Opportunity to Develop Virtues

When I say that moral character is an integral part of who we are as athletes, this seems incontestable. Of course, our training centrally addresses the embodied aspects of the sport—our aerobic conditioning, physical strength, agility, and ability to ascend and descend mountains with minimal muscle strain. These are important things. But *we* are the one running these races—all of us, and not just our legs. Thus, the kind of people we are—the dispositions we have, our motivations, traits, likes and dislikes, and our habits of attention—inform whether and how we can do what we set out to do.

It often seems as though we forget to have explicit conversations in sport about the kinds of interior traits that sustain us as athletes— traits like resilience, joy, and humor. Instead, most of the time when ethics is introduced into athletic conversations, it is because of transgressions: someone took performance-enhancing drugs, cheated, or violated the spirit of the sport in some substantial way. Stated differently, ethical conversations in sport are often framed in terms of the *negative*—what one *ought not* do, without providing a vision for what one ought to *do* or *be* instead.

This wholly negative framing is a mistake because it offers an asymmetrical picture of what athletics (and the good life more broadly) consists of. A good life does not merely consist of the absence of bad actions, such as stealing or lying. It also consists of the good actions we do perform, such as acts of justice or courage. Likewise, a good athlete is not the athlete who simply fails to cheat or disrespect competitors. The good athlete is also marked by great feats, perseverance, courage, and a dedication to "not letting one's capacities lie fallow."[42] Virtue ethics can provide us with a vocabulary and a means of discussing these positive qualities and help provide athletes with a vision for what a rich athletic life can look like.

In summary, to forget about character is to miss a unique opportunity that sports provides to reinforce the development of qualities that make our lives, inside and outside of sport, a lot richer. Second, as I have argued in this chapter, to forget about character is to leave on the table a significant means of performance improvement. The set of virtues I named, as well as others (such as patience, courage, and grit), offer a constructive impact on an athlete's ability to run far, over those who lack these virtues.

Track and Fielding Objections

I anticipate there being two kinds of objections to describing virtues in these terms—as performance-enhancing, or as amenable to athletic improvement. The first kind of objection is motivational, and the second is developmental.

The Objection from Motivation

The motivational objection goes like this: We have already described, earlier in this chapter as well as in Chapters 1 and 2, how important having a suitable motivation is for the presence of a virtue. The idea is that, it is not simply *whether* and *how* we do an action that make it a good action. We also need to do the action for a fitting reason.[43] For example, if we act kindly in order to manipulate a foe, then this is not a virtuous action. If we persevere—remaining long in a task—in order to avenge a petty work dispute, this does not make us virtuous in the given respect. Part of what is admirable in a good action is the motivation for doing so.

Well, if motivation matters for the presence of a virtue, then do we undermine the process of developing virtues by acquiring a virtue *in order to improve our athletic performance*? Is this an unsuitable motivation for developing these qualities? This is a good question.

First of all, no. It is not necessarily true that athletic improvement is an unsuitable motivation for good actions. In fact, two contemporary virtue ethicists, Julia Annas and Matthew Stichter, describe the "drive to aspire" as a fitting motivation for virtue.[44] Athletic improvement would fall under this characterization. It is not ill-placed to aspire, or to seek improvement, in the good endeavors to which we are engaged. This includes running. In fact, it would be odd if we did not desire to do well. Passivity with respect to improvements would signal a bigger motivational problem than the drive to aspire does.

Second, athletics is an incomplete means of virtue development anyway. It offers practice in doing good actions, such that they can become habits, or stable features of our character. However, on its own, athletics is insufficient for the development of these qualities because we still need to do the internal work to align ourselves with good ends.

In the classical tradition, athletics (alongside poetry) served as a propaedeutic to (or preparation for) formal learning.[45] Students would participate in sport as a means of forming good habits and affections, and this would make them disciplined enough to be teachable. But the idea was not that this was the end of, or sufficient for, their character development. It was just the beginning. Students would continue developing virtues as they matured and entered more formal learning spaces. They grew as citizens, were exposed to stories of heroes who exemplified good lives, engaged with reasons for actions, and learned how to choose well for themselves—consistently and for the right reasons. Students developed agency with respect to their own actions, and they took ownership for the habits they already had in place because of their early formation (formation which was not entirely their choice, since much of our early development is dictated by the habits formed in us by caretakers). This kind of internal work, which often consists of self-reflection and motivational revisions, is also a critical part of virtue acquisition.[46]

Why this matters is that, even if the motivations for developing virtues in the context of sport were unsuitable, this would not be a problem. It is not unprecedented to think that motivational revisions can happen later. It is valuable that sports offer us the space to practice the right habits of thinking, feeling, and acting. This is true even if our virtue-tracking[47] actions are not motivated by, and ordered to, all of the right things. So, yes, motivations matter. But athletics need not bear the responsibility for developing them.

The Objection from Development

The objection from development goes like this: Certainly, character is an important part of racing success. However, the performance-enhancing virtues I described, if indeed valuable for performance, will be developed incidentally to the process of athletic development. Therefore, we need not pay them any additional attention.

This is a stronger objection. An example is this: Consider a girl who runs outside every day. Year after year, she develops the ability to run for longer periods of time. Since perseverance is the virtue of staying in place, does this mean she has already developed this virtue without even intending to? And, if so, can we assume the same thing for other virtues that support good performance? It seems that the virtues that support success in distance running, such as courage, patience, and practical wisdom, will already be reinforced in practice. Therefore, we need not address them.

Frankly, yes. This is a helpful insight. Insofar as a given character excellence supports good performance, there is a sense in which it may be naturally reinforced in practice. Its development becomes incidental to the process of training, and this is, in part, what makes athletics such a great tool for character development. Sports offer practice in virtue in the context of the activities we love. For example, running farther is, under another description, practice in perseverance. I agree with this insight. However, I contend that it is still valuable to talk about character *explicitly* as a goal alongside, and as an asset to, peak performance. This is for two reasons.

First, that virtue development is incidental to distance training seems to be the case for some performance-enhancing virtues more so than for others. For instance, patience is a natural complement to distance training, and we can see how this excellence would be regularly reinforced in practice. For example, a runner must slowly, patiently mete out her efforts in a track workout. This way, she is capable of completing all of her assigned repetitions. She develops this virtue as a means of improving her performances on the track. However, other virtues are a less natural part of distance training, unless explicitly addressed. An example is joy. We defined joy as a kind of happy alignment with one's good purpose that offers internal stability. It is an asset in races, particularly in long races, and it shields us from despair in times of difficulty. However, it is unlikely that joy will be a natural part of the conversation of daily training. Conversations of this nature—such as probing the condition of one's spirit, or reflecting on the interior goods that sustain an athlete—are not ones often addressed in a training log. So for virtues such as joy, their development is unlikely to be incidental to the process of training. A concerted effort will be needed to develop them.

Second, being able to name character excellences and deficits is a valuable way to identify deficiencies in practice and in performance, with greater precision and honesty. For example, oftentimes when an athlete cannot "stay in place"—continuing to run at a given pace—he is inclined to think in terms of the physical. Maybe he thinks he has a training weakness or is suffering from fatigue from school or work stresses. He may be correct. However, it might also be the case that he is internally busy, having trouble staying present, and this is his impediment to running further. Having a vocabulary to describe good and bad features of character can be clarifying for helping us to identify strengths and defects. Thus, while character development is incidental to the process of training to a certain extent, the process of developing these virtues can be enriched and strengthened by naming and speaking about these virtues directly.

6

Bad Competition

Performance-Enhancing Vices

My first contact with the World Anti-Doping Agency (WADA) happened the day before my first World Championships in the Netherlands in 2013. My husband, David, and I were reading in the team hotel's business lounge. I was quaking with fear because, just a few minutes prior, I had been locked into the hotel restroom. The restroom had three access doors to pass through until you were in the inner sanctum of it, for the most heroic level of bathroom seclusion I have ever encountered. Entering the bathroom was like entering Narnia.

In any case, the innermost door became jammed. Ultrarunners are not known for their brawn, so I could not exactly muscle it open. My best bet would be to use my endurance to whittle the door down with my body over time by repeatedly *running* at it (i.e., employing my only physical skill), and that could take years. So there I was, trapped inside of the triple-door Narnia bathroom where no one could hear my screams. I did scream.

I am not exactly sure how it happened, but somehow my underdeveloped noodle arms wrenched the door open. I ran out of the restroom shaking and alive, like I had just been given a second chance at life and this would be my renaissance. That was when a WADA agent began calling my name and said I needed to come with her for a pre-competition drug test. I asked her if I could bring my book and my husband. The four of us (the WADA agent, my husband, my book, and I) piled into a tiny car and headed to the athlete village drug testing area.

After waiting in a small room with runners from several different countries, the agent presented me with a form to declare any drugs or supplements I was taking. (I had nothing to declare.) Next, I was presented with a set of factory-sealed bottles with serial numbers on them. I chose which two bottles I wanted to hold my samples (one for an "A" sample, one for a "B" sample), in case of false positives or other testing errors. Also, I was instructed to secure the caps on the bottles myself, so I was confident that the security of my samples would not be compromised. It was all very interesting for someone studying to be an ethicist—to participate in cheating detection. My only concern was that they took a bit of my blood, and I was planning to use it in the race the next day.

The following day was the championship. It went well enough that I was selected for a second drug test. This time, the WADA agent located me moments after the race. She was one of the first people I spoke to after twenty-four hours of running. I was exhausted and shivering in the cold rain, draped in an American flag, and she helped me to my feet and escorted me to the drug-testing facility. There, the other top finishers and I exchanged weary smiles as we awaited our turns for testing.

The Drug Testing Pool

I thought all of this was behind me after that day, but every year, WADA selects a batch of athletes to include in the International Testing Pool. These athletes record their whereabouts on a weekly basis, including a 60-minute daily time window when they will always be available for a test. The process is inconvenient, particularly for ultramarathoners. We are asked to provide a "training site," which is not something an ultrarunner has. Instead, I supplied lists of zip codes I planned to run through each day. But this process also keeps the sport honest, and I personally do not want to race against people who cheat.

There are many ways that people cheat. Performance enhancement (or "doping") is a category term for various kinds of cheating violations in sport. Examples in distance running include the use of anabolic steroids (synthetic testosterone); various kinds of hormones, such as erythropoietin (EPO), human growth hormone (HGH), and insulin; stimulants, such as cocaine, epinephrine, or high levels of caffeine; and narcotics, such as morphine and oxycodone. On WADA's banned list are many over-the-counter cold and flu medicines, asthma inhalers,[1] and marijuana in competition, although permissions can be granted for certain medicines (such as inhalers) through a process known as a "Therapeutic Use Exemption" (TUE) for athletes with a demonstrated medical need.

Alongside these banned substances, certain *processes* are also banned in sport. One is called "blood doping"—the "manipulation of blood and blood components"[2]—such as by removing blood, allowing the body to regenerate, and then injecting the original blood back into the body to achieve greater blood volume. This method was infamously employed by American cyclist Lance Armstrong.[3] Another banned process is the use of intravenous (IV) infusions of more than 100 milliliters over a twelve-hour period without medical justification.[4] Athletes sometimes manipulate their plasma volume levels through infusions to mask their use of prohibited substances.

These rules are in place to protect clean athletes from cheaters, and to protect athletes who might be tempted to cheat from themselves. The United States Anti-Doping Agency (USADA) notes, "Doping is both a health issue and an ethics issue. Performance-enhancing drugs can be extremely dangerous and even deadly."[5] An example is that anabolic steroids decrease heart function and are associated with liver damage and an increased risk for tumors.[6] Yes, they may also aid muscle development, but at what cost?

Protecting athletes against doping, however inconvenient, is imperative, and I was grateful for the system in place. For the next three years, I was on WADA's out-of-competition drug-testing list and fell into a rhythm of notifying them wherever I went—to the grocery store, to the library, and on runs. Years later, I remain fastidious about reading labels on my vitamins and asking pointed questions about medicines because having strict liability for whatever you put in your body becomes a sobering notion when you know you could be tested any day, any time.

The ironies of this situation were not lost on me: I was a professional ethicist, being monitored for cheating behaviors. Also, these cheating behaviors concerned athletic enhancements, and I barely possess the muscularity to open a bathroom door.[7]

The State of the Sport

This should not come as a surprise to anyone who has ever participated in distance running, but there is evidence of vice and poor behavior in our sport. Some of it is obvious, like taking performance-enhancing drugs, selfishness, or endlessly boasting about one's feats. Some of it is perhaps less obvious, like intemperance or committing to finish lines even when we ought to stop, which we will examine as "intransigence," a vice of perseverance.

Some of these vices are a consequence of the fact that human beings are the ones who play sports—flawed, confused, complex human beings. But some vices are also selected for, and reinforced by, our participation in sport. They make us more successful performers.

In this chapter, I examine the vices of distance running and argue for the presence of a class of vices called performance-enhancing vices (PEVs). These are defects of character that assist us to be better performers in running. PEVs result from a misalignment between a good life and a good run, and they are a difficult set of vices to root out because of their constructive impact on performance. Having a good character may have a performance cost. This puts athletes and coaches in an odd position.

In the following section, I define these concepts—vices in general, and performance-enhancing vices in particular. Then, I consider several vices, such as intransigence and envy, as candidates for PEVs. Finally, I assess additional vices of the sport, which are reinforced not because of their performance relevance but because of the media and marketing culture in athletics.

Defining our Terms

Vices

Vices are defects of character. It is likely that you can already name several, since these are the words you use when you chastise the people in your life that you find blameworthy or problematic in certain ways. Examples include deceit and fraudulence, which we see in cheating behaviors, as well as envy, pride, sloth, and greed.

There is a fair amount of consensus regarding the traits we consider to be vices. For example, most people agree that dishonesty and malice are bad traits. These are traits we would not want in a neighbor or in a friend. But there are other vices that either in theory or practice are held as good traits in different contexts. The set of vices may also vary depending on one's philosophical or theological commitments.

For example, lust is a vice for Aquinas, in that it opposes chastity. Today, many people do not consider lust to be a problem at all. We appeal to it in marketing campaigns and on television shows and regard it as an asset or good-making feature in entertainment. Greed is a second vice from the classical tradition that is seemingly prized in today's consumerist culture. If pressed, people would likely concede that it is not an excellence of persons, or a quality one would desire in a friend, but we often live and act as though the acquisition of goods is our highest objective. We want big homes, not small homes, and fancy vacations, not modest ones. In colleges, students are pressed into business and marketing majors, rather than humanities and the arts. Money is the good that we seek. In Chapter 7 we examine why this orientation—a life characterized by greed—is an inadequate view of happiness.

Impatience is a third example. In the classical tradition, impatience involves failing to suffer well for a "hoped for good."[8] Today, many regard impatience as an asset. In a work-driven Western world, activity is often confused with meaningful work. We mistake patience for idleness, and we laud impatience as purpose and productivity. To be impatient is to be perceived as driven and goal-directed.[9]

A final example of preexisting commitments informing one's set of vices is how different thinkers discuss pride. For example, Aquinas describes pride—the vice of overvaluing oneself, or of aiming higher than what one really is[10]—as the root of all sins.[11] By contrast, Aristotle does not include a vice of pride. For Aristotle, aiming high is a key part of magnanimity, or of being great-souled. His magnanimous man "deems himself worthy of great things and *is* worthy of them."[12] What Aquinas considers *over*valuing is what Aristotle sees as valuing oneself suitably. Aquinas also describes a virtue of magnanimity, but he describes it in such a way as to exclude those who overvalue themselves. That is, he describes a kind of greatness of soul that is not viciously proud.

These are not insignificant differences. The great-souled man for Aristotle and the great-souled man for Aquinas are not the same person. Put more strongly, Aquinas would conceive of Aristotle's magnanimous man as exhibiting the vice that grounds all other moral deficiencies and prevents us from the end he describes as our greatest good: communion with God.

Thus, in asking the question of what a vice is, one first needs to have a clear vision of what a good life is. Is a good life one of great wealth, power, or wisdom, or is it reaching overwhelming success in sport? Is the good life a kind of rational happiness or flourishing in accordance with virtue, suited to our human nature? Can the good life be achieved all on our own, or do certain excellences need to be infused in us with divine assistance, in the way that Aquinas describes? These are important questions. In fact, they may be the most important questions we ask regarding how we should live.

Defining Vice

In the previous chapters, we defined virtues as acquired excellences of one's character. We said there are many different accounts of what constitutes virtue, and we aligned with a neo-Aristotelian model, describing them as dispositional traits to think, act, and feel in excellent ways that are relevant to that trait. The same features that we described for virtues—stability over time, consistency across situations, meeting a high threshold for acting in terms of the trait, and the central involvement of a motivational component—also apply to vices. The main difference is that vices are just oriented in the opposite direction, toward the wrong goods.[13]

Excess and Deficiency

For Aristotle, there are generally two ways in which one might incline toward vice. For each moral virtue, he describes a vice of *excess* and a vice of *deficiency* with respect to the domain the virtue is concerned with. For example, an excess of fear is cowardice, and a deficiency of fear is recklessness.[14] Both are vices proper to courage. An excess of conversation is buffoonery, and a deficiency of conversation is boorishness. Wittiness is the virtue positioned between these two vices.

In Chapter 2, we explored how, in forming a virtue, we want to err in the direction that opposes our natural bent, to incline ourselves toward the mean. This is an odd prescription, if you think about it. We are being advised to practice one vice, to cure a different vice. This would be like if a doctor prescribed a common cold to cure the flu. Both are bad states to be in. However, this is a developmental prescription, and the prescribed vice is not a final landing spot. Aristotle seems optimistic that a learner is like a piece of warped wood, suitably taut as to resist an opposing pull. Our natures are not pliable like aluminum foil, holding the manipulation in place. The learner who acts rashly, in order to cure cowardice, is unlikely to remain there.

Still, one might wonder about the internal state of a learner while practicing the opposing vice. For example, when I am a boor, trying to cure my boorishness through buffoonery, do I simply *act* like a buffoon—telling too many and unbefitting jokes? Should I *think* buffoonish thoughts and *feel* buffoonish feelings, too? Am I like a method actor, playing the part of a buffoon, and hoping to become a bit more like the character I portray?

In Chapter 3, we explored how *actions* often precede changes in *emotion*. Courageous attempts at a hill workout can change the amount of fear we experience. Maybe when I initially act in terms of the courage I do not yet possess, I still think and feel in cowardly ways. Over time, these thoughts and feelings adjust toward the virtue.

This seems an imprecise science. For example, perhaps in acting rashly to cure my cowardice, I overshoot courage and become reckless. Then I am in no better position! I just have a new vice. Because of this risk—of overcorrecting to develop a new vice—virtue practice is a character development strategy that is incomplete on its own. It should be coupled with other strategies, such as exposure to a role model who exemplifies a virtue. That way, we can keep in mind what the goal is, rather than trading one vice for another.

Not All Vices Have an Excess

An important note is that not all vices are describable as excesses or deficiencies of emotions. For example, philosopher Nathan King points out that the excess of the virtue of fairmindedness is not a vice, but another virtue—intellectual charity.[15] A second example is Aquinas's theological virtues—faith, hope, and love. These virtues have no vices of excess. You cannot be too loving, faithful, or hopeful. The same is true for intellectual virtues. There is no such thing as being too understanding or too wise. For these virtues, to conceive of virtue as a "mean" between two vices does not make sense. There are only vices of deficiency.

For virtue development, this means that there is no opposing vice to err in the direction of. For virtues without a mean, virtue practice just means acting in terms of the virtue—for example, acting more loving to develop the virtue of charity, without concern for hitting an excess.

If You Do Not Have Virtues, Does This Mean You Have Vices?

No, it does not. In the same way that there is a gap between *being in excellent physical condition* and *being out of shape* as a runner, there is a gap between *virtue* and *vice*. Most of us are somewhere in that gap.

In the previous chapter, we defined this gap using Miller's idea of "mixed traits."[16] The idea of a mixed trait is that we act predictably and stably in certain ways, such that we demonstrate the possession of a trait—cheating in certain ways, but not in others, having unfitting motivations toward honesty in some ways, but not in others. Most people do not think, act, and feel consistently excellent enough, across situations, to meet this high threshold of virtue. Furthermore, we do not think, act, and feel unsuitably enough on a consistent basis to meet the threshold for vice. This means most of us are somewhere in the middle—with both virtue-tracking and vice-tracking dispositions, and ample room for moral improvement.

There are other ways to theorize this uneasy, in-between moral space that most of us occupy, aside from Miller's mixed traits view. We could lower the threshold of virtue, denying that virtues require such a high standard of excellence. But in the same way that lowering our athletic standards is an unsatisfactory way to "meet our goals," lowering the standard of moral excellence does not change the fact that virtue is a higher attainment.

We could describe virtues in more granular ways—as "local" or limited traits. For example, someone may be patient in races but impatient at family functions, at the Department of Motor Vehicles, or just in general. We could still attribute to this person the "local" virtue of "patient racing."

But this "local trait" terminology is not what we usually mean when we say someone is virtuous. We think of virtues in a general way. For example, I would be disinclined to call someone patient if I noticed a counterexample—that the person could not wait patiently in roller coaster lines or while sitting in traffic. Defining virtues as global traits, or traits that apply across situations, matches how we speak of virtues in everyday life.

In any case, many of us exist in this in-between moral space, and most of us have ample room for character improvement. In the same way that it is dissatisfying for a runner to remain in the in-between space of *not-unfit* but also *not-excellent*, we should want to close this gap toward moral excellence, too.

First, we need to figure out which vice-tracking tendencies we may be unintentionally reinforcing through participation in our sport.

Performance-Enhancing Vices

It is early in the morning. The skies are dim, and I am tightening my shoelaces for the third time. The race director makes announcements and then calls the runners to the start line. He asks for the fastest runners to come to the front and everyone else to file in behind. This way, the slower runners will not impede the faster ones when the gun goes off, and those in contention will have fair starting positions.

This is an odd moment if you think about it, and I do. Unlike in track races, where runners are given a hip number and assigned a lane, road and trail runners are asked to self-seed, or to position themselves compared to one another before the race starts. To do so, we need to know two things: our own speed and the field's speed. We need to anticipate where we will stack up before the gun goes off.

I want to tuck myself into the middle of the field because I am uncomfortable with the idea of being proud or brash, or even being perceived as such. But I remind myself that humility does not require self-sabotage or mousy behavior. I have trained really hard, and I plan to run fast. I think I can win. Furthermore, I want to win. So I take a deep breath, tighten my shoelaces one last time, and find a spot on the starting line.

Pride

I often wonder whether malicious pride is an asset in distance running. I do not mean proper pride—the feeling of pleasure in a job well done, or the satisfaction with one's own good choices. I do not mean magnanimity either—a pursuit of greatness informed by an accurate self-appraisal and knowledge of which great feats are, in fact, worthwhile. What I am interested in is *superbia*, or the vice of pride—an outsized and unbridled preoccupation with one's own successes, which Aquinas calls the root of all of the other vices. I want to know whether this kind of pride is an asset in distance running. I want to know whether it can make a person run faster. My suspicion is that it can.

I think there are other vices, too, that can make us run faster and compete harder. Envy is an example. It seems that perceiving another person's successes as one's own loss would motivate a runner to push harder. Intransigence—the vice of excess with respect to perseverance—is also reinforced in distance running. It supports the ability to finish, whatever the cost, and as such is performance-enhancing. Selfishness and certain forms of intemperance likely facilitate good performance, too. Also, deception—the vice behind shortcuts like course cutting and taking performance-enhancing drugs—can make us more successful in sport, particularly if one can do so without being caught. I call these traits performance-enhancing vices.

Defining the Concept

PEVs are defects of our character, which help one to be a successful athlete but otherwise detract from a well-ordered, flourishing life. In general, we can identify them by asking ourselves whether certain traits that help us to perform as distance runners also impede our ability to be loving friends or responsible citizens. Other times, performance-enhancing vices can be identified as traits that help us to perform athletically, yet compromise our long-term ability to live full lives outside of sport.

If such a category of traits exists—and I am going to argue that it does—performance-enhancing vices will be an insidious issue, difficult to root out. This is because, in submitting ourselves to athletic objectives, we are inclined to "put on" the traits that support the goods of performance. Sometimes this happens consciously, and other times not. But in the same way that runners are transformed physically by submitting themselves to the goals of distance running, their characters are transformed as well.

As coaches, fans, and participants of the sport, the presence of these traits creates a puzzle for us: Should a sport's commitment *always* be to having a good character, or is it sometimes okay to be vicious in certain ways in order to master a sport? At elite and Olympic levels of running, should allowances be made in a person's character to see what the human form, however corrupt, is capable of?

Clarifications

I have two clarifications about the category of PEVs. The first is that, while we will exclusively examine distance running here, a concern with PEVs is relevant to most social practices. These include other sports and hobbies, various models of schooling, political frameworks, and economic structures. The goods selected for and reinforced by these structures and practices may not match the set of goods selected for in a happy life.[17] An example is that greed is a trait reinforced in certain capitalistic systems. Greed can make a person successful in these contexts—more successful than he or she would have been without this trait—but viewed from the perspective of a happy life, it may be a vice.[18]

In Chapter 5, I introduced Alasdair MacIntyre's approach to virtue. He identifies virtues as constitutive goods of a given practice. Foresight, for example, is a virtue of chess because it helps one to achieve the objectives of a chess game. Patience is a virtue of distance running because it helps one to be successful in running. A note of caution in using practices to identify virtues is that even the best practices are limited or time-restricted aspects of our lives. Independently, practices do not reflect our humanity *in totum*. For example, no person is *just* a runner.

It may sometimes feel as though you are just a runner. You have sneakers everywhere, and there is a "26.2" bumper sticker on your car. People greet you by asking how far you ran that day, and you know the answer to two decimal places because you wear a GPS watch. Even so, you are not *just* a runner. You are a human and a friend, maybe a sibling, a citizen and neighbor, and play various other roles. Maybe one day, you won't be a runner at all. So you might wonder how the practice of running shapes you in ways that impact other areas of your life. You might inquire about which goods running selects for, as compared to the goods ordered to a flourishing life in general.

Stated differently, insofar as the goods of *sport* and the goods of *flourishing* are not a Venn diagram with a perfect overlap—that is, the "sports" circle being entirely contained within the "flourishing" circle—we need to inquire about the ways in which they pull apart. Are there goods of running that are antagonistic toward, or undermine, happiness?

Here is an example. The most high-performing athletes are (understandably) *devoted* to their craft. Or, at least, from the perspective of the sport, they are devoted to their craft. They are *committed*. These are virtues. But in my many years of competing, I have learned to listen to the adjectives that these same runners' families and friends use to describe them. Sometimes they use the same words—*devoted, committed,* or *conscientious*. But often they use different words, like *obsessed, single-minded,* or *stubborn*. Excellence viewed from the perspective of sport—and praised in that context—is conceived differently from the vantage of their loved ones. There are certainly exceptions to this pattern, but sometimes high-performance traits can be antagonistic toward the goods of community.

Running aside, we should investigate the impact of all the practices we engage in. For example, someone may be exceedingly good at a career in finance. Being good at this career may have costs outside of the office, such as on their health, family, or community. If all a person is concerned with is excelling at his job, he may both (1) achieve that end, and (2) in the process of doing so, develop a character ordered toward an unhappy life, all other things considered. Thus, social practices should be examined from both *within* and *without* a practice. Examining a sport from *without* helps us to detect vices.

MacIntyre does assess practices in this way. He specifies that the goods supporting our practices must square with the "good of the whole community."[19] This protects us from the worry I just raised—that a trait, like greed, can make you excel at finance, while also undermining your family life. MacIntyre also takes seriously our human nature—which he characterizes as dependent (or social) rational (or intellectual) animals (or biological beings). We are not *just* runners. We are humans. Thinking broadly about human life helps us to avoid pitfalls of shaping our lives solely in terms of running performance. In Chapters 7 and 8, we explore what it means to take our humanity seriously as athletes.

A second clarification about PEVs is that, while the vices we examine in this section are performance-enhancing, I am going to argue that, in many cases, there are *virtues* that can be substituted in their place—and these virtues are comparable to, or better than, the vices at facilitating peak performance. In part, this is an empirical question. For example, we will investigate whether being maliciously envious is more motivating than admiring an excellent peer. Where no psychological studies are available, I defend the value of certain virtues for performance on conceptual grounds.

Candidates for Performance-Enhancing Vices

You can be both a fast runner and a bad person. In this section, I assess four possibilities for PEVs, examining whether they qualify as such. These vices are pride, intransigence, envy, and selfishness. I selected them on the grounds that they are qualities that seem to both support the performance objectives of distance running—to run far and fast—as well as detract from a well-ordered life, defined in terms of compromising one's integrity, health, or the goods of community.

Let's start where Aquinas would, with the root of all vices: pride.

Pride

There is a certain kind of pride which is not a vice. It is a feeling of pleasure in a job well done, or satisfaction with one's own good choices. We can experience it toward ourselves, when we set our minds on reaching a big goal and then accomplish it, or we can experience it toward others, the way parents often do toward their children. Maybe *pride* is not the best word for this feeling, but it is the word we often use. When we talk about pride as a moral defect, this is not what we are referring to.

However, there is another kind of pride that is a vice. It is destabilizing and damaging to our communities, and it makes us less teachable. It also makes us, for lack of a better description, human commas. There is an expression in Latin—*homo incurvatus in se*—humanity as 'curved in on itself.' This was a phrase coined by Martin Luther, which captures what we act like when we build our lives around our pride. We 'turn in on ourselves' like commas, becoming so preoccupied with our own desires and interests that we are unable to see anything past them.

Obviously, Luther was not speaking literally when he introduced the phrase, such that we all transform into hunchbacks. (although, this would make the error very easy to spot). But there is truth to the idea that our pride crowds out the possibility of a life spent looking outward—of seeing and loving the people around you, responding to their needs, and considering ideas other than your own. If you are proud, your self-importance curves you inward—*incurvatus in se*.

Pride is a vice we often find in sports, for a few reasons. The first is that athletes are humans, and pride is a common vice for people in general, in every endeavor. It would be odd if pride were *not* seen in athletics because it is found everywhere else. But athletics, in particular, is characterized by pride, more so than other domains of public life, and this seems to be for two reasons.

The first is that there is a great deal of social capital to be found in athletics in the Western world. If you are good at sports as a child, this affords you attention and social status. It often seems as though we prioritize athletic prowess over many other goods, like scholarship, kindness, and thoughtfulness. This prioritization bears out in the budgets of many secondary schools and universities. A great deal of money is invested in the spectacle of athletics, to the chagrin of many educators. Developmentally, it seems clear why a talented athlete might develop pride. Pride is a kind of concession to a cultural narrative of one's importance over others, as this person is repeatedly shown favor over peers.

As a coach, I have observed middle school athletes of modest talent with such big heads they barely fit through the door of the school bus on the way home from youth track meets. Pride often presents itself very early in the life of an athlete.

Furthermore, sports are essentially performative. Maybe the outsized social attention that athletics brings permits certain vices to blossom—vices such as vainglory and pride. When fans root for an athlete and speak in overblown terms about her capabilities, it is easy to become puffed up and self-important. Or, at least, it is easier for the athlete than for others in nonperformative roles, who are not regularly shown preference over peers.

Second, over the past few decades, the job of the athlete has become increasingly entangled with marketing. Athletes are expected to not only perform in their sport but also manage social media platforms and share the journey. Bigger contracts are offered to runners with larger social media followings, and athletes are incentivized to value attention.

In certain ways, this makes distance running more professionally viable—that a runner's worth is based on more than just their performances, something which is comforting through periods of injury and as an athlete ages. However, it also means that the attention of an athlete is split between perfecting their craft and managing attention. How an athlete appears to others becomes just as important as who they are and what they are capable of, which should concern us. Cicero notes that this is a human vulnerability in general: "*Virtute enim ipsa non tam multi praediti esse quam videri volunt.*"[20] Few wish to be endowed with virtue rather than to seem so. As athletes interested in character, our objective is to *be* rather than to *seem*. Having a performance orientation inclines us to prioritize seeming, and this does not set us up to be people of good character and substance.

So far, I have offered explanations for why pride is a significant feature in athletics. But I have not described its performance relevance. Setting aside considerations of fame and social clout, is there something internal to the activity of competitive running that would benefit from pride? It seems that there is.

Pride as Performance-Enhancing

Earlier in this chapter, I described a scenario in which I stood on a start line, rattled by the notion of having to self-seed, or to position myself with respect to the competition. I asked whether a proud person—someone with an inflated sense of self—would have handled that moment better. I wondered whether a proud person would have dared greatly and had a performance benefit over an athlete *not* marked by pride, all other things equal. There are two additional concepts—a virtue concept (magnanimity) and a vice concept (pusillanimity)—that can help us to assess starting line postures, but first, we need to clarify the nature of pride.

To determine how pride might support performance, it is important to clarify the kinds of errors pride commits. It commits at least two.[21]

1. The first is an *epistemic* (knowledge) error. The proud person perceives herself to be greater than she actually is. She may imagine she is independent and fail to understand "how one's life is fragile and dependent on many factors beyond one's own control."[22] In short, she is forgetful of her own humanity. Realistically, we all rely on other people to help us to accomplish our goals. Even in a sport animated by the trope of the "lonely long-distance runner," we are not actually alone. We depend on one another for strength and support. We also encounter our own limits and frailties any time we run.

2. The second is an error of *valuing*. The proud person considers herself to be superior to those who aspire to lesser things. She values herself and her interests more than others.

These two errors will have unequal impact on a runner. For the first error, whether a performance benefit occurs depends on the kind of knowledge error made. For the second error, there is likely to be a performance benefit in most cases.

First, committing an epistemic error of pride is not necessarily performance-enhancing. Imagine the athlete who commits to a fast early pace—one that she cannot sustain. She does so because she is wrong about her own limitations. Likely, this would not provide the athlete a performance benefit. Instead, it can be a deficit because the runner may implode before reaching the finish line. In fact, one might argue that the reverse is true: The athlete *better* acquainted with her limitations, or more epistemically sensitive than the average athlete, will see improved performance.

That said, there is one knowledge error of pride a runner could make, which will potentially aid her performances. She could be wrong about the *significance* of her own talents, thinking her abilities as more important than they are. This would position her to perform well because it would incline her to invest in training over other pursuits. Furthermore, this may be a motivating error, since she will want to make good on her investment by racing well.

Second, an error of *valuing* seems beneficial for performance in general. The athlete who considers herself as superior to others is inclined to prioritize her training over a concern for others. This kind of self-directedness can aid an athlete in becoming more singularly attentive to her own goals. It can also lead a runner to compete more aggressively to maintain her inflated self-conception. The proud runner toggles between presumption, thinking herself more important or talented than others, and despair, threatened by the possibility of defeat. Pride's greatest secret is that it is always under threat.

So, to answer the question of whether pride is performance-enhancing, it depends. An error of valuing can offer performance benefit, since crowding out a love of others helps a person to focus singularly on her own goals. Perceiving oneself as superior to others can be profitable in running. However, only knowledge errors that do not interfere with an athlete's recognition of her actual limits may be beneficial.

So where does this leave us? Is there a virtue alternative to pride? And is it still okay to dare greatly and accomplish big feats without falling into these errors? Certainly.

An Alternative to Pride

The running world, and our culture more broadly, has an uneasy relationship with excellence. It seems like we can't decide whether aspiration is presumptuous and cocky, or something we should celebrate as admirable. We often give excellent people a platform and set them up as exemplars. Yet we also sometimes speak as though setting big goals or wanting to be excellent is a bad thing. We speak as if humility requires that we set modest objectives and act as though we have low self-esteem, deflecting compliments and suppressing aspirations. An example is the intense public scrutiny the United States women's national soccer team star player, Megan Rapinoe, endured when she famously asserted, "I deserve this," while holding the World Cup trophy.[23] She did, in fact, deserve it.

As a young athlete, I certainly thought this was the case—that aspiration was a broken part of me that needed repair. So I was pleased to read about the virtue of magnanimity for the first time and to realize that—if done well—it can be an asset to aim for great things. In fact, to do otherwise may actually be a vice.

The Concepts

While in popular discourse today, *magnanimity* has come to mean something like generosity, in the classical tradition, it means "greatness of soul." Magnanimity is a virtue described by Aristotle and revised by Aquinas, among others, and it is a virtue important in athletics because competitive sports are aspirational in character, or concerned with greatness.

For Aristotle, the magnanimous person "deems himself worthy of great things and *is* worthy of them."[24] He knows his relative value as an agent, is aware of his capacity for doing great things, and does those great things.[25] Magnanimity captures the runner whose pursuit of greatness is informed by an accurate self-appraisal and knowledge of which great feats are, in fact, worthwhile. And, Aquinas adds, this pursuit of greatness need not be at odds with humility.[26] We can strive for greatness in ways that do not devalue others. (If you need an example of a magnanimous runner, consider Courtney Dauwalter and others I named as exemplars in Chapter 4.)

The virtue of magnanimity is described in opposition to the vice of *pusillanimity*, or smallness of soul. The pusillanimous person is so meek as to not aspire to excellence.[27] My temptation to slip into the pack, far removed from the starting line at a recent road race, is an example. And while we might be inclined to think that such a person is humble for her modest intentions, the pusillanimous person is animated by two defects: misperception and inaction. She is "ignorant of [herself]" and "otherwise would long for the things [she] is worthy of."[28] She does not realize that she can do great things. Moreover, because she is wrong about her capabilities, she does not live up to them.

I promised I would name virtuous alternatives, when possible, to the performance-enhancing vices under discussion. Aquinas's magnanimity is an alternative to pride. It is certainly performance-enhancing, in that it involves daring for great deeds with acute recognition of one's own limitations. But magnanimity also captures the high-minded aspirations of the distance runner without compromising self-knowledge, gratitude, and love of others. It takes the good, without the bad. We do not need to be maliciously proud to strive for big things.

Intransigence

It is an early morning in August. My athletes have a mile time trial on the track, and I am pacing a seventh grader who requested my help. "Just tuck in," I tell her. The time trial begins, and she positions herself behind me.

To run a time trial well—as opposed to a race situation in which athletes respond to one another's moves—the goal is to mete out one's efforts evenly. It is like slowly squeezing out a tube of toothpaste. The objective is to neither run out of toothpaste before crossing the finish, nor have any toothpaste remaining at the line. This typically means that the first laps feel almost too easy and under control. Then fatigue overtakes the runner in a crescendo as she approaches the finish.

As we run, my athlete's breathing becomes more labored. I remind her to stay tucked in, and I give her what I think is a compelling speech about the vice of irresolution. We want to be steadfast, perseverant people who do not capitulate in situations of difficulty. We want to be Odysseus tethered to the mast or oak trees deeply rooted in our purpose.

We cross the finish together. She sets a new personal best, and we celebrate with the team. "What did you think of my speech?" I ask her, as we change our shoes. "Did it help you to persevere?"

"No, it didn't," she tells me. "I couldn't hear anything you said in the wind. I just heard, 'blah blah blah.'"

Perseverance

Aquinas defines perseverance as "persist[ing] long in something good until it is accomplished."[29] It is the virtue of endurance or staying in place, and if I had to choose a single virtue that is an excellence of distance running, it is this one.

In Chapter 5, we examined perseverance as a performance-enhancing virtue—a trait that is both a good-making feature of running, and one that suits a happy life outside of it. Perseverance is a virtue that supports the development of freedom because it permits us to "remain in place" or commit to a good end, even when rogue desires arise and we want to quit. Instead, we can choose to stay, and this is good practice for remaining in place for the things in life that matter.

Yet, paradoxically, perseverance is a difficult virtue to get right in a sport structured around the task of enduring. Ours is a sport that rewards those who incline toward perseverance's vice of excess—intransigence.

Intransigence

Perseverance's vice of excess is called pertinacity, or intransigence. Intransigence is a good word for this vice, in the context of distance running, because it captures a 'refusal to abandon.' It is like the runner ascending a mountain peak. Conditions change and the weather turns, but the runner nevertheless declines to retreat.

Intransigence involves bullheadedness, "hold[ing] on imprudently,"[30] or a stubborn persistence to a goal that is no longer worthwhile.[31] This vice is likely less common than perseverance's vice of deficiency (irresolution) among the general population. However, it describes a disposition common among ultrarunners. The phrase "death before DNF"[32] is indicative of it. The culture of completing training through injury or illness is another. We are characteristically recalcitrant.

Intransigence is a performance-enhancing vice because erring on the side of excess means we are apt to see more finish lines. Stubbornly persisting even when it is imprudent to do so, and signing up for races that we ought not have signed up for means, straightforwardly, that a runner covers greater distance than the runner without this inclination. In distance running, covering miles is the central measure of success.

There are two errors intransigence makes in distance running:

1. The first error is committing to goals that are not good ones in the first place. For example, sometimes our families are in a busy season of life, or our friends need help. What we ought to do is support them, not sign up for another race. Sure, we can persist and complete the run, but as Aquinas points out, the

virtue of perseverance is only a virtue insofar as it is ordered to something *good*. If a person persists in a life of crime—or if they persist in being an absentee friend or parent for the sake of running—this persistence is not an excellence. It is a vice.

Sometimes life circumstances constrain us such that we ought not sign up for races. But we also might wonder whether distance races of considerable length or difficulty, in themselves, are good ends. I know, I also dislike this question. For example, if an extended run (hypothetically, a 100-mile race) is not a productive activity in terms of health, mental well-being, or worthier competing goods—for finite creatures with limited energy and attention— then enduring toward that end will not be an instance of virtue. It will be an instance of vice.

To be able to answer the question of whether ultramarathons themselves are good ends, we first need to be able to answer the question raised earlier: What constitutes a good life? Is it a long one? Does a happy life have certain health constraints, or is it okay if I compromise my cardiovascular integrity[33] and joints for the sake of an experience now? Is it okay if my life is imbalanced and narrowly directed on an athletic activity, or should I invest in relationships and activities outside of the sport?

If even raising these questions about whether ultramarathons are a worthy investment is uncomfortable to you, congratulations! You may be intransigent.

2. The second error is committing to goals past the point when doing so continues to be healthy or productive. Persisting through difficulty is generally helpful. Indeed, it is one of the best things we can learn to do. But we cross over into pertinacity if we endure past the point of health or danger, or if we compromise worthier goods. What counts as a worthier good? That is a great question. This is something a runner needs to discern, ideally in conversation with family, friends,

and others, both within and outside of the sport. In general, we can assume that worthier goods include long-term health and the love and welfare of other people in our lives.

My Own Intransigence

I started trail racing and ultrarunning in the middle of college when I was unencumbered by responsibilities. I had schoolwork and extracurricular activities, but otherwise, I could run pretty much all the time. That was what I did. In those days, there was very little research on the impact of over-racing on health and longevity in the sport, so the tendency among participants was to race long events multiple times per year. For example, I once competed in a twenty-four-hour race on a Sunday. Six days later, I raced a 50-kilometer (31-mile) trail race. Imprudent? Certainly! Intransigent? Not yet.

At the time, the culture of the sport was to race consistently. I had very few impediments to participating on these terms because of my youth and relative lack of responsibilities. But as I grew older, I acquired responsibilities. I entered graduate school. I married my husband. I had students. My children were born. These were constraints on my time—happy constraints, but constraints nonetheless.

As these responsibilities grew, it became less feasible for me to compete at the scale I had previously, or to commit to those finish lines. Racing competed with what I recognized were worthier goods in a different season of life, so I backed off considerably.

In my life, I have a higher allegiance to my family and my students than to my running. These are my worthier goods, and my love of them constrains the starting lines I show up to. It informs which goals I see as worthwhile. Persevering does not mean making it to just *any* finish line, irrespective of the cost. If I raced at the cost of higher commitments, this would be an instance not of virtue, but of vice.

The Run Streak

One possible instance of intransigence is the common phenomenon of "run streaking." A "run streak" is the attempt to run every single day for months or years on end. For some runners, they cover just a token few miles each day. For other runners, they cover lots of miles. Either way, it is a daily commitment, without exception. There are no rest days.

For many run streakers, doing so is motivating. The commitment to the daily run works like a tether. It creates inertia around the activity, and it gets a runner out the door on days even when it is a challenge to do so. This creates a strong fitness base and can help an athlete perform well. In many cases, this challenge is constructive. Even so, it is possible that a run streak may devolve into intransigence because a runner might make compromises to other obligations. She may run through sickness and work responsibilities. She may persist in her streak even when doing so no longer makes sense.

Certainly, it can be challenging to know whether we have crossed over from perseverance into intransigence. For competitive personalities, it can seem like a concession to call it a day, or to reconsider commitments. Acknowledging our limitations is not generally easy to do, particularly when finishing a race, even at cost to oneself, is generally celebrated in our sport as a marker of success.

Often we ask athletes, "How bad do you want it?" which is more of a challenge than a question. This challenge can be helpful prodding for the irresolute runner, but not the runner who errs in the direction of excess. This can cloud reasoning about when it is appropriate to quit. Our goal is to persevere, not to commit to bad ends, or good ends past the point when they cease to be constructive.

Envy

Over the years, a question I have been asked many times is whether I consider myself to be a competitive person. This is an interesting question to ask a professional runner who also studies moral character, assuming—as people often do—that competition itself is problematic in certain ways. In response, I generally ask them to define what they mean by "competitive" before I reply.

What is interesting is that, what they often describe as competitiveness—being haunted by loss, the desperation to win, an uneasy relationship with competitors—is not actually *competition*. Competition is a neutral form of comparison, neither good nor bad. It just means "striving together." What they are describing is the vice of envy. This vice is so entangled in our current notions of competition that we define competitiveness *as* envy.

Defining Our Terms

The vice of envy is defined as "feeling bitter when others have it better"[34] or "unhappy self-assertion."[35] It has a negative emotional valence and "arises when a person lacks another's superior quality, achievement, or possession and either desires it or wishes that the other lacked it."[36] We said that envy is fueled by feelings of comparative inadequacy, so resolving a perceived imbalance, in whatever way possible, appeases the vice.

Envy perceives the triumphs of others as threatening—that if one person succeeds, this is their loss. It understands success to be a limited good. But what is interesting about this vice in the context of running is that, in a qualified sense, its perception is accurate.

Only one person can win a race. That person's winning intrudes upon the potential victories of all other competitors. In what follows, I will address what I mean by accurate perception "in a qualified sense." But first, we should ask whether envy is performance-enhancing.

Performance-Enhancing Envy

The short answer is, the vice of envy is performance-enhancing. The longer answer is, it is motivating in the wrong ways, and there are better candidates for constructive responses to excellent people, which also offer potential performance benefits.

First, to assess the empirical data on the emotion, it might help us to clarify the landscape of related concepts—*malicious envy* and *benign envy*. Malicious envy is what I have been referring to as the vice of envy. It is marked by negative feelings toward an excellent other. It wants those feelings resolved, in whatever way possible. Benign envy also has negative feelings toward an excellent other, but it aims to correct one's comparative lack by producing a "leveling up motivation."[37]

While other languages have separate words for these two concepts, the English language only has one: envy. However, many philosophers and psychologists argue that benign envy is not a vice at all. Philosopher Linda Zagzebski, for example, considers it a part of admiration. Others align it with Aristotle's notion of *zēlos*, or emulation. Philosopher Kristján Kristjánsson cautions that this is an imperfect alignment, since Aristotle's emulation is a mixed emotional experience. It involves both a painful feeling of lack and "pleasure at the presence of the 'honored thing.'"[38]

On some accounts of envy, what we are calling "benign envy" is seen as problematic. For example, philosopher Robert Adams describes envy as acting from a perceived *lack*, or an anticipated lack, which is the source of its negative feelings.[39] In contrast, admiration acts from the appreciation of a present good and does not act from a place of lacking anything at all. On this definition, benign envy is just as problematic as malicious envy. Both involve acting not from other-directed appreciation but from self-directed inadequacy.

Why this matters is that, in the empirical literature, envy—as a broad category containing *both* benign and malicious forms—outperforms admiration.[40] Envy is more motivating. But once we select out for these two forms, things become more interesting. Benign envy is motivated to move upward to close the gap; malicious envy desires to pull superior others down.[41]

Regardless of whether benign envy should be considered a vice, these are distinct responses with a differing social cost. We can imagine how, in the running context, one of these motivations would be clearly more pernicious than the other. The benign envier other might lose a race, feel bad, and be compelled to train harder to close the gap to the superior other. By contrast, the malicious envier might lose a race, feel bad, and be compelled to criticize or otherwise tear down the superior person, or to sabotage the superior person's future racing. The benign envier improves within the terms of the sport; the malicious envier subverts the terms of the sport to achieve a higher standing.

Furthermore, in the empirical literature, malicious envy is described as leading to "an appraisal of low perceived control over future outcomes."[42] The envier thinks she cannot reach the high standard of the superior. This pessimistic disposition might motivate the envier to perform even worse actions, such as to thwart the terms of success of other athletes by cheating or dismantling course markings.

So, yes, the vice of envy is motivating and may enhance performances in questionable and perhaps unscrupulous ways. Benign envy is a better alternative because of the kinds of responses it motivates.

An Alternative to Envy

Setting both forms of envy aside, the best alternative is admiration—an appreciative perspective on someone's excellences, which does not act from a lack, but which is also performance-enhancing. It motivates agents to imitate the excellent other or to "promote the value that is judged to be present in the object of admiration."[43] This positions the runner to "put on" or practice admired excellences, such that she can develop them for herself. We have already discussed how moral virtues are developed through practice, so this is a productive motivation for character development. Furthermore, as an emotion which does not begrudge the excellences of others but acts from a place of fullness, this response is both the most compatible with sustaining a strong community and the most psychologically agreeable. If you make other people's successes your own delight, you never run out of reasons to celebrate.

Selfishness

In 2020 and 2021, I spent some time away from the sport. In part, this time away was unplanned—the consequence of the COVID-19 pandemic. The pandemic was marked by great loss. It was also a period of social and political tumult in the United States. It seems trivial to mention that, during this period, the professional racing scene was also impacted. It halted for the better part of two years while we collectively discerned what was prudent and socially responsible regarding the virus's transmissibility. But in part, my time away from the sport was planned. I had my first child during the pandemic, a daughter named Lucy Bea, whose presence made a difficult season sweeter.

Pregnancy for a professional runner is interesting. Imagine a nine-month *Transformers* movie in which the protagonist's body morphs into Santa Claus's body by the end of it. This is effectively what happens. Pregnancy is a time as an athlete when your physical agency is compromised, and you temporarily forfeit your ability to move through the world at the paces you are accustomed to. It was worth it, a thousand times over, but when your body of work is your actual *body*, this is also unmooring. There are no promises that you will be able to return to a high level of competition, and these were just my physical concerns.

Among runners, everyone cautions about the physical changes of motherhood—loose joints, an enfeebled core, and the need to rebuild your aerobic base from scratch while sleep is limited. What they often fail to mention are the internal changes that accompany having a child—changes which, to me, seemed more substantial.

Whereas previously, I put myself first in a thousand ways, becoming a mother reordered my loves. I developed a higher allegiance to my daughter than to my training. These were good and necessary changes because there is a priority proper to different loves.[44] Of course, my daughter would come first. But these were also changes that, frankly, have detracted from my ability to compete at a high level as a distance runner.

The Concept

Selfishness is not a classical vice, as envy, pride, and cowardice are. Rather, in the classical tradition, selfishness is captured in terms of the *form* of the moral life, as egoism. The selfish person, or the egoist, judges the value of goods in terms of how they impact oneself, instead of others. For example, if my life is ordered toward my own flourishing, defined narrowly in terms of my personal interests, then I am an egoist.

As a vice, selfishness is the dispositional trait to think, feel, and act in ways that are self-serving and regularly fail to account for the needs of others. The selfish runner consistently prioritizes performance objectives over people and is guarded with her time and attention. And while this will likely profit athletic performance, athletic performance is not the greatest good in our lives.

To be clear, it can be difficult to discern when one crosses the line from taking one's craft seriously into selfishness, and this is true not just in running but in most high-level endeavors. In part, this is due to the fact that egoism hides in plain sight in a culture that prizes radical autonomy and personal achievements over the goods of community. But it is also true that elite performance sometimes requires a certain myopia or single-mindedness to compete well.

Norm Differentiation

Imagine a professional runner, preparing for her first Olympics. Preparing well may mean becoming singularly focused on her own interests, in a way that crowds out a concern for others. Perhaps this athlete conceives of her self-directed activity during this season of life as serving her community or stewarding her gifts well. These are good motivations. In this case, selfishness seems to be an irrelevant consideration. However, if she *is* selfish (genuinely selfish), putting herself and her own interests first from egoistic motivations, there still remains a question of whether this counts as a vice. Why would it? Often, we consider these kinds of situations to be norm-differentiating.[45] A kind of permission is extended to athletes to go "all in" to prepare for the event.

Norm differentiation—in this case, excusing an athlete from certain moral norms—is an important consideration for all vices of sport. In the case of the Olympics, we can see why exceptions are made. It is a short period of time, and we want to see what an athlete can do, without compromise. We want to see what the athlete who goes "all in" is capable of, not the athlete whose attention is divided between training and the mundane responsibilities of ordinary life, like washing the dishes or answering emails. Affording them the space to act selfishly satisfies a curiosity about what a human being is capable of.

Even so, there are at least three worries about this kind of norm differentiation extended to athletes. The first is that it sets an uneasy precedent. Extending permission to athletes, such that they are not bound by the same norms as others, might set them up for thinking other rules do not apply, like anti-doping requirements within sport or traffic laws outside of it. The second worry is the good life concern. Vices are like cavities. They fester and compromise the integrity of the whole mouth. When athletes are selfish, there are likely to be negative repercussions because selfishness is not a constitutive feature of a good life or healthy relationships.

Third, making exceptions for vice in this way, even for limited periods like the Olympic cycle, offers practice in being selfish the rest of the time. The Olympic period is four years long, but the traits we "put on" in training persist beyond it. An athlete may find that self-directed patterns of thinking and acting persist in her life outside of important racing seasons and over the long term, such that she becomes an unreliable friend or someone who fails to see and respond to the needs of her community. Maybe the athlete won't find the selfishness of training translates into her normal life at all, but this would be surprising. It is worth investigating whether it does.

A Virtue Alternative to Selfishness

Is there a virtue alternative to selfishness that comparably aids performance? It seems that there is. The alternative virtue is charity, or love. It has the potential to both aid performance and to contribute to a more meaningful life than selfishness ever could.

Over the past several years, there has been a growing phenomenon of professional athletes in the United States opting to train in groups, instead of on their own. It is difficult to tell from afar the effect this has had on the athletes, but as far as I can see, the mutual support and friendship arising in these groups is genuine and generally constructive.[46]

Often the advice for combatting vices is to form virtues in their place. From a behavioral modification standpoint, this makes a lot of sense. For example, to help someone stop a bad habit, like drinking too much soda, you should not advise them to drink less soda; you should give them an additive goal (such as to drink a certain number of glasses of water per day) instead. That way, they are focusing on a constructive task, and dishabituating the bad habit occurs as the consequence of habituating the good one. Likewise, to become less *dishonest*, we focus on becoming *honest*. To become less *ungrateful*, we focus on building a *gratitude* practice. We form the virtue that opposes the vice.

I point this out because, to combat *selfishness*, we should develop the virtue that opposes it—*charity*, or love. If I were to recommend a means of doing so, I would suggest the very thing that distance runners seem to be doing—forming communities, being present in them, and investing in the people around them. Doing so is good for two kinds of reasons: (1) *aretaic* (or virtue) reasons and (2) performance reasons.

1. *Aretaic* reasons. First, it is better to be loving than selfish. Charity is a trait that supports a higher kind of life than the alternative. Athletic considerations aside, investing in others and willing their good is an excellent way of being in the world. It is a happier way of being in the world, too.
2. Performance reasons. In Chapters 3 and 4, we examined how good and productive it can be to compare ourselves to others in a nonenvious way. We explored admiration and noted that constructive comparison is edifying; it makes us better. Research supports the idea that we can get more out of ourselves in a team environment than we could if we were alone.[47] As far as I can tell, there is no empirical data on whether the vice of selfishness is superior to the virtue of charity in terms of athletic performance. But along with charity come friendships and companions to "strive together" with, and we know this increases athletic potential.

Surely selfishness can be performance-enhancing. However, the virtue alternative—charity, seen here as genuinely willing a teammate's good—also aids performance. Being part of a community of like-minded athletes and pushing each other is a recipe for success. Moreover, unlike selfishness, charity does not require compromising friendships or making one's world both isolated and small.

Vices of Athletic Culture

In the preceding section, we examined four candidates for performance-enhancing vices: pride, envy, intransigence, and selfishness. Other possibilities are dishonesty, which we briefly addressed early in the chapter regarding cheating behaviors, and intemperance. We said that these vices—PEVs—may assist someone in becoming a successful athlete but otherwise detract from a good life. We said that PEVs are vices that support the goals *internal* to a practice.

There is a second set of vices cultivated in distance running that do not support internal goals of the practice, but goods *external* to it. These are the vices of athletic culture—a culture that prizes *seeming* over *being*, wealth, and attention for its own sake. Like PEVs, they support our participation in athletics and undermine our lives outside of it.

In this section, I briefly raise the issue of cultural vices, naming two examples: vainglory and greed.

Mandeville's Bees

In 1714, philosopher Bernard Mandeville published a book entitled *The Fable of the Bees*, containing a poem called "The Grumbling Hive." The poem describes a successful community of bees, with each bee individually motivated by greed. When the bees start to develop virtues, forsaking their self-seeking tendencies, the hive collapses. As it turns out, the hive was sustained by vices, without which, it ceased to function.

"The Grumbling Hive" is satire. Mandeville's target was moralists who desired the goods of consumerism while being unwilling to admit that certain vices sustain those goods. He was not personally endorsing vice but exposing a kind of hypocrisy of the time period.

Mandeville intended to "expose the unreasonableness and folly of those who, wanting to be a flourishing people and wonderfully greedy for all the benefits they can receive as such, are always exclaiming against the vices and inconveniences that have . . . been inseparable from all kingdoms and states that ever were famed for strength, riches, and politeness at the same time."[48]

The idea is that there are certain visions of the good life that conflict with private virtue. A similar idea is echoed in the famous Gordon Gekko "Greed is good" speech from the 1987 film, *Wall Street*. Greed is "good" insofar as it serves the end in question—making a profit. We need to examine one's end to know which traits will be reinforced in support of arriving there.

The Hive: For Runners

Distance running—and ultramarathoning in particular—is changing. I am sure previous generations have made similar remarks. Each generation laments shifting norms and the passing of former modes and orders. And since the past is drenched in nostalgia, it is tough to compete with that, even when the changes are, on balance, good ones.

In the case of trail and ultrarunning, over the past decade, the sport has risen from relative obscurity to gain significantly more media attention. The rise of social media has been a key precipitating factor of the sport's rising profile. Furthermore, among its participants, there is a growing conversation about how to transform ultrarunning to become more like other sports—sports that are profitable and generate fans. In many ways, these changes are welcome.

It is surely a good thing that more people participate in trail running. This means more people can enjoy natural spaces instead of staring at screens, and they can be edified by the daily disciplines of training. Additionally, if more media attention is afforded to ultrarunners, then participation will grow. More competitive fields will follow from increased participation, and improved competition is edifying for everyone involved.

It also seems welcome that ultrarunning is becoming more profitable for athletes who wish to pursue the sport as a full-time occupation, without requiring supplemental income from additional jobs. It means they can get the best out of themselves, without needing to compromise training by splitting energy and attention with other forms of paid work. In these ways, the maturing of ultrarunning so that it resembles other sports is a good thing.

However, these changes also restructure the hive in substantial ways. And, following Mandeville, one might wonder whether new visions of success conflict with private virtue—whether a growing focus on generating media attention and increasing profit in a growing sport will change the internal character of its participants to sustain these ends.[49]

Cultural Vices

I once entered a room where a group of women were arguing about whether I ran 100 *meters*, or 100 *miles*. "Surely, 100 *miles* is wrong," one of the women declared. "That would be strange. Anyway, no one would ever attempt that."

Until recently, ultrarunning was a relatively obscure sport that, if it drew any attention at all, garnered sideways glances and bemused smiles, not esteem. It is odd to see it grow popular. It feels strange to voice a concern about seeking approval from others. But here we are. The sport has become more amenable to media saturation and attention-seeking behavior. And like most other endeavors in contemporary culture, social media seems partially to blame.

There are two major vices we should be concerned about, in light of the rising popularity and cultural changes of the sport. These are greed and vainglory.

Greed

Greed is an excessive love of wealth.[50] This vice was mostly irrelevant in ultrarunning a few years ago because there was so little money in the sport. Now, one might wonder whether increased economic opportunities will generate the wrong incentives for participating and result in the prioritization of income over trail stewardship, which is something ultrarunners have historically valued.

For example, professional runners are frequently incentivized to participate in major competitions, often on different continents, and they receive minimal recognition from sponsors for participating in lower profile races closer to home. What this means is that athletes whose livelihoods depend on the health and continuation of wild spaces are, ironically, encouraged to increase their carbon footprints and thereby contribute to the degradation of these spaces. These financial incentives undermine a previously held value in the sport—stewardship of the environment.

Vainglory

Vainglory is "the excessive and disordered desire for recognition and approval from others."[51] This is a trait entwined in, and reinforced by, social media. It would be unfortunate if the image of the athlete became prized over the athlete's feats, or if an athlete's primary motivation to run far were to garner approval, rather than to challenge oneself.

There is an odd moment in Dante's *Divine Comedy*. Dante is walking through the inferno, and a few dead heroes call out to him, asking whether they are still spoken of in the land of the living. They do not ask about their loved ones or descendants, whether their city-states are thriving, or whether the seeds of their labors on earth bore any fruits long term. They don't even care who Dante is or why a living man happens to be there. They essentially ask, "Are people still talking about me? All press is good press!" The concept here—which Dante chastises as part of a broader cultural critique—is *kleos*.

In Greek, glory or renown is *kleos*, related to 'hearing' or what others say about you. For Homer and Herodotus, *kleos* pertains to our heroes.[52] Achilles is so great that we will 'speak of' him forever. In Dante's inferno, the great heroes of the past are preoccupied with their fame because there is a false sense of immortality in this: If a person is never forgotten, he remains contemporaneous with every succeeding generation. An example in running is the case of breaking a world record. Until that record falls, you are the standard by which everyone holds themselves, so your name remains in the conversation. You have *kleos*.

There is nothing problematic about *kleos* in itself—that we extol and continue to speak about praiseworthy people. In fact, when it is extended toward its proper objects—toward those who are, in fact, praiseworthy—*kleos* is a great thing. There is a collective enthusiasm for, and shared memory of, people who are excellent. But a problem arises when *kleos* is not fixed on the right objects—when we confuse charisma with substance, popularity with goodness, and *seeming* with *being*. Social media is ripe for these kinds of errors, where popularity becomes a false proxy for living a substantial, worthwhile life.

Track and Fielding Objections

The "Much Ado about Nothing" Rebuttal

Someone might argue that there is no need to worry about vices like vainglory or greed in our sport. The heart of the sport is good. The people are good. This worry about bad character is all much ado about nothing.

To a certain extent, I think this objection is well-placed. I am hopeful for the future of the sport and think distance running can weather the storms of greed and vainglory better than most social practices. My optimism is based on the nature of the activity—the fact that it involves a lot of suffering, often on difficult terrain, alone in our sneakers. These features of the sport offer a kind of correction for the damages done by the culture surrounding it.

In the same way that you do not have to wash soap because it is self-cleansing, maybe you don't have to worry about vainglory in a sport that challenges vanity at every turn. If you try to run 100 miles for attention, well, there are easier ways to get attention. Also, the entire time you are training or racing, you can't go on social media anyway. If you try, you may trip on a log. These are promising features.

Even so, it would be a mistake to think greed will not impact the sport, since it already has. Major companies are entering the sport and buying local races. Elite-level athletes are receiving bigger contracts and are urged to assume marketing roles online. Furthermore, social media has the power to disrupt our motivations for performance. It can lead us to become performative and fickle in our orientations, instead of teachable, present members of the community. It can make us care more about what other people say about us than who we actually are.

So, yes, we should worry about, and correct for, these cultural changes. But perhaps due to the nature of distance running, we do not need to worry as much as participants of other activities similarly compromised by the media world.

The "I'm Not So Bad" Rebuttal

You may be inclined to excuse yourself from worrying about the topics under discussion in this chapter, thinking that vices are not relevant to you, a reasonably good person. If this is the case, it is great that you see no need to engage these ideas.

First, you may be half right. Earlier, I directed your attention to Christian Miller's mixed traits thesis—the view, supported by empirical data, that most people have neither *virtues* nor *vices*, but sit somewhere in the middle. They act in some of the right ways, from some of the right motivations, but not consistently well enough to qualify as having virtues or consistently poorly enough to qualify as having vices.

On these grounds, unless you are among the exceptional few, you are probably right that you do not have full-blown vices. However, you are not inscrutable either. You likely have ample room for moral improvement, so it is constructive to examine the ways in which you fall short. If you participate in a sport that sometimes reinforces bad states of character, it is worthwhile to investigate which traits these are and how they might appear in your life.

7

The Happy Runner

Running and the Good Life

It is the day before a race. I am competing in a twenty-four-hour run in Ohio, which will take place on paved loops in an urban park. I love twenty-four-hour events. They are conceptually simple because all you do is run for a day. But they are difficult in execution because all you do is run for a day. A lot can go wrong over twenty-four hours. I am excited to compete and feel well-prepared to do so. Even so, the day before the race, I sit in my car agonizing over the projected forecast. On race day, there will be heavy rain. I am going to get wet, and this is a kind of suffering I did not sign up for.

This is an odd response, if you think about it. I traveled all the way from my home in New Jersey to Ohio to compete in an event which will involve nontrivial forms of suffering. To be clear, the suffering was not, itself, what I signed up for. I was not in pursuit of suffering for its own sake. I signed up to see how fast I could run. But in registering for this event, I certainly understood that suffering would characterize a considerable part of my day. Furthermore, while I would not enjoy the suffering when it arrived, overcoming it would make my performance feel more meaningful than it would feel if the race proceeded without any difficulty.

Therein lies the riddle. I welcome suffering, but not all forms. I want the challenge, but I want it on my own terms. I want to draw lines in the sand, or to raise fences around the forms of suffering I will permit. I want agency in my suffering. I want running, but I don't want rain.[1]

Suffering: The Concept

At its core, suffering is an aversive state. It is not identical to pain.[2] Rather, suffering is a broader phenomenon than pain. Additional forms of suffering include distress, loss, negative physical and emotional states, efforts of various sorts, negative evaluations of your situation (which may or may not adequately reflect reality[3]), tragedies, and so forth.

Some forms of suffering are the negative consequences of our own actions. For example, if I train imprudently and develop an injury, I suffer pains, and this is my own fault. Some forms of suffering just happen to us, such as rain on a race day. And some forms of suffering are chosen, such as the discomfort of running great distances.

All instances of suffering are aversive states. Many instances of suffering are instructive. And few instances of suffering, such as climbing mountains and racing marathons, are enjoyable somehow.[4]

Suffering on the Run

In distance running, we experience suffering of many forms, from sore muscles to injuries, setbacks, and emotional unease of various sorts. We submit to workouts that are, by design, uncomfortable, and we develop an appetite for arduous goods—relishing difficult workouts even though they cause us strain. This kind of suffering can be instructive.

For example, Thomas Aquinas describes the virtue of hope as involving *irascibility*, or an appetite for arduous goods. To become a more hopeful person—someone grounded in and working toward some desired future—we need to develop this appetite, or taste for remaining in difficulty. Running provides the occasion to do so.

"Remaining in difficulty" characterizes what we do as endurance athletes.

A second example is that distance running involves remaining in place through mounting fatigue. Sometimes fatigue grows slowly, like asparagus, which takes three years to grow from seed to harvest.[5] Moment to moment, we can scarcely detect its growth; then, suddenly, we have an herbaceous plant worth of suffering. Other times exhaustion overtakes us like a tidal wave, knocking us off our feet in what feels like an instant. In both cases, we learn to persist through the discomfort of rising fatigue. We suffer, and sometimes it helps us to grow.

Suffering is a topic at home in the world of distance running. It is a unique kind of suffering—mostly chosen and easy to withdraw from, unlike illness, tragedy, and loss (which I address in the final chapter). Nevertheless, it is suffering. Running aside, suffering is a constitutive feature of a good and happy life. In this chapter, I introduce three models of happiness, including one that takes seriously human nature and the role of suffering in our lives. I address considerations of nature, purpose, and sports on this model. I conclude by raising questions of suffering on the run and in a happy life, criticizing some unhelpful ways we often talk about pain.

Three Models of Happiness

For a question as important as "What does it mean to be happy?" we sure do not talk about it enough. And considering the rising rates of anxiety and depression on a global scale,[6] we probably should.

There are three dominant models of happiness, two of which are inadequate. These three models are (1) hedonic, (2) desire satisfaction, and (3) *eudaimonic*.[7] Only the third account, *eudaimonism*, has the conceptual space to take seriously the pleasures, pains, and oddities of a human life.

The Hedonic View

Here is a thought experiment:

> You have the opportunity to be hooked up to a marathon expe-
> rience machine. It stimulates your brain such that you can have
> whatever pleasurable marathon experience you want—a per-
> sonal record, negative splitting, fans chanting your name, and
> that elusive "floating," in-the-zone feeling for a full 26.2 miles on
> smooth, unpuckered pavement, without an ounce of strain. You
> don't even have to move! You can lie on the couch. The crux is that
> none of this is real. If given the choice, would you hook yourself
> up to the marathon experience machine? Or would you choose
> to experience the real thing—including the arduous preparations
> and self-doubt, elation and pride, nervous stomach, edifying
> discomforts, and the messiness of it all?[8]

If you choose the marathon experience machine, congratulations!
You may be a hedonist. If you think something is forfeited in the
marathon experience when it is not real, then you are like most
people faced with this kind of thought experiment. This first account, the Hedonic Model of Happiness, is one that you will find
lacking.

Hedonism means pleasure-seeking. On the hedonic view, our
greatest good is pleasure. A happy life consists of pleasure and the
absence of pain. On this account, happiness has no objective basis;
it is solely a matter of subjective perception, or of what one feels.[9]
A happy life has, on balance, more smiley faces than frowny faces.
What this means is that, if you feel good more often than you feel
bad, then you are in luck! You have a happy life.

Happy feelings are not altogether beside the point. Surely, a good
life has many. But as a solitary metric for determining whether one's
life is a good one, happy feelings are inadequate. Here are three
reasons why.

Feelings Are Ephemeral, or Short-Lived

Feelings tell us how we are doing at the moment, but as a means of discerning the quality of one's life, they are of limited value. For example, in a long race, my emotions have so many highs and lows that, were you to plot them on a graph, it would look like a topographical map of the Andes. My life is not *unhappy*, then *happy*, then *unhappy*. I am just responding to the world around me, which involves the engagement of my emotions.[10]

This emotional rise and fall does not exclusively occur during races either. Sometimes I wake up happy. Then I check the weather report and see that it is rainy. This makes me sad. I eat a waffle. I love waffles. They are pancakes with storage space; they are what I imagine the Container Store would make if they designed a breakfast. Again, I smile. I look at my phone and see a bunch of work emails, and I feel frustrated. Over the course of thirty minutes, my happiness rises and falls, and these feelings have no substantial bearing on whether my life is a good one.

Happy Lives Are Full of Frowns

This is probably not news to a bunch of runners. Running is full of frowns. A marathon is a frown parade. I once drove past the second half of a major metropolitan marathon and observed so many forlorn looks and sunken postures that I would have believed that these were actors in a postapocalyptic zombie film. Running can be exceedingly difficult, yet it makes our lives richer.

Some of the hardest, most "frowny face" moments in our lives are also the most meaningful. Consider parenting, completing difficult projects at work, climbing mountains, and restoring broken friendships. These are meaningful, important parts of life, yet full of sadness and difficulty. They are also an argument against the Hedonic Model. If happiness consisted of maximizing positive subjective states, then meaningful moments that are difficult—such as marathoning but also parenting,[11] scholarship, and arduous friendships—would not be part of happiness, yet they so clearly are.

Many People Find Happiness in the Wrong Things

Not all pleasures are equivalent. On hedonic accounts of happiness—purely based in subjective preference—some people will choose to maximize pleasure in nefarious ways. For example, some people choose to ride bicycles when they could go running instead. How crazy is that! More seriously, philosopher Julia Annas notes that "some people feel happy when helping old ladies across streets; others feel happy when torturing puppies: happiness comes down to whatever you happen to like."[12]

Maybe you are inclined to believe that happiness can be found in *anything* that gives one pleasure, or that a life spent relishing bad actions is equally as happy as one spent enjoying service to others or perfecting a worthwhile craft. But if you do not accept these conclusions, then you need to provide some additional criteria to specify which pleasures are good ones.

Utilitarian John Stuart Mill attempts such a move.[13] He argues that certain pleasures are of higher "quality" than others, since they are more humanizing. For example, reading a good book (a rational pleasure) has a higher quality than eating cotton candy. Volunteering at a soup kitchen (ethical pleasure) has a higher quality than watching television. Higher pleasures are a difference in kind from lower pleasures, and they are preferable to lower pleasures, even when the lower pleasures appear in greater quantity. Mill's account falls short in a couple of ways.

First, for Mill, no pleasures are bad. Certain pleasures are just less good. This means that wicked pleasures, like in Annas's dog-torturing example, are still on the spectrum of happiness.

Second, there is an epistemic, or knowledge, concern: How can we tell which pleasures are the better ones? Mill writes that those who are "competently acquainted" with both higher and lower pleasures prefer the higher ones.[14] It is unclear from where he draws confidence in our ability to distinguish successfully among higher and lower pleasures, or even to distinguish between two higher pleasures, or between two lower pleasures, in a way that would be action-guiding. It is also unclear why he is confident that, if someone were to distinguish correctly among pleasures, she would prefer the ones she ought to prefer, and act on that basis.

In many cases, we do not prefer higher pleasures. For example, sometimes we choose an afternoon of watching television over climbing a mountain, even if the latter is more humanizing. Sometimes certain lower pleasures facilitate rest, and in that way, they can help us to sustain our ability to continue choosing higher pleasures in the long term. Perhaps in a complete life, including lower pleasures is not a moral error.

Furthermore, often there is a space between what we *ought* to desire, think, and do, and what we actually desire, think, and do. Philosopher John Hare calls this a "moral gap"—the distance between the moral demand on us and our abilities to fulfill these demands.[15] Philosopher Christian Miller calls this a "character gap"—the space between who we currently are and the people of good character we should become.[16] Aristotle calls this weakness of will. Sometimes our *knowledge* of what is good, our *desire* for the good, and our *actions* in terms of the good do not align.[17] Maybe higher pleasures are what we should prefer, but it is not clear why Mill thinks we will prefer them.

A purely hedonic account is left with this worry—what to do with those who take pleasure in the wrong things. It seems clear that not all pleasures contribute equally to a happy life.

Final Thoughts on Hedonism

The fact that hedonism is an inadequate view of happiness has a practical bearing on one's life. If the happy life we pursue is constituted by pleasures, this informs the kinds of choices and self-assessments we make. It can discourage us from making long-term investments that come at the cost of present happiness, and it can lead us to believe that negative feelings are inherently problematic.

This view has repercussions for our relationships as well. On a hedonic account, negative feelings like sadness, guilt, and anger are to be avoided since they detract from an elevated subjective state. But these negative-valence emotions have a significant bearing on how well we can love and invest in the lives of others. If I lose a loved one, the suitable response is sadness. If I perceive an injustice impacting my neighbor, it would be wrong *not* to experience anger on their behalf. Negative emotions help us to construe situations adequately and to respond accordingly. They are part of being human and make a life a good one, more so than a life consisting of lots of pleasure for pleasure's sake.

Again, I probably do not have to tell these things to a runner. Each day, you put your sneakers on and pursue an arduous, edifying, uncomfortable craft. Somehow, doing so makes life richer So, let's keep looking. What other models of happiness are available?

The Desire-Satisfaction View

Shortly after crossing the finishing line of one of the biggest races of my life, I thought, "This is what I have been waiting so long for" . . . followed by a question: "*This* is what I have been waiting so long for?" Leading up to the event, I thought the race would fill me up and satisfy my itch to achieve. But on the other side of that finish line were many, many more finish lines. The first question I was asked afterward was, "What race is next for you?"

On the Desire-Satisfaction Account,[18] happiness is the fulfillment of goals or desires. The account assumes that those who are positioned to fulfill their desires are, on balance, happier than those who are not. On this model, upon crossing the finish line of my big race, my net happiness level will have improved.

In certain ways, the Desire-Satisfaction Account is an improvement over the Hedonic Account. This is because desire satisfaction has space for goals that do not involve pleasure. For example, I desire a marathon finish, which will involve pains of various sorts. Still, I find it fulfilling. On the Desire-Satisfaction Account, if marathoning is what I desire, it can contribute to my happiness.

Second, many, though not all, of our goals and desires involve the engagement of our rational faculties. In this way, the Desire-Satisfaction Account takes human nature more seriously than the Hedonic Account. We are feelers but also thinkers and planners.

Some goals, like the achievement of race objectives, can require long-term planning of training and thoughtful execution on race day. Meeting goals can also involve stewarding one's natural talents and developing skills, which supports a common intuition about the happy life—that it involves "not letting one's capacities lie fallow."[19] Certainly not all desires involve the development of one's capacities or self-improvement, but the ones that do are surely part of a happy life. Engaging in the process of meeting goals can be meaningful and satisfying to us.

There are also limitations of this model. We have said that a central complaint of the Hedonic Account is that some people take pleasure in the wrong things. The same complaint can be made of the Desire-Satisfaction Account.

Not All Desires Are Good Ones
Philosopher Julia Annas writes:

> One thing the desire-satisfaction account disables us from doing is making judgments about the happiness of people whose desires are in obvious ways defective. Notoriously, some desires are based on radically faulty information or reasoning. Some desires are unresponsive to the agent's reasoning powers because of the force of addiction or obsession. At a deeper level, some desires are themselves deformed by social pressures.[20]

The point is that desire fulfillment does not necessarily contribute to a happy life. Some of our goals and desires are problematic. (Consider the athlete whose objective is to embarrass a competitor.)

Some of our desires control us. (Consider addictions.) Some of our desires conflict with other desires. (Consider the runner who both wants to sleep in and skip training *and* become a world-class athlete.)

Some of our desires are also mistaken, or the consequence of inadequate knowledge. In fact, as we explored in Chapter 2, for Plato, all instances of vice are explainable in this way. If we truly knew what was good for us, we would choose our good. The problem is that we often are mistaken about what our good is, so we make bad choices. An example is the person who dedicates his life to the pursuit of great wealth, convinced that wealth will make him happy. He is mistaken about which desires he should pursue; pursuing them will not elevate the quality of his life.

There Is Life on the Other Side of Our Goals

A common belief is that after we accomplish some big goal, then we will have arrived, and this will substantially change something about us or our position in the world. This is precisely what I thought, perhaps not consciously, but as a working assumption while I trained to win my fifth national title. As it turns out, this is just not true. Almost immediately after I crossed the finish line, I was met with the reality that life would proceed as usual despite having reached my big goal. There would be training frustrations, self-doubt, and bad workouts. There would be new events to register for and new mountains to summit. Regardless of what a runner accomplishes, almost immediately upon meeting their big goal, someone will ask them what their next race is.

I am not unique in feeling sad following the completion of a major goal. Over the past several years, led by American Olympic swimmers Michael Phelps and Missy Franklin, American Olympic 1,500-meter runner Heather MacLean, and Greek Olympic 10,000-meter runner Alexi Pappas, athletes have been more forthcoming in sharing their experiences with a phenomenon called the "post-Olympic blues." This is a depression that follows the completion of a major goal—namely, competing well at the Olympics.[21] This is a goal that, in many cases, consumes an athlete's attention for years. Naturally, once the event is over, the athlete can feel unmoored and aimless.

The post-Olympic blues is common among Olympians. According to a 2021 study in the *British Journal of Sports Medicine*, 24 percent of athletes reported high or very high psychological distress following the Olympic Games.[22] This may be surprising because it seems like athletes would be happier following the fulfillment of their greatest ambitions. But achievement is like a trick escalator that never arrives at its destination. It proceeds infinitely upward without relief.

Desire satisfaction is a faulty model because meeting our desires can never satisfy us, even when we meet them constantly. This insatiability is captured by Plato in the Socratic dialogue, *Gorgias*. Socrates and a Sophist, or paid teacher, named Callicles are engaged in a dispute about temperance, the virtue that governs desires. Socrates proposes that temperance involves self-rule, or self-restraint, and Callicles contends that a ruler should not restrain himself. A ruler should maximize pleasure—fulfilling all of his desires—because he can. For Callicles, this is what a happy life consists of—desire satisfaction. In response, Socrates provides two helpful metaphors: He compares this ruler to a leaky jar, which is continually refilled but never full. He also uses the imagery of a person itchy their whole lives, scratching without relief.[23]

The athlete who continually attempts to satisfy herself with goals or desires, however noble they seem, is like a leaky jug or an itchy tyrant scratching without relief. Completing running goals, while part of a rich life, can never satisfy us.

This View Favors the Wealthy and Talented

A final complaint about the desire-satisfaction view of happiness is that it implies that people with means are better positioned to be happy. This could mean wealth, power, or—for runners—natural talent. Given his affluence, Bill Gates would be happier than just about anyone on the planet. The Kardashians would be positively giddy. Moreover, the same can be said of runners with high natural ability. They are better equipped to fulfill performance objectives than those of lesser ability. If happiness means the ability to satisfy one's desires, then talented runners are in luck. They are not only naturally faster than other runners; they are happier, too.

The question of whether happiness levels are higher for those with more resources or natural ability is ultimately an empirical one, but it is a difficult question to study. This is for a few reasons. The first difficulty is that many happiness studies operate by self-report. Study participants are asked to rate their happiness on a scale of 1–10, and we are not great at rating our own happiness.[24] This is because recent experiences often intrude upon our global self-evaluations. For example, try introspecting about how happy your life is overall after a bad morning workout. The recent sour experience makes it tough to think about your life as good or happy overall, even when it really is. And it is not just a bad run that can alter how we evaluate our lives.

In a classic study by psychologist Norbert Schwarz (1987), participants were asked whether they were happy. Those who were asked this question after finding a dime on a copy machine reported higher life satisfaction than those who did not find a dime.[25] Finding a dime (however trivial) lifted their spirits enough that it impacted self-reported well-being. In another study, participants reported they had happier lives on sunny days than rainy days.[26] Surely, dimes and sunshine do not substantially increase overall life happiness. Surely, a bad run does not tank your happiness either, even though it may feel that way in the moment.

Beyond the deficiencies of self-reporting, there is a more insidious difficulty in using psychological studies to learn about happiness: Many studies *assume* what they profess to *measure*. For instance, to observe the relationship between *running talent* and *happiness*, we must first define these concepts, to specify what we are looking for. Often, researchers define happiness in hedonic or desire-satisfaction terms.[27] This means that what is being measured is talent's relationship to *positive subjective feelings*, or to the *ability to fulfill one's desires*—the two views we are challenging here. We assume what we profess to measure. Moreover, in defining happiness as desire satisfaction, we may identify resources (like wealth or talent) that support happiness. But it is only trivially true that they do. Certainly resources help us to fulfill desires, but whether desire fulfillment constitutes happiness is a separate question.

To summarize, whether resources like wealth or talent increase happiness—in the way that we might expect them to, given the truth of the Desire-Satisfaction Account—is an empirical question. But it is a difficult question to study, and many happiness studies will not be helpful to us. Regardless, as we explored earlier, there are additional reasons to find this model unsatisfactory: Not all desires are good ones, and, in the athletic space, the fulfillment of our major objectives seems not to satisfy us.

It turns out both the Hedonic and Desire-Satisfaction models of happiness are inadequate. So what is next?

Eudaimonism

The most promising account of happiness is one you may have never heard of. It takes seriously our humanity and the place of suffering in a good life, and it outshines both hedonism and desire satisfaction in that it centrally involves reason, though not at the expense of the emotions. On this account, happiness is an ongoing activity, rather than a singular event, and it involves an assessment of one's life as a whole, rather than moment to moment. It is called *eudaimonism*. *Eudaimonia* is a Greek word introduced by Aristotle that literally means "good spirit." While this word has no perfect translation into English, *eudaimonia* is often defined as "flourishing," "living well," or—simply—"happiness."

Since this account of happiness is stronger than the others, and because it helps us to understand the place of both virtue and suffering in a good life, we will spend extra time examining it, starting with how Aristotle arrives at the concept.

Key Considerations of *Eudaimonia*

What Are People for?

If I asked you why you went running outside this morning, you might answer something about maintaining fitness. Or maybe you would respond that you needed to hit your weekly mileage. And if I asked why you needed to hit your weekly mileage, you may say something about preparing for a race. Why do you need to race? This inquiry might proceed for a while, but it would not proceed indefinitely. It is not turtles all the way down.[28] At the end of the line of inquiry, you would express some vision you have of a good or happy life. Running is a means by which you progress toward that *telos*, or end—a happy life.

At the beginning of the *Nicomachean Ethics*, Aristotle asks what sort of end is suitable for a human being. Or, stated differently, what are people for?[29] This is a difficult question. Aristotle examines many of the answers supplied by his culture—such as wealth, pleasure, and honor. Whether or not we do so consciously, many of us orient our lives toward these ends. We act as though they are our greatest good.[30] Aristotle points out that these ends are incomplete. Wealth, for example, is a means by which we buy things. It is not an end in itself. The same is true for power. Power has only instrumental value as a means to secure something else we perceive as good. Aristotle concludes that, if there is a greatest good, or ultimate end of humankind, it would need to be self-sufficient. This good would be desirable in itself, rather than as a means to something else.[31]

Aristotle names happiness as our great good. It is self-sufficient and desirable in itself. It is the turtle on which all the intermediary turtles stand. It is a special kind of happiness, which he calls *eudaimonia*. There are further questions we need to ask here. First, what makes *eudaimonia* special? And what, exactly, does happiness consist of? (Tighten your shoelaces! This is where the big disagreements come in.)

Defining Our Terms

According to Aristotle, *eudaimonia* is "an activity of the soul, in accordance with virtue, and if there are several virtues, in accordance with the best and most complete . . . and in a full life."[32] There is a lot to unpack here. Crucially, happiness is an activity for Aristotle. It is not something that just happens to someone, like winning the lottery, but something a person is actively engaged in. To put it in a way a runner would understand, if smart watches tracked activities of the soul, they would report "productive" rather than "detraining."

But what kinds of "activities" is Aristotle referring to? He means the development and expression of virtues. We already know what a virtue (*areté*) is. It is an excellence that makes something a good instance of its kind. In the same way that sharpness is an excellence of a knife, since it permits the knife to cut well, we also have several virtues—perseverance, fortitude, wisdom, and temperance, for example—that make us good instances of our kind, as humans. Our activities are constituted by thinking, feeling, and acting excellently, exhibiting these virtues, such that we are good instances of humankind.

But what is a good instance of humankind? This is a matter of serious debate. Accepting, as we are, Aristotle's idea that happiness is an end suited to our human nature, we still need to define the terms of human nature. What does it mean to be human? What does a flourishing human life look like? These are philosophical, psychological, biological, sociological, and often theological questions. But they are athletic questions, too. The more we learn about our minds and our bodies—how they move through space, conditions of thriving, natural limits, and competencies—we refine our understanding of human nature. Sports play a role in helping us to see ourselves more clearly and to learn our natural limits.

Aristotle defines our nature as rational,[33] so a good human life will be characterized by excellences of reason. He also defines our nature as social, or political,[34] so it will involve excellences of community, like liberality and justice. He reports that we are creatures for which both excesses and deficiencies of pleasures are damaging, so he describes the virtue of temperance.[35] Additionally, Aristotle claims that life should not be cut short or involve too much suffering—claims which we will assess in the final chapter. A happy life is a long one with certain material constraints, like sufficient health and wealth.[36] So, again, desire satisfaction is not irrelevant to happiness. We desire food, shelter, and social esteem, for example. But meeting these desires is not sufficient for a happy life.

For Aristotle, in the same way that there are natural facts about rocks and trees, there are facts about humans. There is such a thing as a good human, just as there is such a thing as a good cat and a good sycamore tree. Virtues are excellences suited to our rational, social, appetitive natures. They make us good humans.

Two Kinds of Lives

Of course, these descriptions of flourishing are unspecific. Even in accepting Aristotle's account, many questions remain about what a good life might involve, and where athletics fits in.[37] For example, is a well-rounded life happier than one fixated on a singular pursuit, such as running at a high level?

The All-In Runner

Even for the professional athlete, running can never be someone's *exclusive* daily focus. Responsibilities of daily life—like washing dishes, grocery shopping, and paying the bills—get in the way. But by "all-in running" I mean to capture a mindset. The all-in runner sets running as her highest priority and ambition. If given a free hour, she will probably run or do running-adjacent tasks, like stretching and lifting. Unoccupied, her thoughts often return to the sport. This runner has a singularity of focus on running that outshines her commitments to many other things.

For the sake of performance, the all-in runner can maximize her potential. She won't have to wonder what she could have done had she invested more of herself into the sport. But like most pursuits taken seriously, there are opportunity costs involved in this kind of relationship with running. While we are running, we are not reading, horseback riding, or practicing an instrument. We are not memorizing poetry or becoming more competent chefs. Humans have limited energy and attention. So to focus on running is—under another description—to *not* focus on other crafts. This idea is captured by the expression "much, not many." When you have *much* of one thing, you sacrifice *many* things.

In a lot of cases, "much, not many" is rewarding. To commit to something—rather than to flit off to do whatever happens to capture your attention from moment to moment—involves a kind of self-mastery. Consider the violinist who practices daily, rather than permitting her attention to turn to the many diversions that pass her way. Her ability to do so is an expression of two kinds of freedom.

The first kind of freedom is self-governance, or freedom from roving desires or the lower parts of herself that want to quit. We also see this freedom in long-term committed relationships and in a runner's decision to finish a long race through mounting fatigue.[38] Remaining in place is simple, but simple and easy are not the same thing. Committing to stay with a task is one of the hardest things we do, and we know this as runners.

The second kind of freedom is the ability to *do* or to *be* something great, which may be unavailable to those who do not commit. Consider again the serious violinist. She is *free* to play difficult music that is not an option for those who do not practice with the same singularity of focus. A standard of excellence is available to her that is not available to the lukewarm musician. Likewise, a world of opportunities, commensurate with one's abilities, can avail itself to a committed runner. The committed is *free* to run further and faster, to reach more mountain summits, and to compete more successfully when she focuses on training.

So the all-in runner's deep investments come at the cost of breadth of experience, but they certainly engage our freedom and can facilitate a high level of attainment in running. Is this a good tradeoff? Maybe. Again, "meeting performance objectives" and "happiness" are not necessarily the same thing. Perhaps the happier life is one that is well-rounded.

A Case for Well-Roundedness

The well-rounded runner is characterized by having a few interests, sufficiently nurtured. An example is a runner who is also a full-time student, plays the piano, and is an amateur chef. Another example is a runner who works as a nurse, makes watercolor paintings, and has a young family to care for. Each runner has various investments—yet not so many that her attention is frayed, or that she merely dabbles, free-floating of any commitments to a particular craft.[39] There are reasons to think well-roundedness may better support a happy life than being "all in" on running.

The first reason is that well-roundedness provides more stable footing (literally) than all-in running does. Statistically, between 37 and 56 percent of recreational runners become injured annually.[40] Thus, it is likely that you will be injured soon if you are not injured already. (I am sorry to hear about your current or forthcoming injury. Get well soon.) Because of her singularity of focus, when the all-in runner experiences injuries or setbacks, she can feel purposeless. Well-roundedness provides a cushion of other activities to occupy an athlete's attention through setbacks. In the long term, the well-rounded runner also has vocational prospects, or a history with interests outside of the sport, should she decide to do something non-running-related upon retiring from competition.

Second, unlike someone who merely dabbles, a well-rounded runner is sufficiently invested in certain activities, such that she is edified by the process of attempting to master various crafts. Throughout this book, we have discussed the growth in character that can accompany participation in running. A well-rounded runner can benefit from character growth in running but also in reading, knitting, and so forth—whatever practices she decides to invest attention into. This means she can become broadly excellent—intellectually, artistically, athletically, and otherwise (rather than only in sports-relevant ways)—taking seriously many aspects of human nature. She can acquire a broad set of virtues.

But what does Aristotle think? Is the well-rounded life more compatible with the virtue-rich vision of happiness, or *eudaimonia,* we discussed earlier?

Aristotle on the All-In Runner

In Chapter 3, we explored how many theorists think that certain virtues have an interdependent relationship with one another—that to be courageous, for example, depends on having other virtues in place, such as patience, practical wisdom, and humility. If it is true that many virtues depend on one another, then we might think that a well-rounded, broadly excellent life better supports one's possession of *any* virtues at all—that to be excellent, we need to be broadly excellent.

However, this is not exactly the message we get from Aristotle. Again, he defines *eudaimonia* not as being constituted by *all* the virtues, in the sense that someone might try to be excellent in every respect. Instead, he writes, "and if there are several virtues, in accordance with the best and most complete."[41] We are supposed to know which virtue (or virtues) is (are) the most important and instantiate it (them). Many theorists think Aristotle is referring to the virtue of wisdom here, which he later calls the highest virtue.[42] We should be sure to acquire wisdom if we wish to be happy.

Another clue that Aristotle does not think happiness is necessarily well-rounded is that he describes the philosopher as admirable. The philosophical life is decidedly imbalanced. Aristotle calls the philosopher godlike in his ability to contemplate eternal things without interruption. This kind of life seems both impractical (Who will pay the bills or cook dinner while you contemplate the cosmos?) and asocial (Contemplation is a solitary activity). Aristotle notes that some socializing and practical action is necessary for the philosopher, since he is a human being, but that "worldly goods may almost be said to be a hindrance to contemplation."[43]

Thus, for Aristotle, it is not the *narrowness* of a life singularly dedicated to a craft (such as running) that is problematic. He seems okay with going "all in" on something, within reason. Even so, Aristotle does speak ill of an athletics-driven life for two reasons: physical and intellectual.

The *intellectual* reason is an issue of what the runner is focused on. The issue is not that the athlete is all-consumed; it's what she is all-consumed by. For Aristotle, since human nature is distinctively *rational*, the athletic life is not the highest or happiest kind of life one might choose, insofar as it crowds out an interest in intellectual goods. For Aristotle, growth in wisdom is more important than aerobic development.

You may disagree with Aristotle's reasoning here. (I often do!) Regardless, perhaps you will find his second reason more compelling.

The *physical* reason against all-in running is the potential for long-term damage to the body in high-level sport. Aristotle raises this concern in the *Politics*. He writes,

[G]ymnastic exercises should be employed in education, and that for children they should be of a lighter kind, avoiding severe regimen or painful toil, lest the growth of the body be impaired. The evil of excessive training in early years is strikingly proved by the example of the Olympic victors; for not more than two or three of them have gained a prize both as boys and as men; their early training and severe gymnastic exercises exhausted their constitutions.[44]

Whether you accept this case against all-in running will depend on two things: (1) whether serious athletic practice *does* indeed exhaust one's constitution in the long term, and (2) whether you are willing to compromise long-term health for what you may deem higher aims.

Physical Health
After high school, I briefly ran for my college's National Collegiate Athletic Association (NCAA) Division I Cross Country team before venturing into the world of trail and ultrarunning. I say "briefly" because my competencies were a poor fit for the training style. The program involved more high-intensity training than my younger body was able to absorb. I was frequently injured and impatient—a perilous combination—so I repeatedly returned too quickly to high-level training before sufficiently recovering from each injury. I would agitate the injury again, and again, and again. The myth of Sisyphus is a story about my life.

There were two things I learned my freshman year of collegiate running. The first was how to walk noiselessly in a stress fracture boot so as not to disturb my fellow students on the quiet floor of our university library. The second was that injuries are sad, but they are not lonely. I was never the only member of my team who was injured. Rather, a good portion of the team was injured at any given time—with tendon issues, plantar fasciitis, sprains, strains, low iron, and good old-fashioned bone stress injuries. I had plenty of company in my suffering.

The point is, I do not have to tell a group of runners that there is the possibility of damage from high-level participation in running. If you are like me, you already know.

Ultimately, the extent to which our physical bodies can be damaged by committed athletic practice is an empirical question. Interestingly, the data here are mixed. Moderate aerobic exercise is widely touted as beneficial, improving heart and metabolic health, reducing cancer risk, and supporting cognition.[45] Moreover, regular running is considered a cost-effective tool for maintaining mental wellness, such as by reducing anxiety.[46] Compared to nonrunners, one study found runners to have a 30 percent reduced all-cause mortality, and runners have been assigned a three-year life expectancy benefit.[47] This is great news. We have three more years to spend running.

Of course, moderate running does not characterize what many of us do. While some studies claim that all participation in running, regardless of dose, is linked to better health outcomes as compared to no running at all,[48] others indicate there may be adverse consequences to running in high doses. These consequences include pathological structural remodeling of the heart and arteries (changing the size, shape, or structure of the heart muscle—such as through scarring or thickening of the heart walls—in ways that adversely affect cardiac function in the long term) and increased risk for bone and tendon injuries.[49]

Of course, personal factors should be taken into consideration—how much you train, how resilient your body is, and how much of a gamble you feel comfortable making regarding health. Something to keep in mind when you make these calculations is the *Base Rate Fallacy*. This is a failure of reasoning in which we mistakenly ignore statistical information, in favor of individuating information.

For example, only 5 percent of applicants are accepted to this university, but my daughter is exceptional! She will certainly be admitted. Lifelong cigarette smokers are 20 to 40 times more likely to develop lung cancer than those who do not smoke.[50] But I eat vegetables and have good genes, so I will be okay. Or, of relevance here, a given percentage of distance runners develop long-term heart issues, but I am an exceptional athlete. I will be fine.

For runners who are especially talented, the Base Rate Fallacy is an appealing error. This is because talented runners are often described as exceptional, or distinct from other people.[51] In fact, they *are* physically distinct. They have a higher ceiling for performance than others do. But their exceptionalism with respect to talent does not mean they are an exception to statistical norms regarding long-term health outcomes for athletes. Insofar as they are part of the endurance athlete population, the base rate applies to them.

With these things in mind, my advice regarding making decisions about endurance training when it comes to health and wellness is two-fold. First, gather information from experts about the plausible impacts of endurance training on long-term health outcomes. Be sure these are experts, not "experts." (Start with peer-reviewed studies and credentialed clinicians, rather than running influencers or content creators online.) Furthermore, ideally some of these experts will not be participants in the running community. This will help you to avoid blind spots and motivated reasoning. Second, when reflecting upon this information, advise yourself as you would advise an acquaintance. This will reduce the temptation to excuse yourself from the data and view yourself as an exception.

Health and Happiness

So you gathered high-quality information about the probable impacts of running far on your long-term health, and you are taking seriously its relevance to you. Now what? Well, you may decide the risks of getting injured or the worst-case scenario health outcomes are not worth the gamble. Maybe you stop running and take up bull riding or football instead. (These sound safer from an injury standpoint.) Or maybe you decide to train more moderately than you currently do to mitigate negative impacts. You may not be able to maximize your performance potential in doing so, but you could be healthier in the long term.

Alternatively, perhaps you decide the risks are worth it for the richness that running far brings you. You decide you are willing to (potentially) compromise long-term health for what you deem higher aims, like maximizing athletic potential. You think making this trade-off will contribute to the richness and happiness of your life overall.

To a certain extent, we make these kinds of trade-offs all the time. If my highest life goal were longevity, I would live a very different kind of life than I do now. I would not stay up late writing papers. I would not bear the emotional burdens of my friends (too tiring!). I would say goodbye to sweet treats and to my children (to reduce blood sugar levels and stress, respectively), and I would walk around in bubble wrap (to avoid injuries). Sure, endurance training may have costs, but then again, so does everything else I love.

Furthermore, health and longevity—while constitutive features of many good lives—are often beside the point as markers of flourishing. Consider doctors who treat sick people and compromise their personal health as a result. Also consider those who die prematurely for noble causes, such as humanitarian workers, soldiers, and religious martyrs. These are people whose lives often seem good and admirable to us. They are not living longevity-focused lives.

Now consider the case of the Olympic athlete who competes with otherworldly ability while young, but lives with a compromised physical constitution thereafter. Maybe the life of an Olympic athlete is this kind of life—one potentially compromised in terms of health, yet still good and admirable. Why should we claim that a life marked by moderate athletic pursuits and unimpaired physical capacity into old age is happier? And who gets to decide?

I am not sure there is a standard way of answering these questions, such that it is always better to make one choice rather than another—or that one kind of life is happier than another. We are different people, with different interests, abilities, and opportunities. It is clear that very different kinds of lives can constitute excellent instances of human nature. For this reason, it can be valuable to surround yourself with exemplars, or virtue role models (as described in Chapter 4) to demonstrate a range of possibilities for flourishing lives. Ideally, you will have a mix of athletes and nonathletes, demonstrating various ways of being excellent and thriving in the world. With a backdrop of these people, we can self-examine about how our present activities square with our long-term health and the visions we have of a good life. We need to self-examine because we only have one life to get it right.

To potentially compromise your health for sport (or for anything else you commit to at a high level) is a personal decision. It is one I hope athletes will make with loved ones and friends who will their good. It is also a decision I hope will be made with foresight and empathy extended to the future versions of yourself. It can be easy to fall into a kind of presentism regarding athletic performance, wanting to maximize outcomes now, without thinking for the long term.

Personally, now that I am in my thirties, the only regrets I have about running concern the short-term trade-offs I made as a teen without thinking about this version of me, now. I wonder if I would feel stronger had I taken rest days and not pushed myself so hard as a sixteen-year-old. And I wonder if I would currently have a more diverse set of interests and deeper friendships had I made more space for these things.

I can't go back and change the ways I occupied the sport at age sixteen. However, I can raise these questions for young runners. And I can use this acquired perspective to examine what the fifty-year-old version of me will think about the bargains I may be making for performance reasons currently. I hope she will be pleased with me, and I hope she will be happy.

Thinking More Seriously about Nature

Earlier, I said that inquiries about human nature—what we are and what people are *for*—are interdisciplinary. They are philosophical questions but also psychological, theological, biological, anthropological, and *athletic* questions. Each of these domains has something to say about what it means to be human.

Disputes about human nature are especially important in the context of sports, where we often negotiate and attempt to extend our natural limits. This makes it prime territory for a fruitful discussion about what a human is and what a human is not. Theoretically, these are interesting conversations, but these are also considerations that practically inform how we participate in sport.

Often, we tread on our natural limits, in ways that make sports exciting. We brush up against, and sometimes exceed, efforts our bodies can withstand. Culturally, we tend to celebrate these things. We praise fast times and incredible feats. But drawing close to, or exceeding, natural limits can be costly—like flying too close to the sun. It can also involve a fair amount of suffering for both the athlete and her community. So the risks of doing so should be made explicit. They should be talked about so that athletes do not find themselves making bargains with their long-term health or happiness by accident, and being pressed by the culture of sport to do so. This is part of what it means to take humanity seriously in sport, as a consideration in a happy life.

In the final chapter, we examine two key features of *eudaimonism* particularly relevant in the athletic context: suffering and limits. But first, let me anticipate your objections.

Track and Fielding Objections

The Egoism Argument

A common argument against *eudaimonism* goes like this: For Aristotle and other *eudaimonists*, the happy or flourishing life is constituted by virtues. But framing the good life in terms of personal flourishing is egoist, or selfish.

In *Justice in Love*, philosopher Nicholas Wolterstorff challenges the *eudaimonist* principle "that one should seek to promote the well-being of another as an end in itself only if doing so promises to enhance one's own well-being."[52] He reminds readers that there are many situations in which helping others comes at the cost of personal well-being. For example, maybe we invest in younger athletes, and this is a time-intensive investment. Doing so may come at the cost of pursuing personal goals, since we are limited creatures with limited time.

Whether *eudaimonism* is egoistic is an important concern. There are two kinds of responses one might give to this concern. First, we can say that our good is inseparable from the community's good on a *eudaimonist* framework. Aristotle moves seamlessly between ethics and politics—or the individual and the collective—because, by nature, we are social creatures. There are certain excellences of humanity, such as generosity and justice, we cannot acquire apart from one another. (I cannot be generous to myself!) So, when we say we are interested in flourishing, this can be understood as compatible with loving our families, our running clubs, the other competitors on the start line beside us, and spectators of the sport.

Second, just because an action happens to be for our own good does not mean that our *motivation* for that action is egoistic. Maybe my motivation for helping younger athletes is altruistic. I want them to succeed. I also happen to live a fuller, happier life because I help these athletes. Both statements can be true. In this case, there is no conflict between caring about others and my own happiness.

That said, it is always a good idea to inspect our motivations. Returning to the example of helping younger athletes—even though it may be to my benefit to help them—I want to help them from an altruistic motivation, making the action about caring for *them*, rather than making the action about *me*. This is important for the reasons we discussed in Chapter 1—that our motivations change the character of an action.

The "Virtues Don't Make Us Happy" Argument

Someone might still be unconvinced by the terms of *eudaimonism*. Maybe virtues are morally good ways of being in the world, but how could they possibly make us happy?

Let's look at a couple of examples. Temperance is a virtue that concerns taking proper pleasure in food and drink. This does not mean deprivation, or even self-restraint. It involves enjoying these pleasures but not to the extent that you are consumed by the task of consumption. If you are temperate, this frees you up to pay attention to worthier things—like the people present at a meal, conversations, or anything else beyond the acts of eating or drinking.[53] You are not governed by your appetites, and this is a kind of attentional freedom that affords you the opportunity to do other things and think other thoughts. This seems like a happier kind of life than the intemperate alternative.

A second example is intellectual virtues like wisdom and fair-mindedness. These also contribute to a happy life. They help you think clearly and make good choices. You can align yourself to worthwhile ends, and you are less likely to be duped by those who wish you harm.

Virtues help us to self-govern well, and they eliminate a major frustration—the fact that we often lack freedom with respect to our own appetites and get in our own way. My students report that, when they fail to hit their goals, it is not generally that they have been impeded by others or lack the opportunities to do so. Rather, they often lack the perseverance to remain on task, the patience to stay committed through moments of little progress, the resilience to proceed through setbacks, or the practical wisdom to know what steps to take to advance toward their objectives. Virtues correct for these defects. The virtuous life is indeed a happier one.

The "Too Much Disagreement" Objection

This objection goes like this: There are too many disagreements about what a human being is and what constitutes a good life. So we should stay in our own (track) lane and avoid these conversations, lest we disagree. This is an important point in a pluralistic society marked by values conflicts and the struggle to get along. I have two responses.

The first is that, even in a society in which there are many disagreements, there is often more consensus than we think regarding character. There are many virtues on which we broadly agree, such as honesty, integrity, perseverance, and patience, that are relevant in the context of sport. We can prioritize these broadly agreed-upon virtues together in our training and racing without offending many, if any, people at all.

Second, disagreements about virtue and happiness provide an opportunity to examine what we find most important in our lives. Without these discussions, one of the most important questions in life—what it means to be happy—is passed over in silence. In a culture marked my aimlessness, malaise, anxiety, and depression, taking happiness seriously is not just a theoretical exercise; it is a social imperative. Certainly, we will disagree. Regardless, we should persist in having discussions—employing the same perseverance we have worked hard to develop in our sneakers—in inquiries about the good life. We should take happiness seriously. We should live an examined run.

8

Limitless

The Pitfalls of Faustian Running

Nature

A couple of years ago, I was part of an advertising campaign for a shoe company centered on the concept of limitlessness. *We have no limits. We are boundless. There is no ceiling on our potential.* With the camera on, I was asked to give a soundbite on the topic, and I could not do it. This was one of the few occasions in which my two vocations—runner and philosopher—came directly into conflict. I have theoretical qualms about the idea of being limitless. I could not make that claim.[1]

These qualms concerned our nature. I had been working through questions of *eudaimonia*, wondering about how my running ambitions either supported or undermined a good life. What I was coming to understand was that, while I had athletic ambitions—big ones—maybe considering myself "limitless" in potential did not align with my shifting understanding of a good life.

Sports and Limits

The language of limitlessness is not new to athletics. Sports have always been about overcoming limitations. We—as individual runners—press against our own limits, real or perceived. We—as a community of runners—stand on the shoulders of runners from previous generations and surpass the standards they have set. For example, the four-minute mile was once believed to be the outer limit of human physiological capacity. Then in 1954 Roger Bannister broke it. Now the four-minute mark is broken by milers regularly, and even periodically by talented high schoolers. The very best runners now aim to break 3:50 in the mile, and Hicham El Guerrouj holds the world record at 3:43. The original limit was demolished. Shattering limits has been a collective enterprise.[2]

The notion of limitlessness appears in numerous sports-marketing campaigns. Athletes often declare that they will not place limits on their own potential. Moreover, the closest person we have to a sage in running—marathon world record holder, Eliud Kipchoge—is known for the catchphrase "No human is limited." We often speak in this way. So what is the problem?

Faustian Bargains

There is an essay entitled "Faustian Economics" by Wendell Berry.[3] To describe our current rates of economic consumption, waste, and greed, Berry draws on the German legend of Faust. As the legend goes, Faust was a scholar who made a deal with the devil. He traded his soul for unlimited knowledge and worldly pleasures. Faust received these things at great cost: he lost his self-possession, and his life was cut short.

From this legend comes the concept of a Faustian bargain. The Faustian bargain is trading long-term considerations for short-term satisfactions. Berry explains our treatment of the environment in these terms. He describes "prodigal extravagance," "assumed limitlessness," and a pattern of consuming too many resources without regard for the future.[4] We ignore our limits to our peril because, over the long term, there are consequences. Realistically, over the short term, there are consequences, too. By overstepping limits in one area of life, we are apt to neglect responsibilities in others.

Berry's essay concerns the precariousness of overstepping environmental limits, but the same posture toward limitlessness pervades competitive athletics. One might wonder what kinds of Faustian bargains we are making and what the repercussions will be.

Faustian Running

In general, I assume that those who use the concept of "limitlessness" do not mean that we are literally without limits. For example, I do not know anyone who supposes that, one day, we will run a zero-minute mile. Likely, when they make claims of limitlessness, they mean to capture something softer, like this: "You are wrong about where your biological potential lies, and you can probably squeeze better performances out of yourself. How much better? Who knows? Maybe a lot better! Keep trying." But that slogan does not fit neatly on a t-shirt.

Even so, there are compromises made in trying to overstep limits, and these compromises should be made explicit in a sport where limit-pushing is our standard mode of being. For example, we often see runners enter the sport, overtrain, undereat, or both, become ascendant figures on the racing scene, and then disappear shortly after. They have made a kind of Faustian bargain. It is profitable for a limited amount of time, but it costs them healthy running over the long term.

So, for the sake of balancing out the assertions of limitlessness we hear frequently in the world of sport, I contend that we do, in fact, have limits. To be human is to have limits. At times, we should press these limits, as we do in athletics, because this allows us to get the best out of ourselves, to build confidence, and to learn, in a more fine-grained way, what our capabilities are. But we should also be aware of these limits and respect them. We have *biological* limits—meaning we are bodily creatures, involving matter and physical restraints. We also have *cultural* limits—meaning we have friendships, family ties, and "self-restraints implied by neighborliness."[5]

Why Our Limits Matter

You May Want to Use Your Legs When You Are Old

In the present, you can run an unsustainable number of miles, decrease body mass,[6] lift extra weights, and pay undue attention to the sport. At first, it may even benefit you. You might run faster or farther than you ever have. But eventually, your Faustian bargain will catch up with you. You will find yourself in a hole. Hopefully the hole is not so deep that you can't claw your way out of it.

There are limits to the amount of training we can absorb, and our bodies require rest—lots of it. We can either be annoyed by this fact—that we are embodied beings who need to step away from hard work to refuel, sleep, and recover—or we can find a way to make peace with our physical restraints as part of the rhythm of training.

Some of Our Limits Are the People We Love

Often, when we speak of "not putting limits on our potential," it seems the kinds of limits we have in mind are the imaginative and the physical. We are not going to underestimate what we can achieve, and we are going to work physically in such a way that we can accomplish something extraordinary. We intend to free ourselves from these self-imposed limits. But, if you think about it, many of the limits in our own lives are the people we love, to whom we have obligations.

For example, Berry points out that, in friendship, there are "implied restraints of faithfulness and loyalty."[7] Friendships take time and attention. We also have obligations to our families and neighbors, and we have obligations as community members and citizens. Usually when I am unable to train at the level I want to, it is not my body that limits me. Rather, the responsibilities I have to my family and to my students limit me. These are happy, humanizing limits. My life is richer because of them.

On these grounds, when we make claims about being limitless in our athletic pursuits, these claims ignore the ties that bind us, whether or not we intend for this to be the case. When we are "all in" on our athletic performances—not willing to put a cap on our potential— our families and communities are the first limit we step over.

Extension Is a Narrow Way to Conceive of Sports and Life

My greatest worry is the one I am having the hardest time articulating, but it goes something like this: It often seems like we talk about surpassing human limits without really caring about what a human is, or about how to live a rich life and run beautiful races within the limitations we have. Berry frames the worry this way: He calls his readers to think about limits in the way an artist does. An artist does not generally focus on extension—requesting a bigger canvas. Rather, she fills in the canvas that she has and makes something beautiful.

A second example is a potter who makes pots. There is way of conceiving of the potter as limited by the constraints of her craft— material constraints (the use of clay), formal constraints (the shape of a pot), and so forth. But these limits are not restrictions; they are a framework that gives coherence to the craft. A good potter works within his constraints, rather than begrudging them—wishing, instead, that he were making tin mugs or porcelain buckets, for example. A pot is what it is by nature of its limits.[8]

In the same way, we either can frame our participation in sports as being exclusively about extension—surpassing limits and systematically accomplishing greater feats. Or we can create something beautiful within the limits we have. This would demand that we think about sports and life in richer, broader ways than the rhetoric of limitlessness affords us.

More specifically, if we frame sports solely in terms of the overcoming of limits, this positions us to be inhospitable to those who cannot participate in sports under those terms. It positions us poorly to notice beauty and value in sports beyond breaking barriers. It makes the athlete disposable after her days of peak performance are over. Moreover, limitlessness can motivate a desire for performance at any cost—be that through advanced shoe technologies that distort natural limits increasingly with every carbon-plated iteration of racing flats, through doping, or by other inappropriate means of extension.[9]

Call to Action

Recently, I found myself panting in the grass on the far side of my neighborhood. I was struggling to hit paces I wanted to in a workout—paces which had been easy for me a few years prior— and I was annoyed with my body for not complying.

In the past few years, my life has changed considerably. I graduated from a doctoral program and began a full-time teaching position. My research load increased. I had two children, the youngest of whom was six months old and not yet sleeping through the night, when I struggled through that workout. These are all changes that fill my proverbial canvas with new textures and colors; they make life and running richer. But they also make it less plausible for me to even feign limitlessness in my running.

To be clear, I do not think my best days of running are behind me. There are several big goals I intend to meet, and I am not naïve in thinking I can meet them. There are many examples of female runners who have come back stronger after having children.[10] But in a busy season of life, I am learning how to broaden the ways I measure success. My miles can be *beautiful* even if not maximally fast. I can run with *integrity* and *fullness* in the stage of life I am currently in, rather than begrudging myself for failing to meet performance standards that made more sense when I had fewer obligations.

What would it be like to look happily upon our constraints as people, or to live full lives within our means? How would our sport need to change? When we talk about flourishing as indexed by human nature—taking seriously the kind of thing we are as humans—this means we need to be mindful of our limits, physical and cultural. It might mean thinking creatively about how we occupy sport, measuring success in broader terms, and embracing the fullness of a life that is invested in performance but also our loved ones and communities. Doing so, in some cases, may have a performance cost.

Conversations about balance and limits are not popular in athletics. Limitlessness and breaking barriers are more exciting and make better marketing slogans. But there are reasons to take our limits seriously—for the sake of our bodies, communities, and flourishing—presently and over the long term. Athletics provides the opportunity to have these conversations, and we need to be having them if we want to take our happiness seriously.

If discussions of limits are challenging, the next topic is even more so.

Suffering

It is the first week of cross-country practice. Our team is sitting in the shade of a gazebo outside of the school, writing down season goals on index cards. A runner raises the idea of team t-shirts, and conversations erupt about all of the possible colors, styles, and slogans. Some of the slogans are very bad, and I look over at my assistant husband (my full-time husband, who serves as my assistant coach) and grimace. I want the athletes to take ownership of the team and its culture, shirts included, but I have a deep-rooted antipathy for bad running t-shirt slogans.

The greatest offenders to me are "No pain, no gain," "Pain is weakness leaving the body," and other variations on this theme. It should go without saying, but not all forms of pain or toughness are constructive. A problem with these slogans is the lionizing of physical damages, which, even if only rhetorical in most cases, is alarming.

Ruling Out Unproductive Forms of Suffering

In the previous chapter, I introduced some riddles of suffering. I pointed out that suffering is part of a good life. It is involved in some of our richest, most meaningful experiences, like maintaining friendships, having children, building careers, and racing marathons. But it is also not always constructive, nor always part of a good life. Certainly, if we live by the "No pain, no gain" slogan, it could not be. This slogan fails to rule out imprudent forms of suffering—like running through injury, making Faustian bargains with our health, or even self-harm for the sake of self-harm. All forms of suffering are not productive. So how can we tell the difference between productive and unproductive forms?

The short answer is, this is a difficult question. The long answer is, trying to answer this question concisely in this book has been a form of suffering for me that has surely exceeded constructive limits.

The question of what forms of suffering are beneficial for us in a good life is not one that can be answered with precision or a standard response across individuals or situations.[11] Regardless, we can make general claims about there being dosing limits for the quantity of suffering that is profitable for a good life. Aristotle assumed there were. He wrote that happiness was contingent upon not only *internal* factors, such as one's emotional constitution and virtue, but *external* factors as well—"factor[s] of fortune or nature."[12] If a person faced sufficient hardship, poverty, or difficulty, or if his life were cut short for some reason, this would prevent him from being happy.[13]

One might reject Aristotle's claims here. Many people do. For example, they might point to the lives of martyrs or to those who die in battle, who suffer for the sake of some higher aim. While these people suffer and their lives are cut short, there is a sense in which, however pitiable they appear to us, in achieving their purpose, they are happy.

However, others may be inclined to resist considering a life wholly characterized by suffering a good or happy one, as Aristotle does. Those who resist doing so need to consider how much the suffering we endure in distance running may detract from a happy life. Likely the optional suffering of athletic activity is weighed differently than the suffering we undergo without choice in the matter, such as from plague, famine, or rain on a race day. Still, it must count for something.

In Chapter 7, I described how discomfort experienced for the sake of distance running is more welcome to me than the heavy rainfall I am exposed to while I run. I do not think I am unique in bracketing off welcome and unwelcome forms of suffering in this way. There is a lot that a person is willing to endure for the activities and the people they love, and this willingness transforms how the suffering appears to us. Furthermore, regardless of how this suffering appears to us, there is a significant objective difference at play. For something like a marathon, at any point, you are free to step off the course and take a nap—an option that may not be available in nonelective suffering, like tragedies or financial hardship. For these forms of suffering, you may not have the option of relief.

Even so, regardless of how welcome elective suffering is to us, surely it can also have a negative impact on one's life if it occurs in large doses. For example, if someone were to willingly imperil their long-term physical health for the sake of athletic performance, perhaps this would detract from a happy life.[14] And if an athlete were to train to an extent such that it dulled her intellectual sensibilities or impeded her ability to sustain meaningful relationships, this may also detract from overall happiness.

There is also a question of whether one's elective suffering in training is always beneficial for running itself. We should not take for granted that it will be. In running, the only training that counts is the training the body can absorb. What this means is that adding training stimulus in the form of workout stress is not constructive past a certain point. Past this point, fatigue and injury risk increase.[15] This is an Aristotelian point. In the *Politics*, Aristotle observes of the person who plays sports too intensely that there are long-term negative repercussions for his physical constitution.[16]

In Chapter 3, I described how our bodies and our characters are inseparable—that how our bodies move through the world shapes our characters, and that our characters inform how we move our bodies through the world. Unsurprisingly, then, there are also concerns about the intensity and dosage of athletic suffering for our characters, not just our bodies.

In Plato's *Republic*, Socrates describes the education of the guardians, a military class in his imagined city, who have the important task of guarding against threats to justice from within and from outside the city. As preparation for more formal learning, Socrates describes how athletics (which he calls "gymnastics") can be employed alongside poetry to shape the guardians to serve the city well and to love the right things.

The goal of gymnastics is to cultivate spiritedness, which manifests itself in "savageness and hardness."[17] The goal of poetry is to soften the guardians and to make them philosophic. Through a combination of poetry and gymnastics, the souls of the guardians are "tuned to the proper degree of tension and relaxation."[18] They become well-ordered. But the key is that the guardians need to participate in the right kinds of activities, at an appropriate intensity. Socrates observes of the person who spends too much time focused on athletics that he becomes too spirited and is "like a wild beast . . . he lives ignorantly and awkwardly without rhythm or grace."[19] He becomes angry or warlike.

Surely the proper degree of tension and relaxation for a person outside of the guardian role, and outside of the imagined city, will be different. Even so, we can draw on the Platonic metaphor of tuning our souls and wonder how much athletic strain is profitable in our formation as persons, and the impact it has, not just on our marathon times but also on who we are at the dinner table and among friends. But how do we know how much strain is too much strain?

Training in Suffering

I once had a middle school athlete run a personal best in the mile by 60 seconds in one race. This is a massive margin of improvement in a marathon, let alone a mile. And he improved because I told him before the race to pay attention. Previously, he never focused. I am not sure where, mentally, he would go. I wager it's the same place many of us go when we get lost in our own heads at various moments of racing and training. It is probably the same place where our missing socks are—somewhere in the abyss. Regardless, this time he focused, and he saw a massive improvement as a result. He drew closer to his potential than he ever had in the past.

Sometimes improvement is that simple—paying attention. But, for many of us, it is not. For many of us, we have to go to difficult places when we race, squeezing out every bit of ourselves to improve by narrow margins. It is an uncomfortable process, one in which you negotiate with yourself to draw closer to your limits, inching toward your body's distress signals. It feels like you are blindly navigating through your own suffering—gritting your teeth, feeling your way toward your limits, and hoping you don't push yourself further than what you can take.

I wish I could claim that you will know when you cross the line into unproductive strain. But if there is one thing I have learned through my own suffering, and the suffering of the young athletes I have coached, it is often difficult to locate this line.

It is difficult to know whether a discomfort is edifying—the fruits of a constructive athletic practice—or the beginnings of an injury. It is challenging to recognize where our limits actually lie. There are extreme efforts and obvious instances of overstepping limits; these are easy to detect. Examples include increasing mileage abruptly or attempting massive efforts an athlete is unprepared for. But often our mistakes are gradual—like an athletic sorites paradox (the paradox of the heap). Every crumb of difficulty we add to our training load is like an additional grain of sand, and it is unclear at what point the grains form a heap.

Sometimes we straddle unsustainability and lean too far in the wrong direction. Sometimes we cannot discern whether we are making a Faustian bargain or are just getting the most out of ourselves in a reasonable way. Sometimes we only know this in retrospect, after stepping too far. This is especially so since, as fitness waxes and wanes, the locations of our physical limits shift. An athlete's breaking point is not something one can learn once and then assume it will remain the same thereafter. It changes, even over the course of a single season.

Young athletes especially struggle to know the difference between productive and unproductive forms of suffering. They tend to err in one of two directions: Some find *all* discomforts alarming and want to back off. They may lack an appetite for arduous goods and choose to be comfortable instead. Otherwise, they might think suffering, in itself, is a problem. These athletes often train only up to the point of difficulty. Then they slow down. Other runners have the opposite issue. They fail to back off when they should and either overcook themselves like cafeteria ziti, or they end up injured. For this second group of runners, it can be confusing to know whether backing off from a workout is prudence or laziness, so they choose neither.

It is important to coach these athletes differently, pressing the risk-averse to make peace with difficulty, and encouraging the tough ones to self-assess and speak up about discomforts. Returning to the "warped board" imagery from Chapter 2, we can coach the athlete toward virtue by pulling them in the opposite direction of their natural warp, to incline them closer to the mean.

Furthermore, it can help athletes to look to an exemplar—what Aristotle calls the *phronimos*, or the person marked by practical wisdom—for guidance on how to suffer excellently. Often professional runners serve this role, but tread carefully. Elite-level athletes are (of course) *elite*. Their abilities typically far exceed our own, and their incentive structures are different. Sometimes taking cues from elite and professional runners about stress and rest is not helpful for the nonelite runner. The time and resources professional runners devote to recovery impact how well they can absorb the suffering they endure in the sport, and they often have teams of people helping them monitor progress and regress in training. It can be helpful for nonelite runners to look to other runners similarly positioned to themselves instead—athletes with school or jobs, families, and other hindrances to rest—for guidance in how to draw lines regarding their elective suffering in the sport.

Suffering and Meaning

In *The Adventures of Tom Sawyer*, Tom is sentenced to whitewash his Aunt Polly's fence as punishment for skipping school. He is not pleased to do so, but he pretends he is having a great time—so convincingly that his friends pay him for the privilege of completing the chore on his behalf.[20] Twain writes that Tom has "discovered a great law of human action, without knowing it—namely, that in order to make a man or boy covet a thing, it is only necessary to make the thing difficult to attain."[21]

In recalling this scene, cognitive scientist Paul Bloom expands on Twain's sentiment, writing that "effort sweetens the value of the products of labor."[22] The difficulty of a task is part of what makes the outcome worthwhile to us. It makes the work feel more meaningful. We know this as runners. The satisfaction we feel in the wake of a long run is buoyed by the knowledge of how difficult it was. Our major triumphs in the sport are often accompanied by reflections about the work it took to accomplish them, and having done this work is what makes the result a triumph.

Interestingly, while suffering can increase the meaning we find in an activity, the opposite is also true: Meaning can sustain our ability to suffer well. This is something we learn from Viktor Frankl in *Man's Search for Meaning*. He describes how those who had a purpose, a meaning, or a hope in the Nazi concentration camps were more likely to survive.[23]

Of course, the kinds of suffering most of us experience pale in comparison to what Frankl endured. But the insight that finding meaning amid difficulty can sustain us is valuable for everyone. As runners, this should also be unsurprising. It is challenging to complete a difficult race if you lack a clear sense of purpose, or do not know why you are there. This seems to be why runners often talk about knowing their *why*.

Generally, our *why* (or reason for enduring) needs to be something bigger or broader than race objectives. This way, when running feels trivial or too challenging, some deeper purpose can tether you to the task. To select a suitable *why* means we will proceed through the same kind of inquiry Aristotle does: *Why am I running this mile? To finish the race. Why should I finish this race?* and so on until we arrive at something solid to stand on. This *something* should have value or be connected to our vision of a good life. Among my running friends, some examples of their *why*s include stewardship of physical talents, making their families proud, curiosity for their limits, self-improvement, to be in community, and theological objectives, like honoring God. These are sufficiently broad such that, even long after our days of running are done, our activities can have continuity and coherence, in serving the same end we chased in our sneakers. For the "all in" runner we examined in Chapter 7, having this continuity in our pre- and post-running lives is especially important.

So *meaning* increases *suffering*, and *suffering* increases *meaning*. This is not a relationship of identity. Meaning and suffering are clearly not the same thing. This is not a necessary relationship either; it does not always hold. Sometimes we suffer (stubbing a toe) without it being meaningful. Other times, we experience something meaningful (watching a good film) without suffering. These are generic claims, meaning they often but not always hold true.

Furthermore, perhaps it should go without saying, but sometimes the meaning we derive from suffering is incorrect. When I, as a college professor, ask students to interpret a text, sometimes the meaning they glean does not follow from the words on the page in front of them. It is a faulty interpretation, and my task is to help them see what meanings are actually supported by the text. Likewise, sometimes we misinterpret the meaning of discomfort.

For example, we train too hard and become ill, and we think this means we are tough instead of imprudent. Or we finish an ultramarathon that we should have dropped and think this means we are perseverant, as though perseverance is indifferent to the kinds of ends to which we commit ourselves. In fact, not every instance of suffering supports our flourishing. Many of our actions—and some of the ways we inhabit the sport—undermine our happiness, and many of the meanings we derive from this suffering are incorrect.

Suffering and Growth

Thus far, I have challenged the "pain is weakness leaving the body" mentality as misguided. This is because not all pains are beneficial, and this sentiment inclines us to participate in sport without sensitivity to whether our bodies are absorbing the workload. But there are additional issues here. One is the (potential) myth of "posttraumatic growth."[24]

Psychologist Eranda Jayawickreme and his colleagues point out that the idea that adversity is a source of strength is a uniquely Western framing. It is a narrative that we tend to adopt, reflected in the aphorism "What doesn't kill you makes you stronger."[25] Jayawickreme points out that, while there is empirical support for this idea—that we come away stronger after a setback—these findings may be more a reflection of flawed studies than any fact of the matter. Often the way we frame questions about suffering in psychological studies implies a redemptive arc—that one will have learned from a difficult event or period of suffering. In many cases, it is possible that nothing good resulted from a struggle at all. Maybe the difficult time was just that—difficult.

Why this matters is that we may be inclined to receive other people's bad news (their injuries, personal struggles, or losses) with hopeful themes of future growth and progress. Maybe their suffering will be a constructive force in a flourishing life, and they will grow stronger and acquire perspective because of it. Maybe suffering *is* broadly instructive, and all of the "can't wait for the comeback" comments we send to injured runners will be well-placed.

But this reception can also impede our ability to empathize well. It may diminish the significance of the suffering someone is undergoing in the present moment, or function like a hand-waving that shirks off responsibilities to help. And it may be untrue that their suffering will be productive in the long term. Not all forms of suffering are constructive. Not all forms of suffering have a happy ending on the other side.

Track and Fielding Objections

The "It's a Correction" Argument

Someone might argue that, surely "No pain, no gain" and its sister slogans are problematic. However, we live in very comfortable world, full of laptops, microwaves, and air conditioning. These slogans offer a needed correction to a world of comforts, where we often fail to value difficult goods and lack the motivation to pursue them.

This is a good argument. Returning to the language of warped boards, for those who find discomfort alarming, it seems this culture of celebrating pain in itself can incline them in the opposite direction, toward virtue.

My response is two-fold. First, for those not marked by suffering avoidance, a culture that praises pain can reinforce or strengthen preexisting tendencies to persist in difficulty. It can warp their figurative boards further in the direction of embracing too much elective pain to their detriment. But these messages reach more than only one kind of person, with one kind of inclination. A slogan like "No pain, no gain" can be more narrowly directed to those who actually need to hear it.

Second, corrections should not be fundamentally misguided. For example, more than once I have seen injured runners start and finish races on crutches, to the applause of others. Maybe there are personal reasons for doing so, which I am not privy to, but this sends an odd message to young runners. It demonstrates that suffering, even at the cost of one's body, is praiseworthy.

Surely there are more balanced ways to communicate that some forms of suffering are edifying. For example, to redirect an athlete who is discomfort-avoidant altogether, we can direct their attention toward someone who suffers well. We might give them gentle leadings when discomfort strikes, to try to remain longer in that difficulty. Alternatively, we might help them recognize what is of value and worth persisting for. That way, they will have something to tether them in place when efforts become hard. Not only might this clownish rhetoric about pain be unhelpful; it might actually deter discomfort-avoidant runners from entering the sport altogether. This manner of speaking makes the sport inhospitable to those who do not naturally share that leaning.

The "This Is Just Pride" Objection

Someone might argue that all of this bravado around suffering is not about suffering itself, or any qualities that inhere in suffering. Lauding our suffering is just another expression of pride, or a means of feeling self-important.

This is a great point. Given, as Aquinas states, that pride is both the root of all other vices and present in those vices,[26] we can generally assume that when we act poorly, our pride is playing at least a supporting role. In fact, further support for this kind of argument is seen in a phenomenon James Dawes refers to as "depth larceny." We sometimes brag about, not even our own suffering, but our proximity to the suffering of others.[27] We take on another's suffering as a point of pride for ourselves.

An example of depth larceny is provided by Holocaust scholar Eva Hoffman. She recounts an episode at a dinner party in which guests boasted about their friendships with Holocaust survivors.[28] The horror was turned to fashion. Even though these people had no personal experiences of the Holocaust, they adorned themselves in proximity to this suffering as though (a) it was of great value and (b) that its value was transferrable to themselves.

It is unclear why we might assume someone else's suffering reflects well on us. A more mundane example of the depth larceny phenomenon is how runners who did not themselves experience the horrific weather year at the Boston Marathon in 2018 nevertheless recount with pride how their friends and training partners fared in the cold winds and driving rain. They have become co-owners of this suffering. It is a shared asset within the community.

Pride explains why depth larceny occurs *now*: Suffering is a valued commodity, so we associate ourselves with it, pinning it to our chests like a merit badge. However, pride does not explain why suffering became a commodity in the first place. For explanations about that—why suffering was initially seen as valuable—it helps to investigate the nature of suffering itself, as we have done here. We need to examine what goods we associate with suffering.

An additional counterpoint to the "this is just pride" argument is that pride does not correlate directly with the celebration of suffering. There are some instances in which we explain away the amount of suffering we experienced for the sake of pride. For example, sometimes we brag that a run did not hurt at all. "I barely felt a thing!" When a runner makes such a claim, he or she diminishes the amount of suffering experienced for the sake of expressing superiority over those who found the effort challenging.

Conclusion

I still remember the pain of my first-ever cross-country race. I was a sophomore in high school, and, although I had played sports my entire life, I had never experienced the lung burn and desperation I felt running across the grass fields that day at full speed for five kilometers. I thought I must be doing something wrong because the discomfort was almost more than I could take. When my coach congratulated me at the finish line, all high fives and smiles, and asked me how my first race went, I leaned on a pole, my whole world spinning, and I said, "It was nice."

It was nice. It was also uncomfortable.

When I first started running, I used to wait on the glorious day when racing hard wouldn't hurt anymore—when I would become so strong and well-trained that *fast* would feel easy. I am still waiting.

As that season progressed and my fitness grew, and then years passed, and finally a decade, I gave up on the idea of progressing beyond discomfort because discomfort is a part of the process—not always, but sometimes, and definitely when you are pressing your limits. The truth is, *fast* is a moving target. Over time, you become better at distinguishing discomfort from pain and at perceiving where your personal limits are. You lose that feeling of desperation and realize you are not actually in a state of physical emergency when your heart rate rises. But the difficulty of fast running never completely goes away. Fitness is feeling like you're dying at a faster pace than you used to feel like you were dying at.

So, no, I couldn't outrun the discomfort. But the difficulty of the sport would be an occasion for growth, and I would be edified through those uncomfortable moments, depending on how I responded to them. I would train my body and learn my limits, and it would shape my character. This would be part of my education.

What I Aimed to Accomplish

In this book, I placed running in conversation with the classical tradition of inquiry about character and the good life. I described the process of developing virtues and how we might learn from exemplary athletes. I explored emotions and competition, natural limits, happiness, and the nature of suffering.

I also argued for two new classes of traits relevant to the sport: performance-enhancing virtues, the carbon-plated shoes of the soul; and performance-enhancing vices, traits that make us successful performers but otherwise detract from a good life. The presence of the latter category puts us into an interesting dilemma. To become the best athletes we could possibly be, we might need to make compromises to our character. Or, we could be good people, but maybe not get everything out of ourselves on race day. I argued against compromising character for the sake of athletic performance, even for elite-level competitors. I also argued against norm differentiation in sport—the tendency to extend permission to high-level athletes to be selfish, envious, and so forth.

These days, the way we speak about ethics in athletics is often one-sided. We talk about what one *ought not* do, like doping, course cutting, and violating the spirit of the sport. We talk about misdeeds and consequences, violations, and rule-breaking. These conversations are valuable because we should know which actions are objectionable. Runners can be held accountable for these bad actions. But on its own, talking about what we ought *not* do without providing a vision of what to *do* or to *be* instead is incomplete. A good life (and a good run) is more than the bad actions we do not perform. It also consists of the good actions we do perform, acts of perseverance, integrity, and justice. In focusing on questions like virtues, exemplarism, and happiness, this book attempts to restore to sport a vision of the good life and how running fits in.

The Examined Run is the beginning of a conversation about how to take our happiness seriously and live good lives in and out of the sport. I hope that my readers will continue to ask these questions and to live an examined run.

Notes

Preface

1. Plato, *Symposium* 210a–211a.
2. Plotinus, *Ennead* V.2.1.
3. J. C. Gerstner, "In First 18 Months, USOPC Mental Health Task Force Has Made Strides for Team USA Athletes," TeamUSA.org, May 19, 2022, https://www.teamusa.org/News/2022/May/19/In-First-18-Months-USOPC-Mental-Health-Task-Force-Has-Made-Strides-For-Team-USA-Athletes
4. J. Longman, "Simone Biles Rejects a Long Tradition of Stoicism in Sports," *New York Times*, July 28, 2021.
5. Kristján Kristjánsson, *Flourishing as the Aim of Education: An Aristotelian View* (London: Routledge, 2020), 5.

Chapter 1

1. An early version of this section first appeared in Sabrina Little (2018), "Pride Ran-eth Me into a Shed," https://www.irunfar.com/pride-ran-eth-me-into-a-shed
2. The "City in Speech" is a thought experiment in Plato's *Republic*. Socrates describes how justice fits into a city to better understand what it means to have a just soul.
3. Plato, *Republic* 410d.
4. Plato, *Republic* 412b.
5. Plato, *Protagoras* 325c4–326e5; see also Sabrina Little, "The Trivium: Revisiting Ancient Strategies for Character Formation," *Journal of Character Education* 17, no. 1 (2021): 113–124, for additional assessment of this passage.
6. Plato, *Protagoras* 326b6.
7. Plato, *Laws* 793e–798e.
8. Plato, *Laws* 795d.
9. Aristotle, *Politics* 1338b3.

10. Amy Freeman, "Remedies to Acedia in the Rhythm of Daily Life," *Christian Reflection: A Series in Faith and Ethics*, edited by Robert K. Kruschwitz (2013): 36–37.

11. Robert F. Rhodes, "The *Kaihōgyō* Practice of Mt. Hiei," *Japanese Journal of Religious Studies* 14, no. 2–3 (1987): 185–202.

12. Aristotle, *Nicomachean Ethics* II.2.6.

13. Julia Driver, "Modesty and Ignorance," *Ethics* 109, no. 4 (1999): 827–834.

14. Kant, *Metaphysics of Morals* 6.390.

15. See John Hare's *God and Morality* or Anscombe's "Modern Moral Philosophy."

16. For more on this, see Sabrina B. Little and Molly Reed-Waters, "Virtue Ethics," in *Ethical Leadership: A Primer*, second edition, ed. R.M. McManus, S.J. Ward, and A.K. Perry, pp. 48–70. (Northampton, MA: Edward Elgar Publishing, 2023).

17. Be right back. I am going to go write this book.

18. "How Does a Substance Become Prohibited?" USADA, retrieved June 14, 2014, from https://www.usada.org/spirit-of-sport/substance-become-pro hibited/

19. Aristotle, *Nicomachean Ethics* II.2.4.

20. This is Swedish for 'speed play.' It is a common early season workout for distance runners.

21. Rosalind Hursthouse and Glen Pettigrove, "Virtue Ethics," in *The Stanford Encyclopedia of Philosophy* (Winter 2018 edition), ed. Edward N. Zalta, https://plato.stanford.edu/archives/win2018/entries/ethics-virtue/

22. Hursthouse and Pettigrove, "Virtue Ethics," pp. 1–3.

23. Jennifer Frey, "What Is Virtue and Why Does It Matter?," retrieved November 18, 2021, https://fordhaminstitute.org/national/commentary/what-virtue-and-why-does-it-matter

24. Susan Wolf, "Moral Saints," *Journal of Philosophy* 79, no. 8 (1982): 419–439, p. 419.

25. Wolf, "Moral Saints," p. 410.

26. This view seems to be informed by religious notions of virtue, as popularly understood. In this book, I am writing about secular virtue, in the Aristotelian vein. However, this critique is not fair for religious virtue either. Two counterexamples from the Catholic tradition include Saint Philip Neri, the patron saint of laughter and joy, and Saint Francis of Assisi, who was known for his joyful spirit. Thomas Aquinas described joy as an infused virtue of Christianity. Søren Kierkegaard also noted that Christian saints can laugh more than others because of the commitments of the

faith and the freedom it affords them. (See Robert C. Roberts, "Smiling with God: Reflections on Christianity and the Psychology of Humor," *Faith and Philosophy* 4, no. 2 (1987): 168–175. See also C. Stephen Evans, "Kierkegaard's View of Humor: Must Christians Always Be Solemn?" *Faith and Philosophy* 4, no. 2 (1987), https://place.asburyseminary.edu/cgi/view content.cgi?article=1143&context=faithandphilosophy.) There is a lot of misery in the Christian tradition. Consider the descriptions of the "suffering servant" (Isaiah 42:1–4, Isaiah 52–53), but there is space for joy, too.

27. For Aristotle, wittiness is among the virtues, and virtues are constitutive features of the good life. This is neither humorless nor unhappy.

28. Aristotle, *Nicomachean Ethics* II.1.3.

29. See Mary Nichols, *Citizens and Statesmen* (Lanham, MD: Rowman & Littlefield, 1992), p. 18, for a discussion on virtue as the fulfillment of nature in Aristotle.

30. For more on this, see Sabrina B. Little and Molly Reed-Waters, "Virtue Ethics," in *Ethical Leadership: A Primer*, second edition, ed. R.M. McManus, S.J. Ward, and A.K. Perry pp. 48–70 (Northampton, MA: Edward Elgar Publishing, 2023).

31. I discuss this in Chapter 6, "Bad Competition: Performance-Enhancing Vices."

32. Aquinas names three kinds—moral, intellectual, and theological. Both the kinds of virtues named, and the set of virtues listed under each kind, are a function of how one defines our greatest good, or the human end. For Aquinas, communion with God is the greatest good, so there are more virtues included (namely faith, hope, and love). Many virtues are also defined in different ways. For example, Aquinas says Aristotle's definition of magnanimity involves misvaluing—overvaluing oneself and undervaluing others. Both thinkers define the virtue in light of what they perceive to be the greatest good.

33. Nathan King, *The Excellent Mind: Intellectual Virtues for Everyday Life* (New York City: Oxford University Press, 2021).

34. Like most other contemporary theorists of intellectual virtue, Nathan King (2021) expands the set of intellectual virtues beyond Aristotle's set (*nous*, *sophia*, *phronesis*), to include virtues such as intellectual humility and intellectual courage. In so doing, he includes virtues that centrally involve emotions. This expanded set of virtues is often defined in terms of a mean with respect to an emotion (pp. 22–25). Thus, what is a point of contrast between intellectual and moral virtues for Aristotle ceases to apply to much of the contemporary virtue theory literature.

35. R. Roberts, "Humor and the Virtues," *Inquiry* 31, no. 2 (1988): 127–149, 142.

36. Aristotle, *Nicomachean Ethics* 1103a.

37. Aristotle, *Nicomachean Ethics* II.2.4.

38. Plato, *Crito* 49a–d.

39. E. Schwitzgebel, "The Moral Lives of Ethicists, or How Often Do Ethics Professors Call Their Mothers?" *Aeon Magazine*, July 14, 2015, <https://aeon.co/essays/how-often-do-ethics-professors-call-their-mothers>

40. There are limitations to the skill comparison, which I examine in Chapter 2, "Practicing Courage in My Sneakers: Virtue and Development."

41. Aristotle, *Nicomachean Ethics* II.2.4.

42. K. A. Ericsson, "Deliberate Practice and Acquisition of Expert Performance: A General Overview," *Society for Academic Emergency Medicine* 15 (2008): 988–994, https://onlinelibrary.wiley.com/doi/full/10.1111/j.1553-2712.2008.00227.x.

43. Malcolm Gladwell, *Outliers: The Story of Success* (Little, Brown & Company, 2008), pp. 37–40.

44. I see now that I did not practice my violin enough.

45. K. A. Ericsson, "Training History, Deliberate Practice and Elite Sports Performance: An Analysis in Response to Tucker and Collins's Review—What Makes Champions?" *British Journal of Sports Medicine* 47 (2013): 533–535.

46. Christian Miller describes growing in character in this way—as closing a "character gap between (1) how we really are, and (2) the people of good character we should become" (xii). Christian B. Miller, *The Character Gap: How Good Are We?* (New York City: Oxford University Press, 2018).

47. "Comparison is the thief of joy" is a quotation often attributed to Theodore Roosevelt, but the source is unknown. Runners love this quotation. In Chapter 3, I argue that most forms of comparison are prosocial and constructive. Envy is the thief of joy.

Chapter 2

1. This is an illustration Aristotle uses in the *Physics* to describe hylomorphism, or the composite nature of body and soul.

2. If my physical therapist is reading this, I am just kidding. The exercises did not seem inconsequential.

3. "World Athletics," Twitter. @WorldAthletics, November 6. 2022, https://twitter.com/WorldAthletics/status/1589313917305643010

4. See Chapter 3.

5. L. Giovannone, "The Prevalence of Domestic Violence in the NFL," *Charger Bulletin*, December 7, 2021, https://chargerbulletin.com/the-pre valence-of-domestic-violence-in-the-nfl/

6. P. Skrbina, "When Pro Athletes Are Accused of Abuse, How Often Does Punishment Follow?" *Tennessean*, September 18, 2018, https://www.ten nessean.com/story/sports/nhl/predators/2018/09/19/nfl-domestic-viole nce-sexual-assault-child-abuse-nba-mlb-nhl/1335799002/

7. Brad J. Bushman, "Does Venting Anger Feed or Extinguish the Flame? Catharsis, Rumination, Distraction, Anger, and Aggressive Responding," *PSPB* 28, no. 6 (2002): 724–731; Art Markman, "You Can't Punch Your Way out of Anger: You Can't Let off Steam with Violence," *Psychology Today* (2009). https://www.psychologytoday.com/us/blog/ulterior-moti ves/200909/you-cant-punch-your-way-out-anger

8. See Malcolm Gladwell, "Drugstore Athlete," *New Yorker*, September 10, 2021.

9. An early version of this section first appeared in Sabrina Little (2022), "A Discourse on Freedom," https://www.irunfar.com/a-discourse-on-freedom

10. For more on what makes an emotion ill-fitting, see Chapter 3.

11. Scott Cacciola, "The Impossible Task of Keeping Up with the Ingebrigtsens," *New York Times*, July 14, 2022.

12. I find myself unable to pass over the phrase "*exercise* free choice" without acknowledging the pun.

13. See Chapter 3 for an expanded explanation of suitable postures to take to- ward a coach.

14. For more on the idea of respecting one's limits as an athlete, see the final chapter.

15. Plato, *Laws* 635c.

16. Scott Cacciola, "Eliud Kipchoge Is the Greatest Marathoner, Ever," *New York Times*, September 14, 2018, retrieved June 11, 2019.

17. R. Roberts, "Humor and the Virtues," *Inquiry* 31, no. 2: 127–149 (1988): 142.

18. Aristotle, *Nicomachean Ethics* 1103a.

19. An early version of this story first appeared in Sabrina Little (2023), "Running on Intellectual Virtues," https://irunfar.com/running-on-intel lectual-virtues

20. At the moment, there is a growing debate in virtue theory about the na- ture of practical wisdom—about what it really is and about how we can

develop it. Three possible candidates for what practical wisdom consists of are (1) a character trait, specifically an intellectual virtue, which is required in the possession of all moral virtues but which is not sufficient for the possession of those moral virtues, (2) a master virtue, the possession of which means one possesses all of those traits we refer to as discrete moral virtues, or (3) metaphysically nothing at all. Proposal (3) is the simplest explanation. Rather than saying that there are several different virtues that depend on something else (phronesis), there is just one single virtue that is centrally characterized as phronesis: the ability to navigate moral situations excellently. Proposal (3) is a newer proposal, raised by philosophers such as Sophie Grace Chappell and Christian Miller. It is an eliminativist position which detects no "deep unifying feature" such that there is one thing "practical wisdom" refers to. Stated differently, acting well across situations is nothing over and above moral traits themselves, so there is no additional trait (practical wisdom) to account for. I encourage philosophically inclined readers to investigate this debate and consider which account seems most likely. It will give you something to think about on your next long run.

21. Aristotle, *Nicomachean Ethics* 1103a.
22. See Chapter 7 for these ideas.
23. When we focused on vices, my students affectionately referred to this time as "vice education."
24. Sabrina Little, "Talking about Good Deeds: Elaborative Discourse and Moral Virtue," *Journal of Value Inquiry* 55 (2021): 725–743.
25. To say a trait is "normative" means it is a trait we are accountable to, or responsible for.
26. Snow (2010); Miller (2014). Traits are described as either *local* (as applying to narrow situations, such as honesty while paying taxes) or as *global* (as applying across various situations, such as honesty while paying taxes, talking to one's parents, taking quizzes, and in other situations relevant to the virtue). For Aristotle, virtues are global in that they are relevant across a range of situations.
27. Aristotle calls virtues *hexeis*, or active dispositions.
28. Julia Annas, "Virtue as a Skill," *International Journal of Philosophical Studies* 3, no. 2 (1995): 227–243; Matthew Stichter, "Ethical Expertise: The Skill Model of Virtue," *Ethical Theory and Moral Practice* 10 (2007): 183–194; Matthew Stichter, "Virtue as a Skill," in *The Oxford Handbook of Virtue*, ed. N.E. Snow, pp. 57–72 (Oxford: Oxford University Press, 2018).

29. See Walter Mischel and Yuichi Shoda, "A Cognitive-Affective System Theory of Personality: Reconceptualizing Situations, Dispositions, Dynamics, and Invariance in Personality Structure," *Psychological Review* 102, no. 2 (1995): 246–268. Their proposal—Cognitive-Affective Processing Systems (CAPS)—was proposed as a response to the situationist critique. To some psychologists, the presence of virtuous traits seemed dubious because it seemed that the most salient predictor of one's actions in a given situation was the situation someone was in, rather than any stable features of the person.

30. Plato is an example.

31. Aristotle and Julia Annas are examples. See Julia Annas, *Intelligent Virtue* (Oxford: Oxford University Press, 2011).

32. Rousseau and Hume are examples.

33. Aristotle and Thomas Aquinas are examples.

34. Julia Driver is an example. See Julia Driver, *Uneasy Virtue* (New York: Cambridge University Press, 2001).

35. Michael Slote and Linda Zagzebski are examples. See Michael Slote, *Motives from Morals* (New York: Oxford University Press, 2001). See also Linda Zagzebski, *Exemplarist Moral Theory* (New York: Oxford University Press, 2017).

36. Nancy Snow, *Virtue as Social Intelligence: An Empirically Grounded Theory* (New York: Taylor & Francis, 2010).

37. Christian Miller, *Character and Moral Psychology* (New York: Oxford University Press, 2014).

38. Christine Swanton, "Developmental Virtue Ethics," in *Developing the Virtues: Integrating Perspectives* (New York: Oxford University Press, 2017).

39. Aristotle, *Nicomachean Ethics* 1109b2–8.

40. K. Timpe and C. A. Boyd, "Introduction," in *Virtues and Their Vices*, ed. K. Timpe and C. A. Boyd (New York City: Oxford University Press, 2014), p. 9.

41. Timpe and Boyd, "Introduction," p. 10.

42. See Chapter 1 for more on the gawky stages of virtue development.

43. Homer, *Odyssey* 1.489–491; Plato, *Republic* 516c–517a.

44. Social media has increased the visibility of professional athletes to young runners and the general public. Even so, there is lower name recognition of professional runners than of professional athletes in other sports.

45. H. Han, C. Jeong, W. Damon, and G. L. Cohen, "Attainable and Relevant Moral Exemplars Are More Effective than Extraordinary Exemplars in

Promoting Voluntary Service Engagement," *Frontiers in Psychology* 8 (2017): 7.

46. S. Pinckaers, *Passions and Virtue* (Washington, DC: Catholic University Press, 2015), pp. 42–43.

47. An early version of this section first appeared on Sabrina Little (2020), "The Riddle of Will," https://www.irunfar.com/the-riddle-of-will

48. Aristotle, *EE* 2.10.1126B20–21; Chamberlain (1984): 153.

49. Plato, *Republic* 410d; Aristotle, *Politics* 1338b.

50. C. S. Lewis, "The Necessity of Chivalry," in *Present Concerns*, ed. Walter Hooper (San Diego: Harcourt, 1986).

Chapter 3

1. Names have been changed.

2. An early version of this section first appeared in Sabrina Little (2019), "Competition and Envy: The Examined Run," https://www.irunfar.com/competition-and-envy

3. Tayla Minsberg, "Eliud Kipchoge Smashes His Own Marathon World Record," *New York Times*, September 25, 2022.

4. Mark Agnew, "Why Eliud Kipchoge Smiles during Sub-Two Hour Marathon: The Science behind the Historic Grin," *South China Morning Post*, October 14, 2019.

5. S. Söderkvist, K. Ohlén, and U. Dimberg, "How the Experience of Emotion Is Modulated by Facial Feedback," *Journal of Nonverbal Behavior* 42, no. 1 (2018): 129–151.

6. F. Strack, L. L. Martin, and S. Stepper, "Inhibiting and Facilitating Conditions of the Human Smile: A Nonobtrusive Test of the Facial Feedback Hypothesis," *Journal of Personality and Social Psychology* 54, no. 5 (1988): 768–777.

7. Robert Roberts, *Emotions: An Essay in Aid of Moral Psychology* (Cambridge University Press, 2003), pp. 318–319.

8. Jesse J. Prinz, *Gut Reactions: A Perceptual Theory of Emotion* (Oxford University Press, 2004), p. 6.

9. Benjamin Yetton, Julia Revord, Seth Margolis, Sonja Lyubomirsky, and Aaron Seitz, "Cognitive and Physiological Measures in Well-Being Science: Limitations and Lessons," *Frontiers in Psychology* 10 (1630): 2019.

10. Martha Nussbaum and Hilary Putnam, "Changing Aristotle's Mind," in *Essays on Aristotle's De Anima*, ed. Martha C. Nussbaum and Amélie Oksenberg Rorty (Oxford University Press, 1992), p. 44.

11. For more on cognitive theories of emotions, see Part II of Pia Campeggiani, *Theories of Emotion: Expressing, Feeling, Acting* (New York: Bloomsbury, 2023).

12. Roberts, *Emotions: An Essay in Aid of Moral Psychology*.

13. Kristján Kristjánsson, *Virtuous Emotions* (Oxford University Press, 2008), p. 6.

14. Roberts, *Emotions: An Essay in Aid of Moral Psychology*.

15. See Robert Solomon, "Emotions and Choice," in *Explaining Emotions*, ed. A.O. Rorty, pp. 251–281 (Berkeley: University of California Press, 1980); see also Martha Nussbaum, *Upheavels of Thought: The Intelligence of Emotions* (New York: Cambridge University Press, 2001).

16. Roberts, *Emotions: An Essay in Aid of Moral Psychology*, pp. 1–2.

17. An early version of this section first appeared in Sabrina Little (2022), "Contentment: The Examined Run," https://www.irunfar.com/cont entment

18. It was not 26.2 miles either. It seems to have been about 25 miles between Marathon and Athens, shortly after a sustained effort from Marathon to Sparta and back (150 miles each way). Still, the myth of Pheidippides's run inspired the modern-day marathon.

19. "Pheidippides," in *The Ancient World: Dictionary of World Biography*, ed. Frank Magill, volume 1, (New York: Routledge, 2003), pp. 818–821.

20. Sabrina Little, "Variations in Virtue Phenomenology," *Journal of Value Inquiry* (2022).

21. Amy M. Schmitter (2021), "Ancient, Medieval and Renaissance Theories of the Emotions," in *Stanford Encyclopedia of Philosophy*, ed. Edward N. Zalta, https://plato.stanford.edu/entries/emotions-17th18th/LD1Backgro und.html>

22. Aristotle, *Nicomachean Ethics* II.2.4.

23. Christian Miller, *The Character Gap: How Good Are We?* (Oxford University Press, 2018), p. 71.

24. There are certain emotions that it is challenging, if not impossible, to educate. One example is disgust. Emotions that resist change are called recalcitrant emotions. For more, see Pia Campeggiani, *Theories of Emotion: Expressing, Feeling, Acting* (New York: Bloomsbury, 2023).

25. To "bonk" is to experience low blood sugar during a run.

26. Wait, they're not?

27. Protagoras 80B1 DK.

28. Allen Wood makes this point in a working paper entitled "Relativism," https://web.stanford.edu/~allenw/papers/Relativism.doc

29. J. R. Zadra and G. L. Clore, "Emotion and Perception: The Role of Affective Information," *Cognitive Science* 2, no. 6 (2011): 676–685.

30. This quotation is widely attributed to Theodore Roosevelt, but the source is unknown.

31. C. S. Dweck and E. L. Leggett, "A Social-Cognitive Approach to Motivation and Personality," *Psychological Review* 95 (1988): 256; B. J. Zimmerman, "A Social Cognitive View of Self-Regulated Academic Learning," *Journal of Educational Psychology* 81 (1989): 329; B. C. DiMenichi and E. Tricomi, "The Power of Competition: Effects of Social Motivation on Attention, Sustained Physical Effort, and Learning," *Frontiers in Psychology* 6 (2015): 1282.

32. J. C. Burguillo, "Using Game Theory and Competition-Based Learning to Stimulate Student Motivation and Performance," *Computers & Education* 55(2010): 566–575.

33. R. Le Bouc and M. Pessiglione, "Imaging Social Motivation: Distinct Brain Mechanisms Drive Effort Production during Collaboration versus Competition," *Journal of Neuroscience* 33(2013): 15894–15902.

34. G. J. Kilduff, "Driven to Win: Rivalry, Motivation, and Performance," *Social Psychological and Personality Science* 5 (2014): 944–952.

35. Paul Geroski, "Innovation and Competitive Advantage," OECD Economics Department Working Papers 159 (OECD Publishing, 1995); Stephen Nickell, "Competition and Corporate Performance," *Journal of Political Economy* 104, no. 4 (1996): 724–746; Richard Blundell, Rachel Griffith, and John Van Reenen, "Market Share, Market Value, and Innovation in a Panel of British Manufacturing Firms," *The Review of Economic Studies* 66, no. 3 (1999): 529–554.

36. R. DeYoung, *Glittering Vices* (Grand Rapids, MI: Brazos Press, 2009), p. 41.

37. S. Algoe and J. Haidt, "Witnessing Excellence in Action: The 'Other-Praising' Emotions of Elevation, Gratitude, and Admiration," *The Journal of Positive Psychology* 4, no. 2 (2009): 105–127.

38. R. A. Emmons and M. E. McCullough, "Counting Blessings versus Burdens: An Experimental Investigation of Gratitude and Subjective Well-being in Daily Life," *Journal of Personality and Social Psychology* 84, no. 2 (2003): 377–389, 386.

39. Algoe and Haidt, "Witnessing Excellence in Action."

40. Emmons and McCullough, "Counting Blessings versus Burdens," p. 377.

41. Algoe and Haidt, "Witnessing Excellence in Action."

42. Emmons and McCullough, "Counting Blessings versus Burdens," p. 386.

43. Robert Roberts and Daniel Telech, "The Emotion-Virtue-Debt Triad of Gratitude," in *The Moral Psychology of Gratitude*, ed. R. Roberts and D. Telech, pp. 1–12 (New York: Rowman & Littlefield, 2019); Robert Emmons and Michael McCullough, "Counting Blessings versus Burdens: An Empirical Investigation of Gratitude and Subjective Well-Being in Daily Life," *Journal of Personality and Social Psychology* 84, no. 2 (2003): 377–389, p. 383; Sara Algoe and Jonathan Haidt, "Witnessing Excellence in Action," *Journal of Positive Psychology* 4, no. 2 (2009): 105–127.

44. An early version of this section first appeared on Sabrina Little (2018), "Admiration and Awe: Learning from Redwoods," https://www.irunfar.com/admiration-and-awe-learning-from-redwoods

45. Nietzsche, Friedrich. *Human, All Too Human*. Translated by R.J. Hollingdale (New York: Cambridge University Press, 2004, p. 86).

46. M. Arcangeli, M. Sperduti, A. Jacquot, P. Piolino, and J. Dokic, "Awe and the Experience of the Sublime: A Complex Relationship," *Frontiers in Psychology* 11 (2020): 1340, 1.

47. Roberts, *Emotions: An Aid in Moral Psychology*, p. 270.

48. Robert Roberts and Michael Spezio, "Admiring Moral Exemplars: Sketch of an Ethical Sub-discipline," in *Self, Motivation, and Virtue: Innovative Interdisciplinary Research*, ed. Nancy Snow and Darcia Narvaez, pp. 85–108 (Abingdon: Routledge, 2019)..

49. Linda Zagzebski includes emulation (which is characterized by a negative affect) as a part of admiration (Zagzebski 2015, 2010), but her position seems to be the exception here. See also K. Kristjánsson, "Emotions Targeting Moral Exemplarity: Making Sense of the Logical Geography of Admiration, Emulation, and Elevation," *Theory and Research in Education* 15, no. 1 (2017): 20–37, 24.

50. S. K. Kierkegaard, *The Sickness unto Death*, ed. and trans. E. Hong and H. Hong (Princeton, NJ: Princeton University Press, 1980), p. 86.

51. Alfred Archer, "Admiration and Motivation," *Emotion Review* 11, no. 2 (2019): 140–150, 140.

52. I. Schindler, J. Paech, and F. Löwenbrück, "Linking Admiration and Adoration to Self- Expansion: Different Ways to Enhance One's Potential," *Cognition and Emotion* 29, no. 2 (2015): 292–310.

53. Roberts and Spezio, "Admiring Moral Exemplars," p. 10; Zagzebski (2013, 2015, 2017).

54. D. Harper, "Etymology of Compete," Online Etymology Dictionary, retrieved December 27, 2022, from https://www.etymonline.com/word/compete

55. Aristotle, *Nicomachean Ethics* 1103b20–25.

56. Seneca, *On Favors* 1.1–2.

57. Technically, our feet.

58. Gerald P. Boersma, "Augustine's Immanent Critique of Stoicism," *Scottish Journal of Theology* 70, no. 2 (2017): 184–197.

59. Antoine Bechara, "The Role of Emotion in Decision-Making: Evidence from Neurological Patients with Orbitofrontal Damage," *Brain and Cognition* 55, no. 1 (2004): 30–40.

60. Emphasis is my own.

61. Antonio Damasio, *Descartes' Error: Emotion, Reason, and the Human Brain* (New York City: Penguin, 2005), pp. 53, 54.

Chapter 4

1. Linda Zagzebski, *Exemplarist Moral Theory* (New York: Oxford University Press, 2017).

2. This was a socially acknowledged interaction between older and younger men in Athens, typified by both mentorship and romantic relations.

3. Plato, *Symposium* 174b.

4. Plato, *Symposium* 174b.

5. C. Chavez, "Alberto Salazar Ruled Permanently Ineligible by SafeSport for Verbal, Sexual Misconduct," *Sports Illustrated*, July 26, 2021, https://www.si.com/olympics/2021/07/26/alberto-salazar-permanently-ineligible-safesport-investigation-sexual-emotional-misconduct

6. A. Francis, "Jordan Hasay Discusses Mary Cain, Announces Paula Radcliffe Is Her New Coach," *Canadian Running*, November 20, 2019, https://runningmagazine.ca/the-scene/jordan-hasay-discusses-mary-cain-announces-paula-radcliffe-as-new-coach/

7. Jordan Hasay referred to him as such, and Salazar's relationship with Galen Rupp (Salazar's protégé since Rupp was fifteen) is described in these terms. Both references are found here: https://www.si.com/edge/2019/10/11/alberto-salazar-doping-ban-galen-rupp-mo-farah-hasay-chicago-marathon. Former Olympic marathoner, Kara Goucher, has referred to Salazar as a father figure as well. This reference is found here: https://www.nytimes.com/2019/10/06/sports/salazar-doping-nike-oregon-project.html

8. E. Carlson, "Who Are Moral Exemplars and What Are They Like?" lecture, The Beacon Project, July 2018, Winston Salem, NC.

9. Christian Miller refers to this as "mixed character." Very few people meet the high standards of virtue in every respect, and very few people meet the very low standards of vice in every respect. Most of us are positioned somewhere in the middle—acting for some of the right ways, but not all, from some fitting motivations, but not all. We have enough consistency and predictability to have traits. For example, if I am honest when I speak to my friends, I am likely to keep being honest to my friends. It is just that most of us do not act well enough, or poorly enough, on a consistent basis to possess virtue or vice.

10. Ben Snider McGrath, "Jim Walmsley Runs 6:09:26 for 100K, Misses World Record by Just 12 Seconds," *Canadian Running*, January 24, 2021, https://runningmagazine.ca/sections/runs-races/jim-walmsley-runs-60926-for-100k-misses-world-record-by-just-12-seconds/

11. This was an ironic response from me, considering I had just completed my dissertation—a 305-page tome on moral growth by way of admiration. My response to Jim's heroics was to delight in his performance yet leave unchanged.

12. Søren Kierkegaard, *Practice in Christianity,* trans. H. Hong (Princeton, NJ: Princeton University Press, 1991), p. 241.

13. More about The Steps Foundation can be found here: https://www.thestepsfoundation.org.

14. No, I am not cheesy!

15. See the final chapter, on suffering in distance running.

16. J. R. P. French Jr. and B. H. Raven, "The Bases of Social Power," in *Studies in Social Power*, ed. D. Cartwright, pp. 150–167 (Ann Arbor, MI: Institute for Social Research, 1959).

17. Hyemin Han, Jeongmin Kim, Changwoo Jeong, and Geoffrey L. Cohen, "Attainable and Relevant Moral Exemplars Are More Effective Than Extraordinary Exemplars in Promoting Voluntary Service Engagement," *Frontiers in Psychology* 8, no. 283 (2017): 1–14.

18. Sabrina Little, "The Graded Engagement Model of Admiration," *Theory and Research in Education* 19, no. 1 (2021): 3–18, 1–16.

19. Zagzebski, *Exemplarist Moral Theory*, p. 135.

20. Aristotle, *Poetics* I.iv.

21. R. C. Roberts, "What an Emotion Is: A Sketch," *Philosophical Review* 97, no. 2 (1988): 183–209.

22. Emotions can be wrong. For example, I might become angry at friends for having lunch without me. In reality, they may not have known that I was in town.

Chapter 5

1. In Greek mythology, the myth of Sisyphus is about a man who defies the gods. As punishment, he is sentenced to push a boulder uphill for all of eternity. When he reaches the summit, the boulder rolls back down to the bottom, and Sisyphus must push it back up. I have been assigned a lot of difficult hill repeat workouts over the years, but none of them involved boulders and none of them lasted forever. The philosopher Albert Camus has a famous line about how one must imagine Sisyphus happy. I would like to add that one must imagine Sisyphus very physically fit. See Albert Camus, *The Myth of Sisyphus and Other Essays* (New York: Knopf Doubleday, 2012), p. 123.

2. Nancy Snow, "Resilience and Hope as a Democratic Civic Virtue," in *Virtues in the Public Square: Citizenship, Civic Friendship, and Duty*, ed. James Arthur, pp. 124–139 (London: Routledge Press, 2019).

3. Philip Pettit, "Hope and Its Place in Mind," *Annals of the American Academy of Political Science* 592 (2004): 152–165, in Nancy Snow, *Hope and Resilience*, in *The Virtues of Endurance*, ed. Nathan King Forthcoming.

4. See Chapter 3 for an extended discussion on admiration and the emulation of excellent people.

5. To taper means to reduce mileage while maintaining intensity in preparation for a race. Reducing mileage while keeping the intensity high (such as through short speed work sessions) leaves an athlete feeling fresh, primed, and ready to compete.

6. R. Domínguez, E. Cuenca, J. L. Maté-Muñoz, P. García-Fernández, N. Serra-Paya, M. C. Estevan, P. V. Herreros, and M. V. Garnacho-Castaño, "Effects of Beetroot Juice Supplementation on Cardiorespiratory Endurance in Athletes: A Systematic Review," *Nutrients* 9, no. 1 (2017): 43.

7. A. Kumar, "The Heel and the Heal, Jordan Hasay Is Back," *ESPN*, April 15, 2019, https://www.espn.com/espn/ story/_/id/26531628/boston-marathon-2019-heel-heal-jordan-hasay-back

8. Aristotle, *NE* 195b22–23.

9. For example, medieval philosopher and theologian Thomas Aquinas describes human nature as suited for communion with God. Virtues that help one to fulfill that end, or function, include faith, hope, and love. For philosophers with a different vision of the good life, such as one without a belief in God, the set of virtues may be different.

10. Chapter 7 examines the question of flourishing directly, and asks where running fits in.

11. See Chapter 6 for more on MacIntyre's practices and how he draws in concerns external to practices for considerations of virtue.

12. Alasdair MacIntyre, *After Virtue: A Study in Moral Theory*, 3rd ed. (Notre Dame, IN: University of Notre Dame Press, 2006), p. 188.

13. MacIntyre, *After Virtue*, p. 191.

14. Henry Sidgwick, *The Methods of Ethics*, 7th edition (London: Macmillan, 1907). Part I, Ch. 5.

15. A complete explanation of virtue development is found in Chapter 2. A brief explanation of how to develop performance-enhancing virtues is found later in this chapter.

16. Aquinas, *Summa Theologiae* II.2.137.1.

17. Resilience, joy, perseverance, and humor .

18. Nancy Snow, "Resilience and Hope as a Democratic Civic Virtue," in *Virtues in the Public Square: Citizenship, Civic Friendship, and Duty*, ed. James Arthur (London: Routledge Press, 2019), pp. 124–139.

19. See Chapters 1 and 2 for an explanation of features of a virtue.

20. Snow, "Resilience and Hope as a Democratic Civic Virtue."

21. Snow, "Resilience and Hope as a Democratic Civic Virtue."

22. See Chapter 3 for an extended account of emotions, as related to moral virtues.

23. An example is that some moments we consider the happiest moments of our lives, at the time when they occurred, felt very challenging. An example is the birth of one's child. Another example is accomplishing an important benchmark at work. It can be stressful or overwhelming in the moment. Still, we are happy. Our feelings offer good feedback about how we are doing in the moment, but they often fail to track happiness and life satisfaction in more global terms.

24. Aquinas, *Summa Theologiae* II.2.28.4.

25. P. E. King and F. Defoy, "Joy as a Virtue: The Means and Ends of Joy," *Journal of Psychology and Theology* 48, no. 4 (2000): 308–331.

26. Servais-Théodore Pinckaers, *Passions and Virtue* (Washington, DC: Catholic University Press, 2015), pp. 42–43.

27. Pinckaers. *Passions and Virtue*, 43.

28. Pinckaers. *Passions and Virtue*, 43.

29. Aquinas, *Summa Theologiae* II.2.137.1.

30. Aquinas, *Summa Theologiae* II.2.137.2–3.

31. Aquinas, *Summa Theologiae* II.2.138.1.

32. Nathan King, "Erratum to: 'Perseverance as an Intellectual Virtue,'" *Synthese* 19 (2014): 3779–3801.

33. Aquinas, *Summa Theologiae* II.2.138.2.

34. King, "Erratum to: 'Perseverance as an Intellectual Virtue.'"

35. DNF means Did Not Finish, a designation for when an athlete has withdrawn from a race.

36. This story first appeared in Sabrina Little, "Performance-Enhancing Virtues," March 17, 2021, https://irunfar.com/performance-enhancing-virtues.

37. John Morreall, *Taking Laughter Seriously* (Albany: SUNY Press, 1983), pp. 4–5.

38. Aristotle, *NE* 1128a3–b12.

39. Robert Roberts, "Humor and the Virtues," *Inquiry* 31, no. 2 (1988): 127–149.

40. Roberts, "Humor and the Virtues," 296, 298.

41. This gap between the people we currently are and the people of good character we should become is called the "character gap." It was introduced by philosopher Christian Miller in his book by that name. See Christian Miller, *The Character Gap: How Good Are We?* (New York City: Oxford University Press, 2018).

42. Kristján Kristjánsson, *Flourishing as the Aim of Education: An Aristotelian View* (London: Routledge, 2020), p. 5.

43. H. Battaly, *Virtue* (Malden, MA: Polity Press, 2015), pp. 17–18.

44. Michael Stichter, "Virtue as a Skill," in *The Oxford Handbook of Virtue*, edited by N. E. Snow (Oxford: Oxford University Press, 2018), p. 69.

45. Plato, *Republic* 376e; Plato, *Laws* 654–655; Aristotle, *Politics* 1338b.

46. See Chapter 2—"Virtue and Development"—for a sustained treatment of the role athletics can play in virtue development.

47. By virtue-tracking, I mean we do good actions at the right times, in the right ways, but lack the internal character (i.e., suitable motivations) to classify them as virtues.

Chapter 6

1. See "The Prohibited List" on the World Anti-Doping Agency (WADA) website here: https://www.wada-ama.org/en/prohibited-list. The United States Anti-Doping Agency (USADA) website has a similar resource here: https://www.globaldro.com/Home.

2. The World Anti-Doping Code International Standard, "Prohibited List," January 2019, https://www.wada-ama.org/sites/default/files/wada_2019_english_prohibited_list.pdf, p. 6.

3. Tim Carmody, "Hacking Your Body: Lance Armstrong and the Science of Doping," *The Verge*, 2013, https://www.theverge.com/2013/1/17/3886424/ programming-your-body-lance-armstrong-and-doping-technology

4. USADA, "Is It Prohibited for Athletes to Use IV Infusions for Rehydration and Recovery?" https://www.usada.org/spirit-of-sport/education/is-it-prohibited-or-dangerous-for-athletes-using-iv-infusions-for-re-hydration-and-recovery/

5. USADA, "Why Clean Sport Matters," https://www.usada.org/choose-usada/choose-usada-why-clean-sport-matters/

6. NIDA, "What Are the Side Effects of Anabolic Steroid Misuse?" 2023, https://nida.nih.gov/publications/research-reports/steroids-other-app earance-performance-enhancing-drugs-apeds/what-are-side-effects-anabolic-steroid-misuse on 2023

7. An early version of this section first appeared in Sabrina Little (2018), "A Discourse on Cheating," https://www.irunfar.com/a-discourse-on-cheating

8. Tully De Invent, "Rhet. ii," in Aquinas, *Summa Theologiae* II.2.136.5.

9. S. A. Schnitker, B. Houltberg, W. Dyrness, and N. Redmond, "The Virtue of Patience, Spirituality, and Suffering: Integrating Lessons from Positive Psychology, Psychology of Religion, and Christian Theology," *Psychology of Religion and Spirituality* 9, no. 3 (2017): 264–275, p. 265.

10. Aquinas, *Summa Theologiae* II.2.162.1.

11. Aquinas, *Summa Theologiae* II.2.162.7.

12. Aristotle, *Nicomachean Ethics*, trans. R. Bartlett and S. Collins (Chicago: Chicago University Press, 2011), p. 1123a35.

13. Christian Miller, *The Character Gap: How Good Are We?* (Oxford University Press, 2018), p. 15.

14. A note is that there is no such thing as an excess of the virtue (e.g., "You are too courageous.") The excess and deficiency are with respect to the *emotion* that the virtue concerns. So, for example, a person cannot be too courageous; they would just be rash. My students often make this mistake when they describe the virtue mean.

15. Nathan King, *The Excellent Mind: Intellectual Virtues for Everyday Life* (New York City: Oxford University Press, 2021), p. 240.

16. Christian Miller, *Character and Moral Psychology* (New York City: Oxford University Press, 2014).

17. See Chapters 7 and 8 for discussions and debates on happiness and the distance runner.

18. See Chapter 7.

19. Alisdair MacIntyre, *After Virtue: A Study in Moral Theory*, 3rd ed. (Notre Dame, IN: University of Notre Dame Press, 2006), pp. 190–191.

20. Cicero, *On Friendship*, Little, Brown, and Company, 44, p. 98.

21. C. A. Boyd, "Pride and Humility," in *In Virtues and Their Vices*, ed. K. Timpe and C. A. Boyd (Oxford University Press, 2014), pp. 248–250. See also Herdt (2008), 42.

22. Boyd, "Pride and Humility," p. 250.

23. Phil Mushnick, "Boorish Megan Rapinoe Unfit for Presidential Medal of Freedom," *New York Post*, July 7, 2022, https://nypost.com/2022/07/07/megan-rapinoe-didnt-deserve-presidential-medal-of-freedom/; Tom Joyce, "Megan Rapinoe Doesn't Deserve a Medal of Freedom," *Washington Examiner*, July 5, 2022, https://www.washingtonexaminer.com/opinion/megan-rapinoe-doesnt-deserve-a-medal-of-freedom

24. Aristotle, *Nicomachean Ethics*, trans. R. Bartlett and S. Collins (Chicago: Chicago University Press, 2011), p. 1123a35.

25. Boyd, "Pride and Humility," p. 248.

26. Aquinas, *De Malo* VIII.2.ad.16.

27. Aristotle, *Nicomachean Ethics* 1125a18–28.

28. Aristotle, *Nicomachean Ethics* 1125a22–25; DeYoung (2006, p. 215), in Boyd, "Pride and Humility," p. 248.

29. Aquinas, *Summa Theologiae* II.2.137.1.

30. Aquinas, *Summa Theologiae* II.2.138.2.

31. Nathan King, "Erratum to: Perseverance as an Intellectual Virtue," *Synthese* 19 (2014): 3779–3801.

32. DNF means "did not finish."

33. Duck-chul Lee, Carl J. Lavie, and Rajesh Vedanthan, "Optimal Dose of Running for Longevity: Is More Better or Worse?" *Journal of the American College of Cardiology* 65, no. 5 (2015): 420–422.

34. R. DeYoung, *Glittering Vices* (Grand Rapids, MI: Brazos Press, 2009), p. 41.

35. S. K. Kierkegaard, *The Sickness unto Death*, ed. and trans. E. Hong and H. Hong (Princeton, NJ: Princeton University Press, 1980), p. 86.

36. Parrot and Smith (1993, p. 906), in N. van de Ven, M. Zeelenber, and R. Pieters, "Why Envy Outperforms Admiration," *Personality and Social Psychology Bulletin* 37, no. 6 (2011): 784–795, p. 785.

37. Alfred Archer, "Admiration and Motivation," *Emotion Review* 11, no. 2 (2019): 140–150, p. 147.

38. K. Kristjánsson, "Emotions Targeting Moral Exemplarity: Making Sense of the Logical Geography of Admiration, Emulation and Elevation," *Theory and Research in Education* 15, no. 1 (2017): 20–37, p. 24.

39. R. M. Adams, *Finite and Infinite Goods: A Framework for Ethics* (New York: Oxford University Press, 1999), p. 134.

40. N. van de Ven, M. Zeelenberg, and R. Pieters, "Why Envy Outperforms Admiration," *Personality and Social Psychology Bulletin* 37, no. 6 (2011): 784–795.

41. J. Lange and J. Crusius, "Dispositional Envy Revisited: Unraveling the Motivational Dynamics of Benign and Malicious Envy," *Personality and Social Psychology Bulletin* 41, no. 2 (2015): 284–294, pp. 284, 286; N. Van de Ven, "Envy and Admiration: Emotion and Motivation Following Upward Social Comparison," *Cognition and Emotion* 37 (2017): 193–200.

42. Lange and Crusius, "Dispositional Envy Revisited," p. 286.

43. Alfred Archer, "Admiration and Motivation," *Emotion Review* 11, no. 2 (2019): 140–150, p. 140.

44. This is an Augustinian idea. He describes this as the *ordo amoris*, or order of loves.

45. Terry Price, *Leadership Ethics* (New York City: Cambridge University Press, 2008), pp. 5, 35–36.

46. Consider the Emma Coburn "Team Boss" group in Boulder, Colorado; Puma Elite in Raleigh, North Carolina; Bowerman Track Club in Eugene, Oregon; and HOKA Northern Arizona Elite in Flagstaff, Arizona.

47. See Chapter 3.

48. Bernard Mandeville, *The Fable of the Bees or Private Vices, Public Benefits*, Early Modern Texts (1732), https://www.earlymoderntexts.com/assets/pdfs/mandeville1732_1.pdf, pp. 1–2.

49. An early version of this section first appeared on Sabrina Little (2022), "The Grumbling Hive," https://www.irunfar.com/the-grumbling-hive.

50. DeYoung, *Glittering Vices*, p. 100.

51. DeYoung, *Glittering Vices*, p. 60.

52. "Herodotus," *Perseus Encyclopedia Online*, Annenberg Project, retrieved December 25, 2018, from https://www.perseus.tufts.edu/hopper/text?doc=Perseus:text:1999.04.0004:entry=herodotus&highlight=kleos

Chapter 7

1. An abbreviated version of this article first appeared in October 2022 on iRunFar.com.

2. Antti Kauppinen, "The World According to Suffering," in *Philosophy of Suffering*, ed. David Bain, Michael Brady, Jennifer Corns, pp. 19–36 (London: Routledge, 2019).

3. An example of a negative evaluation of one's situation that is inaccurate is a student believing an exam to be unfair when, in fact, the exam *is* fair; the student just did not study.

4. There is clearly a spectrum regarding how much pleasure people are inclined to take in suffering of various sorts. On one end are those who are entirely pain-aversive, avoiding even moderate discomforts. This inclination can narrow the kinds of experiences someone is able to participate in. (Even writing a difficult email can involve suffering!) On the opposite end are those who take pleasure in unfitting kinds of suffering (e.g., enjoying self-harm) or taking too much pleasure in suffering. Consider conditions such as masochism and sadism, both of which appear in the *Diagnostic and Statistical Manual of Mental Disorders*, 5th ed. (*DSM-5*)—the definitive and most current guide to classifying mental disorders used by mental health professionals in the United States. These conditions are noted as potentially clinically significant—or as disordered forms of pleasure-seeking that can place patients and others at physical and mental risk. Most people are somewhere along this spectrum between these outliers—neither entirely discomfort-avoidant nor taking outsized or unfitting pleasure in suffering.

5. Asparagus, *Almanac* (Dublin New Hampshire: Yankee Publishing, 2022). https://www.almanac.com/plant/asparagus

6. Theresa Gaffney, "Rates of Depression and Anxiety Climbed across the Globe in 2020, Analysis Finds," *STAT*, October 8, 2021; Shmuel Fischler, "The Rise of Anxiety over the Past 100 Years," *CBT Baltimore*, March 16, 2021; Aubrianna Osorio, "Research Update: Children's Anxiety and Depression on the Rise. Georgetown University Health Policy Institute," March 24, 2022; World Health Organization, "COVID-19 Pandemic Triggers 25% Increase in Prevalence of Anxiety and Depression Worldwide," March 2, 2022, https://www.who.int/news/item/02-03-2022-covid-19-pandemic-triggers-25-increase-in-prevalence-of-anxiety-and-depression-worldwide

7. Julia Annas, "Happiness as Achievement," *Daedalus* 133, no. 2 (2004): 43–51.

8. This is a modification of Robert Nozick's famous pleasure machine thought experience, which appeared in his 1974 book, *Anarchy, State, and Utopia*. It is employed as a refutation of ethical hedonism.

9. Kristján Kristjánsson, *Flourishing as the Aim of Education: A Neo-Aristotelian View* (Philadelphia: Taylor & Francis, 2020), p. 6. Jennifer A. Frey, "Taking Humanity Seriously," *Fare Forward* (2020). https://farefwd.com/index.php/2020/09/30/taking-humanity-seriously/#:~:text=Draw

ing%20on%20Robinson%27s%20essay%20collection,lonely%2C%20 anxious%2C%20and%20unfulfilled (accessed December 25, 2022).

10. For a complete explanation of emotions and their relationship to happiness, see Chapter 4.

11. Paul Bloom points out that parents often report a decline in life satisfaction when their children are young, but if you ask them to reflect on their greatest sources of happiness, children are the first thing that comes to mind. See Paul Bloom, *The Sweet Spot: The Pleasures of Suffering and the Search for Meaning* (New York: HarperCollins, 2021).

12. Annas, "Happiness as Achievement," p. 45.

13. Mill, *Utilitarianism* II.1.

14. Mill, *Utilitarianism* II.5.

15. John E. Hare, *The Moral Gap: Kantian Ethics, Human Limits, and God's Assistance* (Oxford: Clarendon Press, 1996).

16. Christian Miller, *The Character Gap: How Good Are We?* (New York City: Oxford University Press, 2018).

17. See Chapter 3 on virtue development.

18. This account is introduced by Annas, "Happiness as Achievement," as a rival to the hedonic account, yet still insufficient.

19. Kristján Kristjánsson, *Flourishing as the Aim of Education: An Aristotelian View* (London: Routledge, 2020), p. 5.

20. Annas, "Happiness as Achievement," p. 46.

21. Ian Costello, Sarahjane Belton, and Áine MacNamara, "Stand Up and Fight: A Case Study of a Professional Rugby Club Negotiating a COVID-19 Crisis, a Talent Development Perspective," *Sports* 10, no. 8 (2022): 124.

22. C. Ranson, S. Leyland, L. Board L, et al., "137 Psychological Distress and Wellbeing in UK Olympic and Paralympic Athletes," *British Journal of Sports Medicine* 55 (2021): A54–A55.

23. Plato, *Gorgias* 479e–527e.

24. See Chapter 2 of John Helliwell, Richard Layard, Jeffrey Sachs, Jan-Emmanuel De Neve, Lara Aknin, and Shun Wang (eds.). (2022). World Happiness Report 2022 (New York: Sustainable Development Solutions Network). See also the Statistical Appendix to the World Happiness Report. https://happiness-report.s3.amazonaws.com/2022/Appendix_1_ SStatiscalAppendi_Ch2.pdf (accessed October 11, 2023).

25. Norbert Schwarz, *Stimmung Als Information: Untersuchungen Zum Einfluss von Stimmungen Auf Die Bewertung Des Eigenen Lebens* (Berlin: Springer, 1987).

26. N. Schwarz and G. L. Clore, "Mood, Misattribution, and Judgments of Well-being: Informative and Directive Functions of Affective States," *Journal of Personality and Social Psychology* 45, no. 3 (1983): 513–523. As found in Paul Bloom, "Happiness and Positive Psychology," Lecture 20: Psychology and the Good Life, Yale Open Courses lecture, https://oyc.yale.edu/psychology/psyc-110/lecture-20

27. Examples are as follows: Daniel Kahneman and Angus Deaton, "High Income Improves Evaluation of Life but Not Emotional Well-being," *PNAS* 107, no. 38 (2010): 16489–16493; Qiong Wu, "Individual Versus Household Income and Life Satisfaction: The Moderating Effects of Gender and Education," *Journal of Comparative Family Studies* 52, no. 4 (2022): 668–688; Carmen Ang, "Charted: Money Can Buy Happiness after All," *Visual Capitalist.* March 1, 2021. https://www.visualcapitalist.com/chart-money-can-buy-happiness-after-all/ (accessed October 11, 2023).

28. "Turtles all the way down" is an expression that captures an infinite regress.

29. This way of framing the question is taken from Wendell Berry. It is what he names a collection of essays, published in 1990.

30. Aristotle, *Nicomachean Ethics* 1095a.

31. Aristotle, *Nicomachean Ethics* 1096a5–10.

32. Aristotle, *Nicomachean Ethics* 1098a15–16.

33. Aristotle, *Nicomachean Ethics* 1098a14.

34. Aristotle, *Politics* 1253a1.

35. Aristotle, *Nicomachean Ethics* 1118a3–10.

36. Aristotle, *Politics* 1131b20; Aristotle, *Nicomachean Ethics* 1098a19.

37. Someone might define the flourishing life in different ways, rather than a life constituted by virtue. For example, Thomas Aquinas defines our greatest good as communion with God. Virtues are involved and make us better instances of our own kind, but we are incomplete apart from God. In fact, three of his virtues—faith, hope, and love—can only be infused by God, rather than acquired on our own.

38. See Chapter 3 for a more complete explanation of freedom in distance running.

39. Dabbling is sometimes appropriate. Sometimes it is an expression of the virtue of curiosity. Also, according to many experts, dabbling in running is preferable to specialization for children in particular. Specializing too early—or going all-in on a sport—can result in overuse injuries and burnout in young athletes. See N. Jayanthi, C. Pinkham, L. Dugas, B. Patrick, and C. Labella, "Sports Specialization in Young Athletes: Evidence-Based Recommendations," *Sports Health* 5, no. 3 (2013): 251–257. See also

J. P. Difiori,, H. Benjamin, J. Brenner, A. Gregory, N. Jayanthi, G. L. Landry, and A. Luke, "Overuse Injuries and Burnout in Youth Sports: A Position Statement from the American Medical Society for Sports Medicine," *Clinical Journal of Sports Medicine* 24, no. 1 (2014): 3–20. See L. D. Wiersma, "Risks and Benefits of Youth Sport Specialization: Perspectives and Recommendations," *Pediatric Exercise Science* 12, no. 1 (2000): 13–22.

40. W. van Mechelen, "Running Injuries: A Review of the Epidemiological Literature," *Sports Medicine* 14, no. 5 (1992): 320–335, doi: 10.2165/00007256-199214050-00004. PMID: 1439399.

41. Aristotle, *Nicomachean Ethics* 1098a15–16.

42. Aristotle, *Nicomachean Ethics* 1141a, 1178b.

43. Aristotle, *Nicomachean Ethics* 1178b.

44. Aristotle, *Politics* 1338b7–1339a.

45. Centers for Disease Control and Prevention (2022), "Benefits of Physical Activity," https://www.cdc.gov/physicalactivity/basics/pa-health/

46. Vedran Markotic, Vladimir Pokrajcic, and Mario Babic, "The Positive Effects of Running on Mental Health," *Psychiatria Danubina* 32, no. 2 (2020): 233–235.

47. D. C. Lee, R. R. Pate, C. J. Lavie, X. Sui, T. S. Church, and S. N. Blair, "Leisure-Time Running Reduces All-Cause and Cardiovascular Mortality Risk," *Journal of the American College of Cardiology* 64, no. 5 (2014): 472–481.

48. Z. Pedisic, N. Shrestha, S. Kovalchik, et al., "Is Running Associated with a Lower Risk of All-Cause, Cardiovascular and Cancer Mortality, and Is the More the Better? A Systematic Review and Meta-analysis," *British Journal of Sports Medicine* 54 (2020): 898–905. For an accessible overview of the research, see Lucy Soto (2019), "Is Long-Distance Running Good for the Heart?" American Heart Association, https://www.heart.org/en/news/2019/03/01/is-long-distance-running-good-for-the-heart

49. See J. H. O'Keefe, H. R. Patil, C. J. Lavie, A. Magalski, R. A. Vogel, and P. A. McCullough, "Potential Adverse Cardiovascular Effects from Excessive Endurance Exercise," *Mayo Clinic Proceedings* 87, no. 6 (2012): 587–595. See also M. Wilson, R. O'Hanlon, S. Prasad, A. Deighan, P. Macmillan, D. Oxborough, R. Godfrey, G. Smith, A. Maceira, S. Sharma, K. George, and G. Whyte, "Diverse Patterns of Myocardial Fibrosis in Lifelong, Veteran Endurance Athletes," *Journal of Applied Physiology* 110, no. 6 (2011): 1622–1626. For lower leg injuries, see D. Sanfilippo, C. Beaudart, A. Gaillard, S. Bornheim, O. Bruyere, and J. F. Kaux, "What Are the Main Risk Factors for Lower Extremity Running-Related Injuries? A Retrospective Survey

Based on 3669 Respondents," *Orthopaedic Journal of Sports Medicine* 9, no. 11 (2021): 23259671211043444.

50. T. Ozlü and Y. Bülbül, "Smoking and Lung Cancer," *Tuberk Toraks* 53, no. 2 (2005): 200–209, PMID: 16100660.

51. See Terry L. Price, *Leadership Ethics: An Introduction* (New York: Cambridge University Press, 2008), pp. 112–113 for a discussion of the uniqueness bias in leaders—how leaders often think of themselves as set apart and unique, and perhaps better than others, because of their position. They are likely to commit the Base Rate Fallacy.

52. Nicholas Wolterstoff, *Justice in Love* (Grand Rapids, MI: Wm. B. Eerdmans, 2015), p. 10.

53. Sabrina Little, "Variations of Virtue Phenomenology," *Journal of Value Inquiry*, forthcoming.

Chapter 8

1. Maybe philosophers should not be on shoe commercials for this reason. Theoretical clarity can come at the cost of sneaker sales.

2. An early version of this section first appeared on Sabrina Little (2021), "Limitless," https://www.irunfar.com/limitless

3. Wendell Berry, "Faustian Economics," *Harper's Magazine*, May 2008. https://harpers.org/archive/2008/05/faustian-economics/ (accessed October 11, 2023).

4. Berry, "Faustian Economics."

5. Berry, "Faustian Economics."

6. B. Sophia, P. Kelly, D. Ogan, and A. Larson, "Self-Reported History of Eating Disorders, Training, Weight Control Methods, and Body Satisfaction in Elite Female Runners Competing at the 2020 U.S. Olympic Marathon Trials," *International Journal of Exercise Science* 15, no. 2 (2022): 721–732.

7. Berry, "Faustian Economics."

8. Thank you to my editor, Peter Ohlin, for this second example.

9. An early version of this section first appeared on Sabrina Little (2022), "Taking Happiness Seriously," https://www.irunfar.com/taking-happiness-seriously

10. Consider Faith Kipyegon, Keira D'Amato, Stephanie Bruce, and Allyson Felix. These women are just as fast, or faster, than they were before having children.

11. Aristotle writes that, in discussing a topic, we should "[achieve] that amount of precision which belongs to its subject matter" (*Nicomachean Ethics* 1094b). Suffering does not afford us much precision.

12. Aristotle, *Politics* 1131b20.

13. Aristotle, *Nicomachean Ethics* 1098a19.

14. See the second half of Chapter 7 for a fuller discussion of health, high-level sport, and happiness.

15. Moreover, this profitability point is not static; it changes throughout the course of a season and a career as fitness waxes and wanes. Athletes need to read their bodies well to discern how much suffering is beneficial for training progress and then adjust this amount as training progresses.

16. Aristotle, *Politics* 1339a.

17. Plato, *Republic* 410d.

18. Plato, *Republic* 412a.

19. Plato, *Republic* 411e.

20. Mark Twain, *The Adventures of Tom Sawyer* (London: Bantam Books, 1981), pp. 10–16.

21. Twain, *The Adventures of Tom Sawyer*, p. 15. As found in Paul Bloom, *The Sweet Spot: The Pleasure of Suffering and the Search for Meaning* (New York: Harper Collins, 2021), p. 130.

22. Paul Bloom, *The Sweet Spot: The Pleasure of Suffering and the Search for Meaning* (New York: HarperCollins, 2021), p. 130.

23. Viktor Frankl, *Man's Search for Meaning* (Boston: Beacon Press, 1962).

24. E. Jayawickreme and L. E. R. Blackie, *Exploring the Psychological Benefits of Hardship: A Critical Reassessment of Posttraumatic Growth* (Cham: Springer International, 2016).

25. E. Jayawickreme, F. J. Infurna, K. Alajak, L. Blackie, W. J. Chopik, J. M. Chung, A. Dorfman, W. Fleeson, M. Forgeard, P, Frazier, R. M. Furr, I. Grossmann, A. S. Heller, O. M. Laceulle, R. E. Lucas, M. Luhmann, G. Luong, L. Meijer, K. C. McLean, C. L. Park, and R. Zonneveld, "Post-traumatic Growth as Positive Personality Change: Challenges, Opportunities, and Recommendations," *Journal of Personality* 89, no. 1 (2021): 145–165.

26. Aquinas, *Summa Theologiae* II.2.162.1–8.

27. James Dawes, *Evil Men* (Cambridge, MA: Harvard University Press, 2013).

28. Eva Hoffman, *After Such Knowledge: Memory, History, and the Legacy of the Holocaust* (New York: Public Affairs, 2011), p. 172.

Works Cited

Algoe, S., and Haidt, J. 2009. "Witnessing Excellence in Action: The 'Other-Praising' Emotions of Elevation, Gratitude, and Admiration." *Journal of Positive Psychology* 4, no. 2: 105–127.

Ang, C. 2021. "Charted: Money Can Buy Happiness after All." *Visual Capitalist.* https://www.visualcapitalist.com/chart-money-can-buy-happiness-after-all/#:~:text=In%20One%20Chart%3A%20Money%20Can%20Buy%20Ha ppiness%20After%20All&text=Previous%20studies%20have%20indica ted%20that,plateaus%20at%20approximately%20%20%2475%2C000%2Fyear.

Annas, J. 2004. "Happiness as Achievement." *Daedalus* 133, no. 2: 43–51.

Annas, J. 2011. *Intelligent Virtue.* Oxford: Oxford University Press.

Aquinas, T. 2017. *Summa Theologiae.* Fathers of the English Dominican Province. Translated and edited by K. Knight. https://www.newadvent.org/summa/

Arcangeli, M., Sperduti, M. Jacquot, A., Piolino, P., and Dokic, J. 2020. "Awe and the Experience of the Sublime: A Complex Relationship." *Frontiers in Psychology* 11: 1340.

Archer, A. 2019. "Admiration and Motivation." *Emotion Review* 11, no. 2: 140–150.

Archer, A., Engelen, B., and Thomas, A. 2019. "How Admiring Moral Exemplars Can Ruin Your Life: The Case of Conrad's 'Lord Jim.'" In *The Moral Psychology of Admiration*, edited by Alfred Archer and Andre Grahle, pp. 233–248. Lanham, MD: Rowman & Littlefield.

Aristotle. 1997. *Politics.* Translated by P. Phillips Simpson. Chapel Hill: UNC Press.

Aristotle. 2009. *Poetics.* Translated by S. H. Butcher. In *Internet Classics Archive.* London: Macmillan. http://classics.mit.edu/Aristotle/poetics.html.

Aristotle. 2011. *Nicomachean Ethics.* Translated by R. Bartlett and S. Collins. Chicago: Chicago University Press.

Asparagus. 2022. *Almanac.* Yankee Publishing. https://www.almanac.com/plant/asparagus

Battaly, H. 2015. *Virtue.* Malden, MA: Polity Press.

Bechara, A. 2004. "The Role of Emotion in Decision-Making: Evidence from Neurological Patients with Orbitofrontal Damage." *Brain and Cognition* 55, no. 1: 30–40.

Berry, W. 2008. "Faustian Economics." *Harper's Magazine.*

Bloom, P. 2008. "Happiness and Positive Psychology." Lecture 20: Psychology and the Good Life. Yale Open Courses lecture. https://oyc.yale.edu/psychology/psyc-110/lecture-20

Bloom, P. 2021. *The Sweet Spot: The Pleasures of Suffering and the Search for Meaning.* New York: HarperCollins.

Blundell, R., Griffith, R., and Van Reenen, J. 1999. "Market Share, Market Value, and Innovation in a Panel of British Manufacturing Firms." *Review of Economic Studies* 66, no. 3: 529–554.

Boersma, G. P. 2017. "Augustine's Immanent Critique of Stoicism." *Scottish Journal of Theology* 70, no. 2: 184–197.

Boyd, C. A. 2014. "Pride and Humility." *In Virtues and Their Vices*, edited by K. Timpe and C. A. Boyd, pp. 248–250. New York: Oxford University Press.

Burguillo J. C. 2010. "Using Game Theory and Competition-Based Learning to Stimulate Student Motivation and Performance." *Computers & Education* 55: 566–575.

Bushman, B. J. 2002. "Does Venting Anger Feed or Extinguish the Flame? Catharsis, Rumination, Distraction, Anger, and Aggressive Responding." *Personality and Social Psychology Bulletin* 28, no. 6: 724–731.

Cacciola. 2018. "Eliud Kipchoge Is the Greatest Marathoner, Ever." *New York Times*, September 14.

Cacciola, S. 2022. "The Impossible Task of Keeping Up with the Ingebrigtsens." *New York Times*, July 14.

Camus, A. 2012. *The Myth of Sisyphus and Other Essays.* New York: Knopf Doubleday.

Carlson, E. 2018. "Who Are Moral Exemplars and What Are They Like?" Lecture. The Beacon Project. July 2018. Winston Salem, NC.

Centers for Disease Control and Prevention. 2022. "Benefits of Physical Activity." https://www.cdc.gov/physicalactivity/basics/pa-health/

Chamberlain, C. 1984. "The Meaning of *Prohairesis* in Aristotle's Ethics." *Transactions of the American Philological Association* 114: 147–157.

Chavez, C. 2021. "Alberto Salazar Ruled Permanently Ineligible by SafeSport for Verbal, Sexual Misconduct." *Sports Illustrated*, July 26. https://www.si.com/olympics/   2021/07/26/alberto-salazar-permanently-ineligible-safesport-investigation-sexual-emotional-misconduct

Cicero. 1887. *On Friendship.* In *Ethical Writings of Cicero: De Officiis (On Moral Duties); De Senectute (On Old Age); De Amicitia (On Friendship), and Scipio's Dream.* Translated by Andrew P. Peabody. Boston: Little, Brown, and Co.

Costello, I., Belton, S. J., and MacNamara, A. 2022. "Stand Up and Fight: A Case Study of a Professional Rugby Club Negotiating a COVID-19 Crisis, a Talent Development Perspective." *Sports* 10, no. 8: 124.

Damasio, A. 2005. *Descartes' Error: Emotion, Reason, and the Human Brain.* London: Penguin.

Dawes, J. 2013. *Evil Men*. Cambridge, MA: Harvard University Press.

DeYoung, R. K. (2009). *Glittering Vices*. Grand Rapids, MI: Brazos Press.

Difiori, J. P., Benjamin, H., Brenner, J., Gregory, A., Jayanthi, N., Landry, G. L., and Luke, A. 2014. "Overuse Injuries and Burnout in Youth Sports: A Position Statement from the American Medical Society for Sports Medicine." *Clinical Journal of Sports Medicine* 24, no. 1: 3–20.

DiMenichi, B. C., and Tricomi, E. 2015. "The Power of Competition: Effects of Social Motivation on Attention, Sustained Physical Effort, and Learning." *Frontiers in Psychology* 6: 1282.

Domínguez, R., Cuenca, E., Maté-Muñoz, J. L., García-Fernández, P., Serra-Paya, N., Estevan, M. C., Herreros, P. V., and Garnacho-Castaño, M. V. 2017. "Effects of Beetroot Juice Supplementation on Cardiorespiratory Endurance in Athletes: A Systematic Review." *Nutrients* 9, no. 1: 43.

Driver, J. 1999. "Modesty and Ignorance." *Ethics* 109, no. 4: 827–834.

Driver, J. 2001. *Uneasy Virtue*. New York: Cambridge University Press.

Dweck, C. S., and Leggett E. L. 1988. "A Social-Cognitive Approach to Motivation and Personality." *Psychological Review* 95: 256.

Emmons, R. A., and McCullough, M. E. 2003. "Counting Blessings versus Burdens: An Experimental Investigation of Gratitude and Subjective Well-being in Daily Life." *Journal of Personality and Social Psychology* 84, no. 2: 377–389.

Ericsson, K. A. 2008. "Deliberate Practice and Acquisition of Expert Performance: A General Overview." *Society for Academic Emergency Medicine* 15, no. 11: 988–994. https://onlinelibrary.wiley.com/doi/full/10.1111/j.1553-2712.2008.00227.x

Ericsson, K. A. 2013. "Training History, Deliberate Practice and Elite Sports Performance: An Analysis in Response to Tucker and Collins' Review—What Makes Champions?" *British Journal of Sports Medicine* 47: 533–535.

Evans, C. S. 1987. "Kierkegaard's View of Humor: Must Christians Always Be Solemn?" *Faith and Philosophy* 4, no. 2: 176–186.

Fischler, S. 2021. "The Rise of Anxiety over the Past 100 Years." *CBT Baltimore*, March 16.

Francis, A. 2019. "Jordan Hasay Discusses Mary Cain, Announces Paula Radcliffe Is Her New Coach." *Canadian Running*, November 20. https://runningmagazine.ca/the-scene/jordan-hasay-discusses-mary-cain-announces-paula-radcliffe-as-new-coach/

Frankl, V. 1962. *Man's Search for Meaning*. Boston: Beacon Press.

Freeman, A. 2013. "Remedies to Acedia in the Rhythm of Daily Life." *Christian Reflection: A Series in Faith and Ethics*, 36–37.

French Jr., J. R. P., and Raven, B. H. 1959. "The Bases of Social Power." In *Studies in Social Power*, edited by D. Cartwright, pp. 150–167. Ann Arbor, MI: Institute for Social Research.

Frey, J. A. 2020. "Taking Humanity Seriously." *Fare Forward*. A Festschrift for Marilynne Robinson. https://farefwd.com/index.php/2020/09/30/taking-humanity-seriously/

Gaffney, T. 2021. "Rates of Depression and Anxiety Climbed across the Globe in 2020, Analysis Finds." *STAT*, October 8.

Geroski, P. 1995. "Innovation and Competitive Advantage." *OECD Economics Department Working Papers 159*. Paris: OECD.

Giovannone, L. 2021. "The Prevalence of Domestic Violence in the NFL." *Charger Bulletin*, December 7. https://chargerbulletin.com/the-prevalence-of-domestic-violence-in-the-nfl/

Gladwell, M. 2008. *Outliers: The Story of Success*. Boston: Little, Brown & Company.

Gladwell, M. 2021. "Drugstore Athlete." *New Yorker*, September 10.

Han, H., Jeong, C., Damon, W., and Cohen, G. L. 2017. "Attainable and Relevant Moral Exemplars Are More Effective Than Extraordinary Exemplars in Promoting Voluntary Service Engagement." *Frontiers in Psychology* 8: 283.

Hare, J. E. 1996. *The Moral Gap: Kantian Ethics, Human Limits, and God's Assistance*. Oxford: Clarendon Press.

Harper, D. (n.d.). "Etymology of Compete." *Online Etymology Dictionary*. Retrieved December 27, 2022, fromhttps://www.etymonline.com/word/compete

Helliwell, J. F., Layard, R., Sachs, J. D., De Neve, J.-E., Aknin, L. B., and Wang, S. (eds.). 2022. World Happiness Report 2022. New York: Sustainable Development Solutions Network.

Herodotus. *Perseus Encyclopedia Online*. Annenberg Project. Retrieved December 25, 2018, from https://www.perseus.tufts.edu/hopper/text?doc=Perseus:text:1999.04.0004:entry=herodotus&highlight=kleos

Hoffman, E. 2011. *After Such Knowledge: Memory, History, and the Legacy of the Holocaust*. New York: Public Affairs.

Hursthouse, R. 1999. *On Virtue Ethics*. Oxford: Oxford University Press.

Hursthouse, R., and Pettigrove, G. 2018. "Virtue Ethics." In *The Stanford Encyclopedia of Philosophy* (Winter 2018 edition), edited by Edward N. Zalta. https://plato.stanford.edu/archives/win2018/entries/ethics-virtue/

Jayanthi, N., Pinkham, C., Dugas, L., Patrick, B., and Labella, C. 2013. "Sports Specialization in Young Athletes: Evidence-Based Recommendations." *Sports Health* 5, no. 3: 251–257.

Jayawickreme, E., and Blackie, L. E. R. 2016. *Exploring the Psychological Benefits of Hardship: A Critical Reassessment of Posttraumatic Growth*. Cham: Springer International.

Jayawickreme, E., Infurna, F. J., Alajak, K., Blackie, L., Chopik, W. J., Chung, J. M., Dorfman, A., Fleeson, W., Forgeard, M., Frazier, P., Furr, R. M., Grossmann, I., Heller, A. S., Laceulle, O. M., Lucas, R. E., Luhmann, M., Luong, G., Meijer, L., McLean, K. C., Park, C. L., and Zonneveld, R. 2021.

"Post-Traumatic Growth as Positive Personality Change: Challenges, Opportunities, and Recommendations." *Journal of Personality* 89, no. 1: 145–165.

Joyce, T. 2022. "Megan Rapinoe Doesn't Deserve a Medal of Freedom." *Washington Examiner*, July 5. https://www.washingtonexaminer.com/opin ion/megan-rapinoe-doesnt-deserve-a-medal-of-freedom

Kahneman, D., and Deaton, A. 2010. "High Income Improves Evaluation of Life but Not Emotional Well-being." *Proceedings of the National Academy of Science* 107, no. 38: 16489–16493.

Kamtekar, R. 2017. Plato's *Moral Psychology: Intellectualism, the Divided Soul, and the Desire for Good*. New York: Oxford University Press.

Kauppinen, A. 2019. "The World According to Suffering." In *Philosophy of Suffering*, edited by David Bain, Michael Brady, and Jennifer Corns, pp. 19–36. London: Routledge.

Kierkegaard, S. 1991. *Practice in Christianity*. Translated by H. Hong. Princeton, NJ: Princeton University Press.

Kierkegaard, S. K. 1980. *The Sickness unto Death*. Edited and translated by E. Hong and H. Hong. Princeton, NJ: Princeton University Press.

Kilduff G. J. 2014. "Driven to Win: Rivalry, Motivation, and Performance." *Social Psychological and Personality Science* 5: 944–952.

King, N. 2014. "Erratum to: 'Perseverance as an Intellectual Virtue.'" *Synthese* 19: 3779–3801.

King, N. 2021. *The Excellent Mind: Intellectual Virtues for Everyday Life*. New York: Oxford University Press.

King, P. E., and Defoy, F. 2020. "Joy as a Virtue: The Means and Ends of Joy." *Journal of Psychology and Theology* 48, no. 4: 308–331.

Kristjánsson, K. 2017. "Emotions Targeting Moral Exemplarity: Making Sense of the Logical Geography of Admiration, Emulation, and Elevation." *Theory and Research in Education* 15, no. 1: 20–37.

Kristjánsson, K. 2018. *Virtuous Emotions*. Oxford: Oxford University Press.

Kristjánsson, K. 2020. *Flourishing as the Aim of Education*. London: Routledge.

Kumar, A. 2019. "The Heel and the Heal, Jordan Hasay Is Back." *ESPN*, April 15. https://www.espn.com/espn/ story/_/id/26531628/boston-marathon-2019-heel-heal-jordan-hasay-back

Lange, J., and Crusius, J. 2015. "Dispositional Envy Revisited: Unraveling the Motivational Dynamics of Benign and Malicious Envy." *Personality and Social Psychology Bulletin* 41, no. 2: 284–294.

Le Bouc, R., and Pessiglione M. 2013. "Imaging Social Motivation: Distinct Brain Mechanisms Drive Effort Production during Collaboration versus Competition." *Journal of Neuroscience* 33: 15894–15902.

Lee, D. C., Pate, R. R., Lavie, C. J., Sui, X., Church, T. S., and Blair, S. N. 2014. "Leisure-Time Running Reduces All-Cause and Cardiovascular Mortality Risk." *Journal of the American College of Cardiology* 64, no. 5: 472–481.

Lee, Duck-chul, Lavie, Carl J., and Vedanthan, Rajesh. 2015. "Optimal Dose of Running for Longevity: Is More Better or Worse?" *Journal of the American College of Cardiology* 65, no. 5: 420–422.

Lewis, C. S. 1986. "The Necessity of Chivalry." In *Present Concerns*, edited by Walter Hooper. San Diego: Harcourt.

Little, S. 2021. "The Graded Engagement Model of Admiration." *Theory and Research in Education*: 19, no. 1: 3–18.

Little, S. 2022. "Variations in Virtue Phenomenology." *Journal of Value Inquiry*. https://doi.org/10.1007/s10790-022-09920-7.

MacIntyre, A. 2006. *After Virtue: A Study in Moral Theory*. 3rd ed. Notre Dame, IN: University of Notre Dame Press.

Magill, F. N., and Moose, C. J. (2003). "Pheidippides." In *The Ancient World: Dictionary of World Biography*, Volume 1, edited by Frank Magill, 818–821. New York: Routledge.

Mandeville, B. 1732. *The Fable of the Bees or Private Vices, Public Benefits*. Early Modern Texts. Edited by Jonathan Bennett. https://www.earlymoderntexts.com/ assets/pdfs/mandeville1732_1.pdf

Markman, A. 2009. "You Can't Punch Your Way out of Anger: You Can't Let Off Steam with Violence." *Psychology Today*. https://www.psychologytoday.com/us/blog/ulterior-motives/200909/you-cant-punch-your-way-out-anger

Markotic, V., Pokrajcic, V., and Babic, M. 2020. "The Positive Effects of Running on Mental Health." *Psychiatria Danubina* 32, no. 2: 233–235.

McGrath, B. S. 2021. "Jim Walmsley Runs 6:09:26 for 100K, Misses World Record by Just 12 Seconds." *Canadian Running*, January 24. https://runningmagazine.ca/sections/runs-races/jim-walmsley-runs-60926-for-100k-misses-world-record-by-just-12-seconds/

Mill, J. S. 2001. *Utilitarianism*. Indianapolis: Hackett.

Miller, C. B. 2013. *Moral Character: An Empirical Theory*. Oxford: Oxford University Press.

Miller, C. B. 2014. *Character and Moral Psychology*. New York: Oxford University Press.

Miller, C. B. 2018. *The Character Gap: How Good Are We?* New York: Oxford University Press.

Miller, C. B. 2021. "Flirting with Skepticism about Practical Wisdom." In *Practical Wisdom: Philosophical and Psychological Perspectives*, edited by Mario De Caro and Maria Silvia Vaccarezza, 52–69. London: Routledge.

Mischel, W. and Shoda, Y. 1995. "A Cognitive-Affective System Theory of Personality: Reconceptualizing Situations, Dispositions, Dynamics, and Invariance in Personality Structure." *Psychological Review* 102, no. 2: 246–268.

Morreall, J. 1983. *Taking Laughter Seriously*. Albany: SUNY Press.

Mushnick, P. 2022. "Boorish Megan Rapinoe Unfit for Presidential Medal of Freedom." *New York Post,* July 7. https://nypost.com/2022/07/07/megan-rapinoe-didnt-deserve-presidential-medal-of-freedom/

Nichols, M. 1992. *Citizens and Statesmen.* Lanham, MD: Rowman & Littlefield.

Nickell, S. 1996. "Competition and Corporate Performance." *Journal of Political Economy* 104, no. 4: 724–746.

NIDA. 2023. "What Are the Side Effects of Anabolic Steroid Misuse?" https://nida.nih.gov/publications/research-reports/steroids-other-appearance-performance-enhancing-drugs-apeds/what-are-side-effects-anabolic-steroid-misuse on 2023

Nozick, R. 1974. *Anarchy, State, and Utopia.* New York: Basic Books.

Nussbaum, M., and Putnam, H. 1992. "Changing Aristotle's Mind." In *Essays on Aristotle's De Anima,* edited by Martha C. Nussbaum and Amélie Oksenberg Rorty, 27–56. New York: Oxford University Press.

Nussbaum, M. 2001. *Upheavals of Thought: The Intelligence of Emotions.* New York: Cambridge University Press.

O'Keefe, J. H., Patil, H. R., Lavie, C. J., Magalski, A., Vogel, R. A., and McCullough, P. A. 2012. "Potential Adverse Cardiovascular Effects from Excessive Endurance Exercise." *Mayo Clinic Proceedings* 87, no. 6: 587–595.

Onu, D., Kessler, T., and Smith, J. R. 2016. "Admiration: A Conceptual Review." *Emotion Review* 8, no. 3: 218–230.

Osorio, A. 2022. *Research Update: Children's Anxiety and Depression on the Rise.* Georgetown University Health Policy Institute. March 24. https://ccf.georgetown.edu/2022/03/24/research-update-childrens-anxiety-and-depression-on-the-rise/

Ozlü, T., and Bülbül, Y. 2005. "Smoking and Lung Cancer." *Tuberk Toraks* 53, no. 2: 200–209.

Pedisic, Z., Shrestha, N., Kovalchik, S., Stamatakis, E., Nucharapon, L., Grgic, J., Titze, S., Biddle, S., Bauman, A., and Pekka, O. 2020. "Is Running Associated with a Lower Risk of All-Cause, Cardiovascular and Cancer Mortality, and Is the More the Better? A Systematic Review and Meta-Analysis." *British Journal of Sports Medicine* 54: 898–905.

Peters, R. S. 1981. *Moral Development and Moral Education.* London: George Allen & Unwin.

Pinckaers, S. 2015. *Passions and Virtue.* Washington, DC: Catholic University Press.

Plato. 1997. *Gorgias.* Translated by D. J. Zeyl. In *Complete Works of Plato,* edited by J. M. Cooper, 791–869. Indianapolis: Hackett.

Plato. 1997. *Laws.* Translated by T .J. Saunders. In *Complete Works of Plato,* edited by J. M. Cooper, 1318–1616. Indianapolis: Hackett.

Plato. 1997. *Protagoras.* Translated by S. Lombardo and K. Bell. In *Complete Works of Plato,* edited by J. M. Cooper. Indianapolis: Hackett.

Plato. 1997. *Republic*. Translated by G. Grube and C. Reeve. In *Complete Works of Plato*, edited by J. M. Cooper, 971–1223. Indianapolis: Hackett.

Plato. 1997. *Symposium*. Translated by A. Nehamas and P. Woodruff. In *Complete Works of Plato*, edited by J. M. Cooper, 457–505. Indianapolis: Hackett.

Price, T. 2008. *Leadership Ethics*. New York: Cambridge University Press.

Ranson, C., Leyland, S., Board, L., Jaques, R., and Currie, A. 2021. "137 Psychological Distress and Wellbeing in UK Olympic and Paralympic Athletes." *British Journal of Sports Medicine* 55: A54–A55.

Rhodes, R. F. 1987. "The Kaihōgyō Practice of Mr. Hiei." *Japanese Journal of Religious Studies* 14, no. 2–3: 185–202.

Roberts, R. 1988. "What an Emotion Is: A Sketch." *Philosophical Review* 97, no. 2: 183–209.

Roberts, R. C. 1987. "Smiling with God: Reflections on Christianity and the Psychology of Humor." *Faith and Philosophy* 4, no. 2: 168–175.

Roberts, R. C. 1988. "Humor and the Virtues." *Inquiry* 31, no. 2: 127–149.

Roberts, R. C. 2003. *Emotions: An Aid in Moral Psychology*. New York: Cambridge University Press.

Roberts, R., and Spezio, M. 2019. "Admiring Moral Exemplars: Sketch of an Ethical Sub-Discipline." In *Self, Motivation, and Virtue: Innovative Interdisciplinary Research*, edited by Nancy Snow and Darcia Narvaez, pp. 85–108. Abingdon: Routledge.

Roberts, R., and Telech, D. 2019. "The Emotion-Virtue-Debt Triad of Gratitude, M. Alfano, Editor. In *The Moral Psychology of Gratitude*, pp. 1–12. Lanham, MD: Rowman & Littlefield.

Sanfilippo, D., Beaudart, C., Gaillard, A., Bornheim, S., Bruyere, O., and Kaux, J. F. 2021. "What Are the Main Risk Factors for Lower Extremity Running-Related Injuries? A Retrospective Survey Based on 3669 Respondents." *Orthopaedic Journal of Sports Medicine* 9, no. 11: 23259671211043444.

Schindler, I. 2013. "Admiration and Adoration." *Cognition and Emotion* 27, no. 1: 103.

Schindler, I. 2014. "Relations of Admiration and Adoration with Other Emotions and Well- Being." *Psychology of Well-Being: Theory, Research and Practice* 4: 14.

Schindler, I., Paech, J., and Löwenbrück, F. 2015. "Linking Admiration and Adoration to Self- Expansion: Different Ways to Enhance One's Potential." *Cognition and Emotion* 29, no. 2: 292–310.

Schindler, I., Zink, V., Windrich, J., and Menninghaus, W. 2013. "Admiration and Adoration: Their Different Ways of Showing and Shaping Who We Are." *Cognition and Emotion* 27, no. 1: 85–118.

Schmitter, A. 2021. "Ancient, Medieval and Renaissance Theories of the Emotions." In *Stanford Encyclopedia of Philosophy*, edited by Edward

N.   Zalta.   https://plato.stanford.edu/   entries/emotions-17th18th/
LD1Background.html

Schnitker, S., Houltberg, B., Dyrness, W., and Redmond, N. 2017. "The Virtue
of Patience, Spirituality, and Suffering: Integrating Lessons from Positive
Psychology, Psychology of Religion, and Christian Theology." *Psychology of
Religion and Spirituality* 9, no. 3: 264–275.

Schwarz, N. 1987. *Stimmung Als Information: Untersuchungen Zum Einfluss
von Stimmungen Auf Die Bewertung Des Eigenen Lebens.* Berlin: Springer.

Schwarz, N., and Clore, G. L. 1983. "Mood, Misattribution, and Judgments
of Well-being: Informative and Directive Functions of Affective States."
Journal of Personality and Social Psychology 45, no. 3: 513–523.

Schwitzgebel, E. 2015. "The Moral Lives of Ethicists, or How Often Do Ethics
Professors Call Their Mothers?" *Aeon Magazine*, July 14. https://aeon.co/ess
ays/how-often-do-ethics-professors-call-their-mothers

Schwitzgebel, E., and Rust, J. 2016. "The Behavior of Ethicists." In *The Blackwell
Companion to Experimental Philosophy*, edited by J. Sytsma and W.
Buckwalter, 225–233. Hoboken, NJ: Wiley-Blackwell.

Seneca. 2011. *On Benefits.* Translated by M. Griffin and B. Inwood.
Chicago: University of Chicago Press.

Sidgwick, H. 1907. *The Methods of Ethics.* Gutenberg Project, produced by
H. Flower. https://www.gutenberg.org/files/46743/46743-h/46743-h.htm

Skrbina, P. 2018. "When Pro Athletes Are Accused of Abuse, How Often Does
Punishment Follow?" *Tennessean*, September 18. https://www.tenness
ean.com/story/sports/   nhl/predators/2018/09/19/nfl-domestic-violence-
sexual-assault-child-abuse-nba-mlb-nhl/1335799002/

Slote, M. 2001. *Motives from Morals.* New York: Oxford University Press.

Snow, N. 2024. "Hope and Resilience." In *Endurance*, edited by Nancy Snow
and Nathan King. New York: Oxford University Press.

Snow, N. 2010. *Virtue as Social Intelligence: An Empirically Grounded Theory.*
New York: Routledge.

Snow, N. 2019. "Resilience and Hope as a Democratic Civic Virtue." In *Virtues
in the Public Square: Citizenship, Civic Friendship, and Duty*, edited by James
Arthur, pp. 124–139. London: Routledge Press.

Solomon, Robert. 1980. "Emotions and Choice." In *Explaining Emotions*, edited by A.O. Rorty, pp. 251–281. Berkeley: University of California Press.

Sophia, B., Kelly, P., Ogan, D., and Larson, A. 2022. "Self-Reported History of
Eating Disorders, Training, Weight Control Methods, and Body Satisfaction
in Elite Female Runners Competing at the 2020 U.S. Olympic Marathon
Trials." *International Journal of Exercise Science* 15, no. 2: 721–732.

Soto, L. 2019. "Is Long-Distance Running Good for the Heart?" American
Heart   Association.   https://www.heart.org/en/news/2019/03/01/is-long-
distance-running-good-for-the-heart

Stichter, M. 2007. "Ethical Expertise: The Skill Model of Virtue." *Ethical Theory and Moral Practice* 10: 183–194.

Stichter, M. 2018. "Virtue as a Skill." In *The Oxford Handbook of Virtue*, edited by N. E. Snow, 57–84. Oxford: Oxford University Press.

Swanton, C. 2017. "Developmental Virtue Ethics." *Developing the Virtues: Integrating Perspectives*. New York: Oxford University Press.

Timpe, K., and Boyd, C. A. 2014. "Introduction." In *Virtues and Their Vices*, edited by K. Timpe and C. A. Boyd, 1–36. New York: Oxford University Press.

Twain, M. 1981. *The Adventures of Tom Sawyer*. New York: Bantam Books.

USADA. 2022. "Why Clean Sport Matters." https://www.usada.org/choose-usada/choose-usada- why-clean-sport-matters/

USADA. 2022. "Is It Prohibited for Athletes to Use IV Infusions for Rehydration and Recovery?" https://www.usada.org/spirit-of-sport/education/is-it-prohibited-or-dangerous-for-athletes-using-iv-infusions-for-rehydration-and-recovery/

USADA. 2014. "How Does a Substance Become Prohibited?" June 14. https://www.usada.org/spirit-of-sport/substance-become-prohibited/

Van de Ven, N., Zeelenber, M. & Pieters, R. 2011. "Why Envy Outperforms Admiration." *Personality and Social Psychology Bulletin* 37, no. 6: 784–795.

Van Mechelen, W. 1992. "Running Injuries. A Review of the Epidemiological Literature." *Sports Medicine* 14, no. 5: 320–335.

Wiersma, L. D. 2000. "Risks and Benefits of Youth Sport Specialization: Perspectives and Recommendations." *Pediatric Exercise Science* 12, no. 1: 13–22.

Wilson, A. T. 2019. "Admiration and the Development of Moral Virtue." In *The Moral Psychology of Admiration*, edited by Andre Grahle and Alfred Archer, 201–215. Lanham, MD: Rowman and Littlefield.

Wilson, M., O'Hanlon, R., Prasad, S., Deighan, A., Macmillan, P., Oxborough, D., Godfrey, R., Smith, G., Maceira, A., Sharma, S., George, K., and Whyte, G. 2011. "Diverse Patterns of Myocardial Fibrosis in Lifelong, Veteran Endurance Athletes." *Journal of Applied Physiology* 110, no. 6: 1622–1626.

Wolf, S. 1982. "Moral Saints." *Journal of Philosophy* 79, no. 8: 419–439.

Wolterstoff, N. 2015. *Justice in Love*. Grand Rapids, MI: Eerdmans.

World Health Organization. 2022. "COVID-19 Pandemic Triggers 25% Increase in Prevalence of Anxiety and Depression Worldwide." March 2. https://www.who.int/news/item/02-03-2022-covid-19-pandemic-triggers-25-increase-in-prevalence-of-anxiety-and-depression-worldwide

Wu, Q. 2022. "Individual Versus Household Income and Life Satisfaction: The Moderating Effects of Gender and Education." *Journal of Comparative Family Studies* 52, no. 4: 668–688.

Zadra, J. R., and Clore, G. L. 2011. "Emotion and Perception: The Role of Affective Information." Wiley interdisciplinary reviews. *Cognitive Science* 2, no. 6: 676–685.

Zagzebski, L. 2010. "Exemplarist Virtue Theory." *Metaphilosophy*, Special Issue: Virtue and Vice, Moral and Epistemic 41, no. 1/2: 41–57.

Zagzebski, L. 2017. *Exemplarist Moral Theory*. New York: Oxford University Press.

Zimmerman B. J. 1989. "A Social Cognitive View of Self-regulated Academic Learning." *Journal of Educational Psychology* 81: 329.

Index

For the benefit of digital users, indexed terms that span two pages (e.g., 52–53) may, on occasion, appear on only one of those pages.

100-mile run, 39, 102–3, 106–8, 162

accountability, xi–xii, 44, 100–1,
    113–114
acedia, xii
Achilles, 58–60, 176–77
Adams, Robert, 166
admiration, admirer, 19, 27, 29, 52,
    58–59, 86–87, 93–95, 96, 97–98,
    99–106, 107–15, 116–17
  mere admirer, 106, 110–11, 114
agency, agent, 32, 40–45, 101, 180
aggression, 18, 36–37
akrasia , 23
Alcibiades, 98, 102
Alighieri, Dante, ix
all-in runner, 195–97
anger, 37, 58, 77–78, 79–80, 81, 102,
    117, 186–87
Anscombe, Elizabeth, 16
applied ethics, 6, 9, 11
Aquinas, Thomas, 10, 16, 128, 129,
    143–45, 146–47, 149, 158–59,
    160, 161–62, 181–82, 226
areté, 17, 122, 194
Aristotle, 2–3, 5, 16–21, 23–24, 26,
    28, 30, 48, 52–53, 54, 63–65,
    74–75, 89–73, 102, 116, 122–23,
    144–46, 158–59, 166, 186, 192–
    93, 194–95, 198–200, 205, 206,
    216–18, 221–23
articulacy requirement, 112–14
asceticism, 3, 20

aspiration, 37–38, 96–97, 158–59
asymmetry (of character), 64–
    65, 103–5
Athens, Greece, 74–75, 99, 132
athletes, professional, 35, 59, 105–9,
    168, 169–71, 176, 196, 221
Augustine, 91
awe, 29, 82, 83, 84–86, 93–94

base-rate fallacy, 201–2
beets, 93, 120–21
Berry, Wendell, 210–13
biology, 20, 47, 112
blithe humility, 132–33
Bloom, Paul, 222
Boston Marathon, 34, 226–27
Bowman, Dylan, 108

Callicles' tyrant, 190
canoes and barges, 89
carbon-plated shoes, 9, 38, 120–22,
    124, 214, 229
cardiovascular system, 162
character, x–xiii, 1–5, 13, 16, 19, 20–
    21, 22, 25, 31–62, 64–67, 68, 79,
    88, 100–1, 102, 103–5, 110–11,
    121–22, 124–25, 133–34, 136–
    38, 142, 143, 147–48, 150, 155,
    179, 186, 208, 218, 228–30
character education, x, 2–3, 22, 32,
    42–45, 46, 49–64, 65–67, 79,
    89–90, 103, 218–19, 228–29
charity, 64, 78, 146–47, 171–72

cheating, xi, 7, 133–34, 140–42, 143, 147, 167, 172–73
Chebet, Evans, 34
chivalry, 65
coach, coaching, 8, 10–11, 14, 21–22, 27, 29–30, 41, 43–45, 49, 51, 53–62, 89–90, 97–98, 99, 100–1, 113, 121, 128–29, 142, 150, 154–55, 220–21
community, 17, 18, 30, 38, 49–50, 60, 151–52, 153, 169–71, 178, 206, 212–13
comparison, 29, 81–83, 165, 172
compete, competition, xi, 1, 7, 15, 23, 29, 37, 47–48, 53, 68–69, 81–88, 92, 93, 109, 120–22, 125–26, 131, 149–50, 151–52, 158, 164–65, 168, 169, 174, 180, 189–90, 197, 203, 206, 211, 229
consequentialism, 7–8, 10, 11–13
constancy, 129
courage, x, 2, 5, 35, 39, 47–48, 51, 53–55, 57–58, 75–76, 86, 91, 94–95, 97, 109, 114, 124, 134, 145, 146, 198
cross country, 6, 14, 47–48, 51, 53–54, 61, 73, 215, 228

Damasio, Antonio , 91
Dauwalter, Courtney, 106–7, 158–59
deontology, 7–8, 9–11, 12
depth larceny, 226–27
Desert Tradition, 3
desire-satisfaction account of happiness, 187–92
discipline, 3, 4, 34–35, 42, 44, 46, 66–67, 89–90, 136, 174
dishabituation, 26–27, 31, 171
distractability , xii, 42
domestic violence, 36
doping, 10, 12–13, 37–38, 45, 101, 139, 141–42, 214, 229–30. See also 'performance-enhancing drugs'

downregulation of emotions, 15, 40
Driver, Julia, 8
drug te⸱.ing pool, 140–42

egoism, 169–70, 205–6
emotions, 15, 19, 29, 37, 40, 42, 44, 69–92, 93–94, 99, 116–17, 127–28, 146–47, 165–68, 181, 184, 186–87, 192, 203, 216–17, 229
    behavioral components, 71–72
    bodily phenomena, 71
    emotions as 'concern-based construals', 72–73, 117
    emotions as educable, 77–79
    evaluative character, 72–73, 74
    expressive character, 72
    subjective experience, 70–71
    veridical emotions, 79, 81
emulation, 35, 58, 82, 87, 93–98, 101–5, 107–8, 110, 111–12, 113–14, 115, 120, 166
enkrateia, 23–24
envy, 29–30, 35, 37, 55, 69, 75, 81–92, 143, 149–50, 153, 164–68, 172–73
ergon, 17, 18
Ericsson, K. Anders, 26
eudaimonia, 19, 123, 192–95, 198–99, 209. See also 'flourishing'
eupatheiai, 90–91
exceptionalism, 202
exemplars, 29, 35, 53, 58–60, 85, 94–115, 116, 158–59, 203–4, 221
experience machine (Nozick), 183

Facial Feedback Hypothesis, 69–70
Faustian bargain, 30, 210–12, 216, 220
feelings, 6–7, 40, 58–59, 63, 70, 71, 78–80, 83–84, 85, 111, 127–28, 146, 165, 166, 183–87, 191–92
flourishing, xii–xiii, 13, 38, 52, 96–97, 123, 124–25, 144–45, 150, 151, 169, 192–95, 203–4,

205–6, 215, 223, 224. See also
  'eudaimonia'
fortitude, 19, 53, 55, 129
freedom, free will, 20, 38–46, 64,
  65–67, 112, 160, 196–97, 207,
  212, 217
friendship, 15, 31, 35–36, 47, 84, 87,
  89–90, 101, 117, 124–25, 143–
  44, 150, 151–52, 161–63, 170–
  71, 172, 184, 203, 204, 211–12,
  216, 226–27

Gallagher, Clare, 107–8
gawky stage of virtue development,
  25–27, 57, 63
Gladwell, Malcolm, 26
God, gods, ix, 3–4, 10, 24, 58, 85–86,
  97, 144, 222–23
Gorgias, by Plato, 190
grateful, gratitude, 33, 83–84, 85, 88,
  121, 171
greed, 143–44, 150–51, 152, 173–76,
  177–78, 210

habit, 2–4, 20–21, 26–27, 32, 47, 51–
  52, 54, 62, 63, 64, 89, 95, 113,
  114, 133, 135–36, 171
Hall, Sara, 109
happy, happiness, 5–6, 11, 19, 30,
  35–36, 80, 91, 123, 143–44, 151,
  182–208, 215, 216–18, 223, 229
health, x–xi, 10, 12, 30, 43, 89–90,
  96–97, 141, 152, 153, 162–63,
  195, 200–5, 211, 216, 217–18
hedonism, hedonic account of
  happiness, 80, 182, 183–
  88, 191–92
hero, heroism, 33–34, 50, 93–94, 96–
  97, 98, 102, 103–5, 136, 176–77
hexis, 19
hill repeats, hills, ix–x, 28, 53, 55, 75–
  76, 81, 114, 146
honesty, xii, 11, 22, 25, 37–38, 51, 77,
  140, 171

humanity, human limits, human
  nature, 2, 4, 7, 10, 16–17, 18, 19,
  37–38, 64–65, 80, 105, 123, 132,
  142, 151, 152, 156, 170, 182,
  186–87, 188, 192, 193, 194–95,
  196, 203–5, 208, 209–10, 211–
  13, 215
humble, humility, 17, 21, 85,
  94–95, 98, 106–7, 111, 132,
  149, 158–59
humor, 16, 19, 69, 106–7, 131–33
hupomoné, 56

identity of the virtues, 56
imitation, imitator, 86–87, 94, 95,
  103, 106, 111–15, 116, 167–68
impatience, 46, 55, 144, 148, 200
impediments to freedom, 41–
  42, 43, 46
imprudence, 5, 46, 125–26, 161, 181,
  216, 223
impulsivity, 15, 33–34, 36–37, 40
Ingebrigtsen, Jakob, 40
injury, 31, 32–33, 35–36, 117, 118–
  19, 125–27, 130–31, 155, 161,
  181, 197–98, 200–1, 202–3, 216,
  218, 220, 224, 225
injustice, 2, 77–78, 117, 186–87
integrity, 37, 38, 39–40, 60, 61–
  62, 82, 101, 109, 110, 121,
  153, 214–15
intransigence, 29–30, 129–31, 142,
  149–50, 159–64
irresolution, 42, 129–30, 160,
  161, 164

joy, 29, 38, 51, 60, 81–83, 121,
  124–25, 127–28, 130, 133–
  34, 137–38
justice, xi, 2, 18, 77–78, 117, 134,
  186–87, 195, 218

kaihōgyō, 3
Kant, Immanuel, 8, 12, 14

Kierkegaard, Soren, 15, 86, 106, 110–11, 114, 132
King, Nathan, 20, 129–30, 146–47
Kipchoge, Eliud, 46, 69–70, 71, 84–86, 210
Kristjánsson, Kristján , 166
Krupicka, Anton, 102–3

Laws, by Plato, 2, 46
laziness, lazy, 25, 42, 55, 220–21
Lewis, C.S., 15, 65
limits, limitless, 30, 35–36, 46, 49–50, 79, 156, 157, 159, 162, 164, 194–95, 196, 205, 209–21, 228–29
Lokedi, Sharon, 34–35
loneliness, lonely, 80–81, 156
longevity, 203
love, 2, 43, 61–62, 65–66, 72–73, 97, 109, 117, 128, 146–47, 157, 159, 163, 169, 171–72, 203, 204, 212–13, 215, 217, 218
Luther, Martin, 153–54
lyreplayers, 5, 20–21, 26, 76

MacIntyre, Alasdair, 124, 151–52
magnanimity, 144–45, 149, 156–59
Mandeville, Bernard, 173–74
McDowell, John, 16
metaethics, 6–7, 9–11
Mill, John Stuart, 185
Miller, Christian, 76, 147, 178–79, 186
misanthropism, 115–16
mixed traits, 147, 178–79
monasticism, 3–4. See also 'Desert Tradition'
moral reasoning, 24–25, 51, 75–76
moral saints, 16, 97
motivation, xii, 5, 8, 14, 27–28, 51, 53–54, 82–83, 95–96, 115, 126, 133, 135–36, 147, 167, 169–70, 178–79, 206
mountain(s), ix, 33, 42, 49–50, 80, 114, 128, 133, 161, 181, 184, 189

mundane exemplar, 97–98
National Collegiate Athletic Association (NCAA), 34, 200
National Football League (NFL), 36
natural law, 7, 8–9
Nicomachean Ethics, 52–53, 89, 193
Nietzsche, Friedrich, 85
"no pain, no gain", 30, 216, 225–26
normative ethics, 6, 7–11, 63
norm differentiation, 169–71, 229

old age, 89–90, 204, 212
Olympic Games, x–xi, 19, 40, 74–75, 93, 100, 150, 169–71, 189–90, 200, 203
post-Olympic blues, 189–90
Other-praising emotions, 81, 83–88

pain, xii, 13, 30, 31, 49–50, 118, 181–82, 183, 187–88, 200, 216, 224, 225–26
paradox of moral education, 42–45
paternalism, 65–67
patience , x, 17, 27, 29, 34–35, 38, 48, 53–54, 55–56, 57, 62, 86, 88, 119, 124–25, 137–38, 144, 148, 151, 200, 207, 208
perception, 72–73, 81, 84, 132, 159, 183
performance-enhancing drugs, xi, 9, 10–11, 37–38, 79–80, 133–34, 142
perseverance, x, 3, 19, 22, 28, 38, 61, 79, 103, 104, 114, 125, 128–31, 137, 142, 149–50, 160–64, 207, 208, 223, 229–30
Pheidippides, 74–75
phronesis, 47. See also 'practical wisdom'
physical therapy, 31, 49–50, 118–19
Pinckaers, Servais-Théodore , 128
Plato, ix, 2–3, 4, 16, 23, 46, 58, 64–65, 99, 102, 189, 190, 218–19
pleasure, 19–20, 23–24, 46, 63, 75, 76, 78, 116, 132, 149, 182, 183, 185–87, 190, 195, 207, 210

Plotinus, ix
poetry and gymnastics, 2–3, 64–65, 136
Politics, by Aristotle, 199–200, 218
post-traumatic growth, 224
practical wisdom, 47–49, 55, 125–26, 130–31, 137, 198, 207, 221
pregnancy, 168
pride, 1, 3, 29–30, 35–36, 55, 149–50, 153–58, 159, 226–27
Protagoras of Abdera, 2, 78
Pusillanimity, 156, 159

reciprocity thesis, 56
relativism, 7, 78
Republic, by Plato, 2, 58, 102, 218
resilience, x, 31, 33, 38, 104, 113, 117, 119, 124–27, 133–34, 201, 207
Roberts, Robert, 72–73, 132
role models, 29, 35, 58–60, 94, 146, 203–4. *See also* 'exemplars'
run streak, 164

sad, sadness, 40, 70–71, 79–80, 81, 90, 115, 117, 125–26, 127, 184, 186–87, 189–90, 200–1
sage, 96–97, 98, 210
saint, 16, 97, 98
schadenfreude, 78
Schwitzgebel, Eric, 24
self-governance, 2, 3, 17, 41, 42, 43–44, 46, 60–61, 130, 196–97, 207
self-importance, 154–55
selfishness, 17, 18, 29–30, 33–34, 142, 149–50, 153, 168–72, 205–6, 229
skills, 26, 51–52, 57, 87, 114–15, 139, 181, 188
Slote, Michael, 16
Snow, Nancy, 119, 125–26
social media, 27, 102, 155, 174–75, 176–77, 178
Socrates, ix, 2, 23, 58, 99–100, 102, 190, 218–19

sophia, 47. *See also* 'wisdom'
Sophie, 94–95, 110
sophist, 78, 190
spirit of sport, xi, 10–11, 12–13, 37–38, 133–34
stoicism, 16, 90–92
subjective experience, 69, 70–71, 78, 80, 183
subjectivism, 78
suffering, xii–xiii, 13, 30, 49, 138, 144, 177, 180, 181–82, 192, 195, 200–1, 205, 215–27, 229

technology, 34–35, 37–38, 120–21
temperance, 19, 20, 37, 42, 75, 149–50, 172–73, 190, 194, 195, 207
Texas, 21, 24–25, 49
"thief of joy", 29, 81–83
thumos, 15
Twain, Mark, 221–22
twenty-four-hour run, 94–95, 140, 163

unity of virtues, 56–57

vainglory, 27, 33–34, 35, 155, 173, 175, 176–78
vice, xi–xii, 3, 7, 11, 13, 16, 18, 19, 22, 25, 29–30, 32, 33–36, 37–38, 42, 49, 50–51, 55–56, 83, 90, 129–30, 139–79, 189, 226, 229
    deficiency and excess, 19–20, 129–30, 145–47, 149–50, 161, 164, 195
    performance-enhancing vice, 29–30, 142–73
violin, 2, 25–26, 196–97
virtue, xiii, 2, 3–4, 5–6, 7–9, 10, 11–30, 32, 34–35, 38, 46–61, 74–75, 89, 102, 104, 112–13, 118–38, 144–48, 152–53, 155, 158, 171–72, 175, 181–82, 190, 193, 194, 198–99, 207, 208, 221
virtue and knowledge, 20, 23–25

virtue development, 13, 14–15,
  21–22, 26, 32, 38–64, 73, 76–87,
  136–38, 147
virtue ethics, xi–xiii, 5–6, 7–9,
  10, 11–14
virtue goals, 39, 60–61
  intellectual virtue, 19–20, 47, 55,
    64, 104
  moral virtue, 19–21, 47, 48, 49–
    50, 55, 64
  performance-enhancing virtue,
    29, 120–22, 124–25
  threshold virtue, 52, 145, 147
  virtue mean, 19–20, 55, 145–46

Walmsley, Jim, 105, 106, 112
warped boards, 28, 54–55, 145–
  46, 221
wealth, 27, 144, 173, 175–76, 189,
  190–92, 193, 195

well-roundedness, 195,
  197–98, 199
will, willpower, 63–64
wisdom, 20, 47, 96–97, 132, 144–45.
  See also 'sophia'
wittiness, 19, 75, 145
Wolf, Susan, 16
World Anti-Doping Agency
  (WADA), 12, 101, 139–42
World Athletics, 5, 34
world championship, 93, 94, 100,
  109, 118, 125
World Cup, 5, 158
world record, 46, 69, 84–85, 105–6,
  176–77, 209–10

youth, 2–3, 21, 59, 61–62, 89, 154–
  55, 163

Zagzebski, Linda, 115, 166